the
Perpetual
Book Fund

A

Bernhard O. Hougen

Perpetual Book Fund
Book

WILLIAMSBURG REGIONAL LIBRARY
FOUNDATION

CONFEDERATE
BUSHWHACKER

JEROME LOVING

Confederate Bushwhacker

MARK TWAIN

IN THE SHADOW OF

THE CIVIL WAR

University Press of New England
Hanover and London

University Press of New England

www.upne.com

© 2013 Jerome Loving

Manufactured in the United States of America

Designed by Mindy Basinger Hill

Typeset in Fanwood

University Press of New England is a member
of the Green Press Initiative. The paper used in this book meets
their minimum requirement for recycled paper.

For permission to reproduce any of the material in this book,
contact Permissions, University Press of New England,
One Court Street, Suite 250, Lebanon NH 03766;
or visit www.upne.com

Library of Congress Cataloging-in-Publication Data

Loving, Jerome, 1941–
Confederate bushwhacker: Mark Twain in the shadow of the Civil War /
Jerome Loving.
page   cm
Includes bibliographical references and index.
ISBN 978-1-61168-465-0 (cloth: alk. paper)— ISBN 978-1-61168-472-8 (ebook)
1. Twain, Mark, 1835–1910. 2. Authors, American—19th century—Biography.
3. Humorists, American—19th century—Biography.
4. Veterans—Confederate States of America—Biography.
5. Soldiers—Confederate States of America—Biography.
6. Grant, Ulysses S. (Ulysses Simpson), 1822–1885. Personal memoirs of U.S. Grant.
7. Twain, Mark, 1835–1910. Private history of a campaign that failed.
8. United States—History—Civil War, 1861–1865—Influence.
9. United States—Social conditions—1865–1918.
10. United States—Race relations—History—19th century.
I. Title. II. Title: Mark Twain in the shadow of the Civil War.
PS1332.L68 2013
818'.409—dc23   2013009641

5   4   3   2   1

TO THE MEMORY

OF

James M. Cox

In time I came to know the Union colonel whose coming
frightened me out of the war and crippled the Southern cause
to that extent—General Grant. I came within a few hours
of seeing him when he was as unknown as I was myself;
at a time when anybody could have said,
"Grant?—Ulysses S. Grant? I do not remember
hearing the name before."

MARK TWAIN

CONTENTS

>⟆×⟅<

Introduction   xi

INTRODUCTION

Mark Twain had already entered his fiftieth year when his magnum opus, *Adventures of Huckleberry Finn,* appeared in England on December 10, 1884. Two months into 1885 the American publication followed. He had finished the book in the summer of 1884 and had set out that fall with George Washington Cable, the New Orleans writer, on what essentially became a book tour for *Huckleberry Finn.* Eighteen eighty-five was a busy year for the writer, whose real name was Samuel Langhorne Clemens. He had formed the publishing house of Charles L. Webster and Company in order to publish his own novel as well as other authors' works. Webster and Company, named for his niece's husband, who was the ostensible director, would publish many books over the next ten years, but its only other success was the *Personal Memoirs of U. S. Grant.* Both became American classics.

Twain idolized Ulysses S. Grant. He stood in awe of his military achievements, as did much of the entire nation twenty years after the end of the Civil War. In July, Grant, a heavy cigar smoker like Clemens, succumbed to throat cancer. At the time, he may have been the most famous man on the planet. His legacy would fade with the First World War, while that of his opposite, Robert E. Lee, grew to mythical proportions with the nostalgia for the Lost Cause. Sam Clemens had also fought for the South as a member of a state militia. He deserted after only two weeks and fled west to the territory of Nevada, where he began his career as a humorist. Since the end of the war, he had become a resident of the North—in Hartford, Connecticut—and the husband of a woman whose father had been an abolitionist (assisting, among others, America's most famous fugitive slave, Frederick Douglass). Mark Twain had kept the Confederate part of his past relatively quiet.

As he and Cable continued on their reading tour in the winter of 1885 and had to keep to the north of the Mason-Dixon Line because of Cable's racial politics if not Huck's abolitionism, he became troubled about that past. He wasn't so embarrassed that as a soldier he had "made a virtue of retreat" and deserted. Some of his fellow soldiers had remained—and died—in the war. But he grew uneasy about the fact that he had once believed in the institution of slavery and had initially set out to defend it in the Civil War. He was also slightly uncomfortable with the fact that he was publishing a memoir by the former head of the army that had won the war and ended slavery. The two-volume set of Grant's *Personal Memoirs* was bound to make money for this former Confederate soldier.

As the "Twins of Genius" tour traveled the country, Clemens saw more and more evidence of the emerging Jim Crow South, whose racial disdain easily washed into the border states they visited on its way to the North, where the ex-slave was not wanted as a neighbor. The freedman was not truly free in 1885, Cable had argued in the January issue of the *Century*. Twain, who had written a book about a runaway slave who was actually free, asked him, somewhat rhetorically, how he hoped to free a people already "free." Unlike his friend Cable, whose views made him persona non grata in his hometown of New Orleans, his fellow Southerner would speak out against the racism of his day only indirectly, if also much more profoundly, in the fiction of *Huckleberry Finn,* and later in *Pudd'nhead Wilson.*

The spirit of reconciliation between North and South was

fully in bloom in 1885. This desire for sectional harmony, however, excluded the ex-slave, for whom the bloody Civil War had supposedly been waged. To take advantage of the national mood between former military combatants, the editors of the *Century* established the series entitled "Battles and Leaders." It ran for the next two years and doubled the magazine's circulation. The editors promised in the October 1884 issue of their magazine a balanced treatment in which "decisive battles, the leading characteristics of army life . . . and the lives of the most prominent commanders [were] to be the subject" of the essays.[1] Of course, the first to participate in this healing history was General Grant. Those who followed were mostly generals, from both sides of the war—including Beauregard, McClellan, and Lew Wallace (by then also the successful author of *Ben Hur* in 1880).

Wallace wasn't the only writer to be asked. Cable, a veteran of the Confederate army, contributed; so did Thomas Wentworth Higginson, who had led the first black regiment for the North. Mark Twain was asked. Originally, he planned to write a straightforward account of his two weeks as a second lieutenant in the Marion Rangers, a Missouri state militia. But the weeklong funeral of Grant that July and other distractions caused him to put off writing the essay until late summer and fall of 1885. "The Private History of a Campaign That Failed," as the story of it that follows in these pages suggests, was viewed as another example of the famous writer's humor by contemporary readers but to later audiences it became an early example of the antiwar feeling that culminated with the horrors of the First World War. In what his official biographer called a falsification, Twain claimed that he had been a Confederate bushwhacker, the name given to the many guerrilla forces in Missouri that remained after the state officially sided with the North.[2] Even though he began the essay with the simple idea of mirthfully apologizing for having fought for the South and the cause of slavery, he ultimately lied to suggest a larger point about the arbitrary nature of war.

The essay appeared in the December 1885 issue of the *Century*—at the close of Mark Twain's annus mirabilis. The year had begun with the installation of Grover Cleveland in the White House, the first Democrat to be elected to that high office since the war. Black lynchings were already on the rise. American Indians in the West threatened to fight to retain lands being poached by cattle ranchers. Chinese laborers were regularly murdered for taking the jobs of white men. The nation was plagued with violent labor strikes that led to the calamitous Haymarket Affair of 1886. In the midst of everything, Mark Twain became not only the author of one of America's greatest novels, but also one of the richest men in America (on paper at least), with the firm expectation of becoming one of the richest in the world because of his investments in the Paige Typesetter. Almost everything he touched up to that year since 1869 had turned to gold.

In this single-year biography, we follow Mark Twain in his concerns from black slavery to wage slavery, as he shifted his sights from *Huckleberry Finn* to *A Connecticut Yankee in King Arthur's Court.* We accompany him through America on the eve of the twentieth century, when Alexander Graham Bell was still in court defending the exclusivity of his invention (probably the reason the telephone wasn't among Twain's many investments), when *Huckleberry Finn* began its first year as a controversial book unsuitable for young people, when the French first delivered their gift of the Statue of Liberty to America, and when triumphant Jim Crow America had first begun to silence the annual black jubilations over Emancipation. Throughout the eight chapters of this slice of the author's life in the shadow of the Civil War, the narrative is peppered with 1885 newspaper citations to submerge the reader in the feel, language, and first-hand concerns of the time. Bushwhacked by his past, enthralled by his present, and doomed to his fate in an unhappy future, Mark Twain remains today America's greatest source of humor in the face of certain adversity. In 1885 he occupied the center of the universe.

><>><

CONFEDERATE
BUSHWHACKER

><>><

><><><

Mark Twain's War Experiences

><><><

His Graphic Recital of Them at the
Dinner to the Boston Ancient
and Honorable Artillery Company.
(*New York Times*, October 7, 1877)

Mr. Samuel L. Clemens was a guest at the dinner given the Boston Ancient and Honorable Artillery Company in Hartford by the Putnam Phalanx[1] of that city, and in responding to a toast said:

"I wouldn't have missed being here for a good deal. The last time I had the privilege of breaking bread with soldiers was some years ago with the oldest military organization in England, the Ancient and Honorable Artillery Company of London, somewhere about its six hundredth anniversary; and now I have enjoyed this privilege with its eldest child, the oldest military organization in America, the Ancient and Honorable Artillery Company of Massachusetts, on this their two hundred and fortieth anniversary. Fine old stock, both of you; and if you fight as well as you feed, God protect the enemy. I did not assemble at the hotel parlors to-day to be received by a committee as a mere civilian guest. No, I assembled at the head-quarters of the Putman Phalanx, and insisted upon my right to be escorted to this place as one of the military guests. For I, too, am a soldier. I am inured to war. I have a military history. I have been through a stirring campaign, and there is not even a mention of it in any history of the United States or of the Southern Confederacy. To such lengths can the envy and malignity of the historian go. I will unbosom myself here, where I cannot but find sympathy. I will tell you about it and appeal through you to justice. In the earliest Summer days of the war, I slipped out of Hannibal, Mo., by night, with a friend, and joined a detachment of the rebel Gen. Tom Harris' (I find myself in a great minority here) Army, up a gorge behind an old barn in Ralls County. Col. Ralls, of Mexican war celebrity, swore us in. He made us swear to uphold the flag and Constitution of the United States, and to destroy every other military organization that we caught doing the same thing, which, being interpreted, means that we were to repel invasion. Well, you see this mixed us. We couldn't really tell which side we were on. But we went into camp and left it to the God of battles. For that was the term then. I was made Second Lieutenant and Chief Mogul of a company of 11 men who knew nothing about war — nor anything, for we had no Captain. My friend, who was 19 years old, 6 feet high, 3 feet wide, and some distance through, and just out of the infant school, was made Orderly Sergeant. His name was Ben Tupper. He had a hard time. When he was mounted and on the march he used to go to sleep, and his horse would reach around and bite him on the leg, and then he would wake up and cry and curse and want to go home. The other men pestered him a good deal, too. When they were dismounted they said they couldn't march in double file with him because his feet took up so much room. One night, when we were round the camp-fire, some fellow on the outside in the cold said: 'Ben Tupper, put down that newspaper; it throws the whole place into twilight, and casts a shadow like a blank.' Ben said: 'I ain't got any newspaper.' Then the other fellow said, 'Oh, I see; 'twas your ear.' We all slept in a corn-crib on the corn, and the rats were very thick. Ben Tupper had been carefully and rightly reared, and when he was ready for bed he would start to pray and a rat would bite him in the heel. And then he would sit up and swear all night and keep everybody awake. He was town-bred and did not seem to have any correct idea of military discipline. If I commanded him to shut up, he would say, 'Who was your nigger last year?' One evening I ordered him to ride out about three miles on picket duty, to the beginning of a prairie. Said he, 'What, in the night, and them blamed Union soldiers likely to be prowling around there any time?' So he wouldn't go, and the next morning I ordered him again. Said he: 'In the rain? I think I see myself!' He didn't go. Next day I ordered him on picket duty once more. This time he looked hurt. Said he: 'What, on Sunday; you must be a — fool.' Well, picketing night may have been a very good thing, but I saw it was impracticable, so I dropped it from my military system. We had a good enough time there at that barn, barring the rats and the mosquitoes and the rain. We levied on both parties impartially, and both parties hated us impartially. But one day we heard that the invader was approaching. So we had to pack up and move, of course, and within 24 hours he was coming again. So we moved again. Next day he was after us once more. Well, we didn't like it much, but we moved, rather than make trouble. And this went on for a week or 10 days, and we saw considerable scenery. Then Ben Tupper's patience was lost. Said he: 'War is not what it's cracked up to be. I'm going home, if I can't ever git a chance to sit down a minute. Why do these people keep us a humpin' around so. Blame their skins, do they think this is an excursion?'

"Some of the other town boys got to grumbling. They complained that there was an insufficiency of umbrellas. So I sent around to the farmers and borrowed what I could. Then they complained that the Worcestershire sauce was out. There was mutiny and dissatisfaction all around, and, of course, at such a time as this the invader must come around pestering us again; as much as two hours before breakfast, too, when no one wanted to turn out, of course. This was carrying the thing too far. The whole command felt insulted. I detached one of my aides and sent him to the Brigadier, and asked him to assign us a district where there wasn't so much bother going on. The history of our campaign was laid before him, but instead of being touched by it, what did he do? He sent back an indignant message and said: 'You have had a dozen chances inside of two weeks to capture the enemy and he is still at large. (Well, we knew that!) Stay where you are this time or I will court-martial and hang the whole lot of you.' Well, I submitted this brutal message to my battalion and asked their advice. Said the Orderly Sergeant: 'If Tom Harris wants the enemy let him come here and get him. I ain't got any use for my share, and who's Tom Harris anyway, I'd like to know, that's putting on so many frills? Why, I knew him when he wasn't anything but a darned telegraph operator. Gentlemen, you can do as you choose. As for me, I've got enough of this sashaying around so's't you can't get a chance to pray, because the time is all required for cussing, so off goes my war-paint. You hear me!' The whole regiment said with one voice, 'That's the talk for me.' So there and then, on the spot, my brigade disbanded itself and tramped off home, with me in the tail of it. I hung up my own sword and returned to the arts of peace, and there were people who said I hadn't been absent from them yet. We were the first men that went out of it anywhere. This, gentlemen, is the history of the part which my division took in the great rebellion, and such is the military record of its Commander-in-Chief, and this is the first time that the deeds of those warriors have been brought officially to the notice of humanity. Treasure these things in your hearts. And so shall the detected and truculent historians of this land be brought to shame and confusion. I ask you to fill your glasses and drink with me to the reverent memory of the Orderly Sergeant and those other neglected and forgotten heroes, my footsore and travel-stained paladins, who were first in war, first in peace, and were not idle during the interval that lay between."

ONE

>ᴙᴙᵪᴙᴙ<

On the Eve of
Huckleberry Finn

>ᴙᴙᵪᴙᴙ<

In the summer of 1884, Mark Twain took off his shirt and sat for the bust of Roman orator or general. An odd photograph shows the bare-chested humorist, in a pose that for a long time no one could make much sense of. The bust makes up part of the front matter in *Adventures of Huckleberry Finn* (1884). It accompanies a warning to critics to keep their hands off the book. The sculptor was Karl Gerhardt. He had only recently returned from Paris, where he had been supported by Clemens to study art since 1881. The story of how Mark Twain came to sponsor this third-rate artist and ultimately include a piece of his work in his literary masterpiece is remarkable for its portraiture of Victorian manners. As a matter of fact, Mark Twain removed his shirt for an artist whose wife had first taken off hers for the famous author.

By the time it happened, he had been married for almost exactly ten years. Mark Twain, or Sam Clemens, was comfortably established with a wife and three children in his "steamboat gothic" mansion in Hartford, Connecticut. It was located in the neighborhood of Nook Farm, in the upscale, genteel part of the town. One of his neighbors was Harriet Beecher Stowe. Another was Charles Dudley Warner, who had coauthored *The*

Gilded Age with him in 1873. Even before *Huckleberry Finn*, Mark Twain was so famous that everybody wanted a piece of him. His second book, *The Innocents Abroad* (1869), sold almost 120,000 copies in its initial run between 1869 and 1877. *The Adventures of Tom Sawyer* (1876) was so popular that he had to resort to a form letter to respond to the clamor for its "sequel." One day his butler, a former slave by the name of George Griffin, announced that there was a lady waiting to see him. Thinking it was another unwelcome book agent, Clemens, who was given to petty domestic rages from time to time, marched into the drawing room and began to assault a young, very attractive woman with "a succession of rude & raspy questions." Not even her delicate manner and ardent beauty could modify his stance against her — at first. Then, as he told his friend William Dean Howells about the "romance" of that moment, "there she stood, with her pretty face bent floorward whilst I inquired, but always with her honest eyes looking me in the face when it came her turn to answer."

Mark Twain was forty-six. Hattie Gerhardt was eighteen and married to a twenty-eight-year-old mechanic at the local Pratt & Whitney machine shop. He was an untrained sculptor who worked away at his avocation in the evenings. His young wife had boldly come to the Nook Farm enclave of famous authors to see whether she could interest any of them in her husband's work, to see if one of them wouldn't pronounce her man a true artist. She evidently went to the Clemens mansion first, where she urged Mark Twain to come downtown to her flat and view one of his works. "I don't know anything about art," the artist and businessman soon to become his own publisher responded, but he was eventually persuaded to examine a statue made of clay that her husband had just finished. And soon after she had departed, he was sorry he hadn't gone home with her to see it that very day. Clearly charmed by the young woman, he told Howells a few weeks later, "Damnation, how can a man be such a hound? — why didn't I go with her *now?* Yes, & how mean I should have felt if I had known that out of her poverty she had hired a hack & brought it along to convey me. But luckily for what was left of my peace of mind, I didn't know that." He also didn't know then that Hattie had subsequently and immediately repaired to his neighbor Warner's house with the same proposal.

Warner did go. He evidently found merit in the statue and urged Clemens to see it, too. But he didn't give him all the details of his visit, saying only that the work, while "crude," showed definite promise. The next day Clemens had his coachman, Patrick McAleer, take him to examine the statue. The Gerhardts lived in the working-class section of East Hartford, on the second story of a small wooden cottage. When Clemens arrived, only Hattie was at home — her husband still at work at the machine shop. Genteel poverty showed everywhere, starting with the small parlor stuffed with a chair and a sofa. Plaster busts her husband had made littered the room, along with a couple of amateur paintings of flowers and birds. There was even a bust of Hattie, but it wasn't the statue she wished to show her visitor. That was in the kitchen. Upon entering it, "the girl," he told Howells in a letter marked *"Private & Confidential,"* "flew around, with enthusiasm, & snatched rag after rag from a tall something in the corner, & presently there stood the clay statue, life size — a graceful girlish creature, (life size) [he repeated himself] nude to the waist." It was the statue of a nymph-like figure interrupted as she was about "to enter her bath."

Actually, it was a statue of a startled bather who was completely nude, but Hattie had been discreet enough to stop disrobing her image at the waist. "Oh, it's *you!*" the reddened Clemens exclaimed. Answering in the affirmative, she proceeded to use a lever to turn the statue around "so as to afford a view . . . from all points." Mark Twain must have been startled himself that day at seeing this married teenager in Victorian America "exhibiting her naked self, as it were, to a stranger & alone." He tried to exempt her of any indecency or indelicacy, but he admitted to Howells that it would "be many a day before I run across another woman who can do the like & show no trace of self-consciousness."

Twain sat down on one of the kitchen chairs and lit his pipe. Hattie told him that she was her husband's only model, that he could afford no other. Gesturing toward the half-nude statue without embarrassment, its flesh-and-blood incarnation talked about her people in Massachusetts, emphasizing that she came from an "old & respectable family" where her father was a doctor. "I am able to believe anything she says," her auditor told Howells. When he discovered that her husband Karl had never taken a single art lesson, he might have attributed the artisan's inspiration solely to his model. As it was already noon, the artist himself arrived home from the factory for lunch — "a slender young fellow with a marvelous head & a noble eye." Twain judged Karl Gerhardt's quiet manner as thoughtful, but he also couldn't help noticing that his wife continued to do all the talking.[1]

Also from Massachusetts, Gerhardt had attended the Phillips School in Boston. By the age of seventeen, he had been apprenticed to a house painter. He spent a year and a half in the Union army that was still basking in the glory of its victory over the South. He landed a job soon afterward as a machinist at the Ames Foundry in Chicopee, Massachusetts, near Springfield in the western part of the state. The company that had built cannons during the war was now dedicated to casting memorials to the soldiers such cannons had killed. Work in the foundry had whetted the young man's appetite for sculpture, which was still only a hobby for him in 1881.[2] Gerhardt's 1940 obituary stated that he had first met Mark Twain in Paris, but in actuality it had been in Hartford and was undoubtedly because of his young wife that Mark Twain then sent him to Paris.[3] As a result of his connection with the famous man, Gerhardt made a name for himself, one of the high points of his career coming with the sculpting of General Grant in 1885, a work that followed soon after the bust of Mark Twain. Without the Mark Twain imprimatur there are serious questions as to what his future as a sculptor might have held.

Mark Twain had been slightly dazed that February day in 1881 when he met Hattie in her working-class boudoir. Whatever pangs of infatuation he took home with him, whatever enchantment still remained of the undraped Hattie, he soon buried in Victorian convention and promptly told his wife about the day's adventure. Sam was utterly devoted to Olivia Langdon, whom he had met shortly after his 1867 cruise on the *Quaker City*, the basis for *The Innocents Abroad*. Yet his head had been turned enough for him to continue his relationship with Hattie Gerhardt, albeit vicariously and through her husband's "art." In his autobiography, it is worth noting, he insisted, perhaps too strenuously, that he had taken "hold of [Gerhardt's] case . . . solely because I had become convinced that he had it in him to become a very capable sculptor. . . . I was merely taking upon myself a common duty — the duty of helping a man who was not able to help himself."[4]

When Sam returned home that day, Livy, as she was called,

was hosting Clara Spaulding, a girlhood friend from Elmira, New York, where they had both grown up and where Mark Twain had written most of *Huckleberry Finn.* The two women went the very next day to see the statue — and Hattie, of course. One can only guess what was in the back of their minds. Whatever it was, Livy managed to regard the couple as innocent "children." Twain and Warner had the sculptor John Quincy Adams Ward come to look at the statue. "Ward came away bewitched with those people & marveling at the winning innocence of the young wife," Sam told Howells. Hattie had "dropped naturally into her model-attitude beside the statue (which is stark naked from head to heel, now — G[erhardt] had removed the drapery, fearing Ward would think he was afraid to try legs & hips)."[5]

Like Mark Twain, Ward was impressed — with both the sculptor and his model. This untrained artist had gone "straight at *nature*" and achieved what a person of average talent could accomplish only after two years of schooling. "Hartford must send him to Paris," Ward exclaimed. Mark Twain sent him there and ultimately gave Gerhardt his first and most important commission. As it turned out, the bust of the Roman general reflected Mark Twain's deep admiration of Ulysses S. Grant, whose memoirs Charles L. Webster & Company would publish along with *Huckleberry Finn.* As part of the frontispiece, the picture of the statue balanced the other image that made up the frontispiece — a pen-and-ink sketch of Huck, the semi-illiterate narrator who thinks he is doing wrong when he assists a fugitive slave. Gerhardt's bust of Mark Twain was matched up with E. W. Kemble's sketch of Huck Finn holding up a shot rabbit, putting flesh on the ungrammatical Huck.

As with Gerhardt, Kemble got his break as an artist with Mark Twain and his *Adventures of Huckleberry Finn.* About the time that the novel was reaching completion, the twenty-two-year-old illustrator published a sketch of a boy just stung by a bee. It caught Clemens's eye, and he had Webster & Company offer Kemble $2,000 to do the artwork for the book. Kemble used the same model as the basis for all the characters in the book, including the fugitive slave Jim. Years later the illustrator recalled: "Jim the Negro seemed to please [his model, Cort Morris] the most. He would jam his little black wool cap over his head, shoot out his lips and mumble coon talk all the while he was posing." As *Huckleberry Finn* became a success, so grew the career of E. W. Kemble. Yet curiously that success came mostly, if not entirely, from Kemble's knack for drawing black people, or their caricatures, in post-Reconstruction America. For these depictions went along with the general caricaturing of the emancipated slave who the North feared would leave the South and invade its cities once Union troops returned home.[6]

One of the clearest examples of this development during and after Reconstruction, which ended in 1877, was the bowdlerization of the best-selling *Uncle Tom's Cabin.* The immense popularity of its unauthorized dramatization, a play that toured the country until the end of the century, turned the heroic Uncle Tom into a black sycophant. "My coons caught the public fancy," Kemble proudly recalled. *"The Century* then engaged me to work exclusively for their magazine. This continued for several years, and all the stories from those charming writers of the South, Thomas Nelson Page, James Lane Allen, Harry Stilwell Edwards, Richard Malcolm Johnson and George W. Cable, were placed in my hands for picture work."[7] Like Twain, these writers were drawn back to the antebellum period for their fictions. Because of the "nigger" in *Huckleberry Finn,* Kemble subsequently became famous for depicting Southern blacks, even though this New Yorker hadn't yet been south of Sandy Hook, New Jersey.

Twain hadn't cared that much for Kemble's first batch of drawings for the book, pronouncing some of them "good, but none of them are very *very* good." He didn't mention any of those of Jim, but he thought that Kemble had made Huck look too much like a member of another unpopular minority in America — the Irish. "Huck Finn," he wrote Charlie Webster, who was running Webster and Company for Sam, "is an exceedingly good-hearted boy, & should carry a good & good-looking face."[8] The character of Huck Finn, Twain insisted, was based on Hannibal's Tom Blankenship, the son of one of the two town drunks. But the Clemens family, especially his wife and daughter Clara, were horrified when the public began to associate the youth of Mark Twain, or Samuel Langhorne Clemens, with that underclass boy. They even insisted that it be mentioned in any magazine articles devoted to the early life of the author of *Huckleberry Finn* that the Clemens family on the Mississippi had been poor but nevertheless respectable enough to own one or two slaves.[9]

* * *

The frontispiece to *Adventures of Huckleberry Finn,* illustrated as it was with the "twin" images of an author who went by two different names, underscores the fact that the magnum opus of America's best-known writer reflected at once the political polarities of the not so United States in the post–Civil War years as well as the personal polarities of the humorist whose jokes were often bathed in tragedy. During the fall of 1884, the presidential election campaign featured James G. Blaine of Maine, the Republican candidate, against Grover Cleveland of New York, the Democrat. Mark Twain and his Nook Farm set had consistently voted the antislavery Republican ticket since the Civil War, but a growing number of supporters of the party were becoming disenchanted with its flagging enthusiasm for the little guy. Its opposition to civil service reform in the late 1870s was one example of its complacency. Another was its withdrawal of federal troops from the South as a way to placate the angry Democrats over their razor-thin loss in the 1876 presidential race between Samuel Tilden and Rutherford B. Hayes. The Republicans were turning their backs on economic and social injustices in favor of big business and America's first aristocrats, the robber barons. Labor unrest in the railroad industry had been steadily increasing since 1877, when it imposed a series of wage cuts. Striking workers brought the number of unemployed in the country to 400,000.[10]

James G. Blaine, as Speaker of the House of Representatives in 1869, had been caught taking kickbacks from a railroad to secure a land grant, allegations he never completely refuted. For those Republicans who favored continued reform, this candidate was unacceptable. Thousands went over to the Democrats in the election, including Mark Twain. Such deserters were called mugwumps, an American Indian pejorative for "holier than thou." The Democratic candidate, even though he had a sound reputation as a reformer, also had his political deficiency. Cleveland, a lifelong bachelor, had fathered a child out of wedlock. The campaign of 1884, therefore, came down to a choice between public dishonesty and private immorality.[11] "Blaine, Blaine, James G. Blaine, / Continental liar from the state of Maine," sang the Democrats, and the Republicans chanted back, "Ma, Ma, where's Pa? / Gone to the White House, ha, ha, ha."

To Mark Twain, this was not a difficult choice. "To see grown men, apparently in their right mind," he told Howells that August, "seriously arguing against a bachelor's fitness for President because he has had private intercourse with a consenting widow!" But most of the Nook Farmers didn't see it that way. Joe Twichell, known by then as "Mark Twain's pastor" (and close friend), had first become a mugwump but was ultimately dissuaded from voting for Cleveland because of his personal behavior. Unable as well to excuse the public thievery of Blaine, the minister threw away his vote on a third-party candidate. Other neighbors held their ground for Blaine in spite of his reputation for graft. "*Isn't* human nature the most consummate sham & lie that was ever invented?" Twain asked Howells. "Take three quite good specimens — Hawley, Warner & Charley Clark. Even *I* do not loathe Blaine more than they do; yet Hawley [former Connecticut governor and one of the owners of the *New England Courant*] is howling for Blaine; Warner and Clark [also *Courant* editors] are eating their daily crow in the paper for him, & all three will vote for him."[12]

Twain thought he was preaching to the choir, but Howells ultimately voted for Blaine, too. Like Twichell, he found sexual philandering worse than plain stealing. He later told a friend that he had "voted for a man *accused* of bribery," but that he would "not vote for a man *guilty* of what society sends a woman to hell for."[13] In fact, the overwhelming pull for Blaine lay not so much in Cleveland's admitted immorality as it did in party loyalty to the Republicans and their record on slavery and the war. "Allegiance to *party*," Mark Twain complained at one of the neighborhood's Monday Evening Club meetings, "plays directly into the hands of the baser sort."[14]

Mark Twain had never completely fit into the Nook Farm society. His Southern birth and his time in the rough-and-tumble West gave him and his writings a coarseness that stood out in this upper-crust world of ministers and former abolitionists. Even his family longed for more elegance in his writings. Until he issued his book on Joan of Arc in the 1890s, their favorite work of his was *The Prince and the Pauper* (1880). Yet by the time he finished *Huckleberry Finn,* this adopted "Connecticut Yankee" was entertaining second thoughts about the morality of man in any part of the country — or the world. *The Prince and the Pauper* told a story of social injustice. Its depictions of cruelties in sixteenth-century England served as more than a backdrop to the amusing mix-up of Prince Edward and Tom Canty in the time of Henry VIII. At least one British critic of the book opined that Mark Twain should stick to humor. Yet this implicit criticism of the British merely hinted at Mark Twain's growing disenchantment with the world, what became to him the "damned human race."

For most of his literary career and well beyond the publication of *Huckleberry Finn,* Mark Twain had been accepted by the literary establishment of his day as mainly a humorist, a "writer of the left hand." That was certainly his "day job." These rudely commercial writers wrote for the masses, not the classes that Henry James and other more serious artists sought out for an audience. Subscription houses instead of mainstream presses were among the outlets for humorists. Their books were sold on a prepaid basis through orders collected by book agents sent into the hinterlands, well beyond the precincts of most bookstores. Scorned by reviewers and editors of the leading magazines and newspapers (because subscription publishers seldom advertised in the press), such books were considered lowbrow reading. Charles L. Webster & Company was a subscription publisher.

The closest Twain came to publishing with a trade press before he handed all his copyrights over to Harper & Brothers at the turn of the century was to bring out *The Prince and the Pauper* with Charles R. Osgood & Company of Boston, heir to the Ticknor & Fields firm that had published such notables as Ralph Waldo Emerson and Henry David Thoreau. Yet even here he forced Osgood to issue the story as a subscription book. With sales that were satisfying enough, he gave the same firm *Life on the Mississippi* (1883). Its sales, however, were relatively disappointing, in part because Osgood was inept as a subscription publisher, but also because that book was a padded extension of the very popular essays in *Atlantic Monthly* entitled "Old Times on the Mississippi." Twain decided that he now knew enough about subscription publishing to start his own publishing house and cut out the middleman. In the winter of 1884, he had enlisted Charles L. Webster, the husband of his niece, to run the day-to-day business of the firm, which would also carry Webster's name. Its first two books — *Adventures of Huckleberry Finn* and *Personal Memoirs of U.S. Grant* — were smashing successes. The other ninety volumes, published between 1887 and 1894, would lead the publishing house slowly down the road to bankruptcy.

Twain was still reading proof for his new book in the summer of 1884. On his "off days" he began yet another story about Huck Finn and Tom Sawyer. *Adventures of Huckleberry Finn* ends with Huck deciding to "light out for the territory." In the antebellum period in which *Huckleberry Finn* takes place, these unsettled wildernesses would have been Kansas and Oklahoma, or Indian Territory. Rather than remain in St. Petersburg and get "civilized" by living with the Widow Douglas, as Huck does at the close of *Tom Sawyer,* he sets out this time with Tom and Jim for the "territory." Twain began the book almost the same way he had *Huckleberry Finn,* using a first-person narration: "That other book which I made before. . . . Maybe you remember about it. But if you don't, it don't make no difference, because it ain't got nothing to do with this one."

And indeed it didn't. For here Tom's love of romance leads to deadly results. During the final chapters of *Huckleberry Finn,* Tom helps Huck in his effort to free Jim from slavery only because he knows that Jim has already been freed in the late Miss Watson's will. Tom looks for adventure at almost anybody's expense, caring little if Jim or anybody else is injured by his shenanigans. In the unfinished "Huck and Tom Among the Indians," Tom insists to Jim, who joins the two on their journey west, that such American Indians are "the noblest human beings that's ever been in the world." Huck, reflecting Twain's dislike of Indians, is skeptical but nevertheless agrees to go on the quest, which ends abruptly with whites being murdered by savages who turn out to be anything but noble. Not only are they murderers in this story, they are also rapists. Before the story breaks off, Huck is satisfied to find Tom in the process of revising his notion of Indians: "Tom was putting the Injuns below the devils, now. You see, he had about got it through his noddle, by this time, that book Injuns and real Injuns is different."[15]

At the close of *Huckleberry Finn,* Huck's plan to "light out for the territory" suggested a romantic escape from the burdens of civilization. Its unrealistic expectations blended well with the romantic ending of the novel, where Jim lives happily ever after as a free black man in a slavocracy. The conclusion to the novel has been heavily criticized for its descent into slapstick humor, but Twain simply had nowhere else to take his romantic plot. He thought he was writing a "boy's book," not an antislavery novel. Yet it was the last truly happy ending he ever wrote. Only in *The American Claimant* (1892), which is a total farce, do things come out satisfactorily for the characters. Every other work of fiction he published after *Huckleberry Finn* — *A Connecticut Yankee in King Arthur's Court* (1889), *Pudd'nhead Wilson* (1894), *The Man That Corrupted Hadleyburg* (1900) — concludes in a dark web of determinism.

The fact is that Mark Twain had nowhere else to go after *Huckleberry Finn.* This novel of adolescence reveals his full awakening to the tragedy of the human condition, his final loss of any illusions about the nature of man. His story about a boy with a good heart and a bad conscience had been a hoax and a romance. This was the beginning of the Age of Darwin and its theory of "natural selection," and even his friend Howells, another social Darwinist who made an exception for a privileged few, was writing himself into the same philosophical corner with *The Rise of Silas Lapham* (1885). It was published at the same time as *Huckleberry Finn.* Both protagonists, Huck and Silas, are innocents who do the right thing at personal expense. Huck chooses "to go to hell" to save Jim; Silas refuses to engage in unethical conduct to save himself from bankruptcy. Both "rise" as they "fall." No wonder Twain warned away critics in the front matter of his fairy tale: "Persons attempting to find a Motive in this narrative will be prosecuted; persons attempting to find a Moral in it will be banished; persons attempting to find a Plot in it will be shot / by Order of the Author / Per G. G., Chief of Ordnance." His motive, moral, and plot were almost as romantic as anything Tom Sawyer could imagine.

* * *

By October 1884 Twain was preparing for his lecture tour with George Washington Cable, the New Orleans writer who had put the antebellum culture of the Creoles and other Southern life into American literature with such works as *Old Creole Days* (1879) and *The Grandissimes* (1880). His courageous writings in favor of civil rights for the freed slaves had already forced him to leave his homeland, where he had fought in the Confederate army, and to relocate in Massachusetts. Their four-month reading tour kicked off in New England on November 5. Howells was in the audience when the duo appeared in Boston on the thirteenth. "I thought that the bits from Huck Finn told the best," he wrote Sam the next day. "That is a mighty good book, and I should like to hear you read it all."[16]

The parts from *Huckleberry Finn* included the scene where Huck is writing a letter to Miss Watson, reporting the whereabouts of her runaway slave Jim. After writing the letter, Huck "felt good and all washed clean of sin for the first time [since he had been helping Jim escape], and I knowed I could pray, now." But he doesn't pray. Instead he lays down the letter and ponders its effect, thinking at first how close he had come "to being lost and going to hell." He then recalls their trip down the river and how Jim had become such a considerate friend. "I couldn't seem to strike no places to harden me against him," he thinks, realizing now that the choice will come down to whomever he likes better — Miss Watson or her slave Jim. "It was a close place." He takes up the letter and tears it up: "All right, then, I'll *go* to hell."

Huck was based on a boy like Sam who had grown up thinking slavery morally right. "In my schoolboy days I had no aversion to slavery," he wrote in his autobiography. "I was not aware that there was anything wrong about it. No one arraigned it in my hearing; the local papers said nothing against it; the local pulpit taught us that God approved it, that it was a holy thing, and that the doubter need only look in the Bible if he wished to settle his mind."[17] This statement is probably true about

Sam Clemens when he was thirteen or fourteen, the approximate age of his protagonist. Yet young Sam could not have long stayed ignorant of the efforts to free slaves in the border state of Missouri. For just across the river, in Quincy, Illinois, lay one of the hotbeds of abolitionism. His own brother Orion, ten years his senior, voted for Lincoln, while Sam voted for John Bell of Tennessee, whose party platform opposed secession but called for a compromise on slavery.[18] Orion was doubtless influenced by Lincoln's popularity in St. Louis with its majority of German immigrants, where Sam's brother had worked as a printer for several years.

Twenty-four years after that crucial presidential election Sam Clemens stood in front of Northern audiences as Mark Twain and recited the dramatic story of Huckleberry Finn's "conversion." He was addressing Americans who had also been "converted" in the sense that they all apparently now agreed that slavery had been wrong. The freedmen's social equality with whites remained a question for the twentieth century. Sam Clemens had traveled a long way to get even this far. He first went out west with his brother in 1861, Orion having been rewarded with a political post in Nevada Territory as the result of his campaigning for Lincoln. Sam had hoped to strike it rich in either silver or gold, but found his fortune and his nom de guerre in newspaper work. He had briefly served in the Confederate army (actually a state militia commanded by a governor who would have chosen secession), but sat out most of the war in the Territory. By the time it was over, he had become a successful humorist ready for a wider exposure on the East Coast. It was at a time when America needed to laugh again. His reformation was complete when he married the daughter of a lumber and coal baron from Elmira who had befriended Frederick Douglass and contributed money to the abolitionist movement, including the Underground Railroad.

After doing his show with Cable in Chickering Hall in New York City in late November, Twain called on General Grant and his family, who resided on the city's east side, not far from the newly constructed Central Park. He told his daughter Susy of seeing all the "swords & medals" that the ex-president and commanding general had collected on his triumphant tour around the globe in 1877–79.[19] It was with this visit that Twain began the successful campaign to persuade the nearly bankrupt general and ex-president to publish his memoirs with Charles L. Webster & Company.

Grant was then in deep financial trouble as a result of his unfortunate partnership with Ferdinand Ward, the "young Napoleon of finance" who had since fled the country to avoid prosecution for schemes in which he pledged the same security for several different bank loans. Moreover, the former president was also beginning a losing battle with cancer of the throat. As he was already committed to writing four essays on the subject of the war for *Century* magazine, such a memoir was essentially under way. This was fortunate because of the general's failing health, but Grant — as his war record amply showed — always worked better under pressure; indeed, the more threatening and deadly it was, the more earnestly and successfully this soldier answered the call to duty. The other incentive was the threat of his family's future indebtedness once he was gone. Clemens was confident that a memoir by Grant would break sales records and so offered him an unprecedented contract that far outbid the magazine's offer of 10 percent royalties to publish the memoir. He would publish the book the same way he was planning to issue his own book — by subscription.

Sam Clemens, the soldier who had "skedaddled" after two weeks in the Civil War, had come to worship its hero Grant. Unlike Robert E. Lee, who personified the "gentleman" in war, Grant had been one of the "roughs." Growing up in Illinois, across the Mississippi River from Clemens, he had stumbled upon his fame much in the way Mark Twain had. It took Twain a little longer to become a folk hero, but by the time of the astounding success of *The Innocents Abroad* with its hilarious irreverence for all things European, he had attained almost the same level of fame as the general. They were America's vernacular heroes — one the quiet warrior; the other the sly quipster.

It was around the time of his negotiations with the ailing Grant that he had decided to include Gerhardt's militaristic bust of himself in the frontispiece of his own book. In the spirit of the general it would be *his* military campaign — an assault against literature as the province of the silver-tongued English, reproduced largely by American writers who wrote in effect like displaced Englishmen. He could write like them. He had proved that in *The Prince and the Pauper,* which had made his own family prouder of him than they had been when he had written irreverent travel books or "children's literature" like *The Adventures of Tom Sawyer.* He didn't want to be remembered as merely a humorist or a travel writer or the author of literature for young people. Something nagged at him to write from the heart, to forget the critics, and that spirit of revolt would finally find its expression in *Adventures of Huckleberry Finn.*

By the beginning of 1884, there had already been much anticipation for this "sequel." In fact, it was announced in the *Dial* in February that the title of the new book would be "Huckleberry Finn, A Sequel to Tom Sawyer."[20] The world expected a continuation of the fairy tale in *Tom Sawyer.* That story takes place almost entirely in boyland, only once indicating that Tom and Huck's childhood sanctuary was also the sanctuary of slave-holders. There are no abolitionists from across the Mississippi threatening their way of life. There are merely grave robbers and a half-breed who dies for his misdeeds. In that book, Twain wasn't even following his ironic paradigm of the good boy and the bad boy in earlier tales, namely, "The Story of the Good Little Boy Who Did Not Prosper," and "The Story of the Bad Little Boy Who Didn't Come to Grief." Tom Sawyer is essentially a good boy, not as "good" as his brother Sid, of course, but somebody who gets a little better as the story progresses, as he grows into his responsibilities as a middle-class resident of St. Petersburg. This was a fantasy, one that promptly tapped into nineteenth-century America's nostalgic fascination with boyhood. But it wasn't nearly so romantic or far-fetched as the story of Huck, the neglected son of the town drunk who goes against the law of his land and gives assistance to a runaway slave.

Evidently, somebody in the printing office of J. J. Little of New York didn't like the introduction of the "peculiar institution" into a book for children. Like *Tom Sawyer, Huckleberry Finn* would have many illustrations. One of them got defaced during production, and the problem wasn't discovered until 250 copies of the prospectus with the mutilated picture had left Webster & Company for distribution among its book agents. (A prospectus contained sample chapters to interest potential buyers of the subscription book.) To this day, we don't know the name of the culprit, but news of his handiwork was soon recounted in a number of major newspapers. "Mark Twain in a Dilemma," announced the *New York World* of November 27, a story that was reprinted three days later in the *Chicago Tribune*. The effaced illustration was a picture of Uncle Silas and Aunt Sally greeting Huck (who they think is Tom) at the Phelps farm. Its caption reads: "Who do you reckon 't is?" This is said by Aunt Sally, who smiles somewhat coyly as she asks the question of her husband. Thanks to a saboteur, Uncle Silas is standing swaybacked with an erect penis protruding through his trousers. Huck is in front looking at the couple with his back to the picture and his right hand on his hip.

While the news of the alteration got out, apparently no details — certainly none suggesting the vulgarity of the defacement — were reported. Rather than stop the canvas for the book, the page of every prospectus with the offending illustration was torn out and discarded. Under the threat of immediate dismissal from the Webster Company, evidently every last book agent with an affected copy followed Charley Webster's instructions. Today only one copy of it remains — in the University of Virginia archives and on its archival website.[21] Indeed, the erroneous description of the illustration in the *World* speaks to the thoroughness of the rescue of Mark Twain's greatest book and his reputation. The reporter obviously never actually saw a copy of the altered illustration, for he described a scene in which Uncle Silas appeared as "a man with downcast head, standing in the foreground of a particularly striking illustration. In front of him was a ragged urchin with a look of dismay. . . . In the background, and standing behind the boy, was an attractive-looking young girl, whose face was enlivened with a broad grin. Something which the boy or man had said or done evidently amused her highly. The title of the cut was, 'In a Dilemma; What Shall I Do?'"

There is no such illustration or caption in *Huckleberry Finn*. In the effaced one, Huck is in fact in something of a dilemma. He has come to the Phelps farm in search of Jim, who has been sold by the two river frauds and is now incarcerated on the farm until his owner can be located. In the original caption, Aunt Sally asks Phelps to guess who he thinks the boy is, and Huck goes along with the answer, which is Tom Sawyer, who has been expected by them. The reporter was clearly working with *some* of the facts of the case, but not all of them. Most likely, he was basing his report on the censored story of the alteration that Webster had given out to the press.

* * *

It was crucial that the whole business be kept as quiet as possible. The *Century* had agreed to publish three excerpts from *Huckleberry Finn* before its official American publication in February. The first one appeared in the December 1884 issue. It focused on the Grangerford family and their feud with the Shepherdsons. Shortly before his return to the river in 1882, when he visited New Orleans and Hannibal, Twain had made a note to remember to stop at New Madrid and ask about the famous Darnell-Watson feud. A microcosm of the Civil War, their feud was based mainly on Southern pride swaddled in the romantic ideology of the Gentleman and the Christian. "They used to attend church on the line (part of church in Tenn. part in Ky.) Both Darnell & Watson went to that church armed with shot guns, & neither party would allow the other to cross the line in that church."[22] The Grangerfords and the Shepherdsons also attend church together and shoot at each other on sight afterward. In fact, young Buck Grangerford, Huck's age in the episode, is shot in the back in the same fashion as a twelve-year-old Watson boy. Both the factual and fictional feuds were like Tom Sawyer adventures that turned deadly.

What began as a boy's book, a sequel to a story that practically ignored "adult issues" like slavery and civil war, became after its initial chapters linking it to *Tom Sawyer* a picaresque novel. This narrative platform allowed Mark Twain to satirize and criticize his society while the runaway slave and his teenaged narrator float down the Mississippi. Twain included in the Grangerford episode a caricature of the poet, or what he had termed the "poet-lariate" in *The Innocents Abroad*. The late Emmeline Grangerford wrote graveyard verse. "Every time a man died, or a woman died, or a child died, she would be on hand with her 'tribute' before he was cold," went the first installment in the December *Century*. "The neighbors said it was the doctor first, then Emmeline, then the undertaker. The undertaker never got in ahead of Emmeline but once, and then she hung fire on a rhyme for the dead person." In the novel proper, we are given an example of her outright doggerel in "Ode to Stephen Dowling Bots, Dec'd."

> And did young Stephen sicken
> And did young Stephen die?
> And did the sad hearts thicken,
> And did the mourners cry?
>
> No; such was not the fate of
> Young Stephen Dowling Bots;
> Though sad hearts round him thickened,
> 'Twas not from sickness' shots.
> . . . .
> O no. Then list with tearful eye,
> Whilst I his fate do tell.
> His soul did from this cold world fly,
> By falling down a well.

> They got him out and emptied him;
>> Alas it was too late;
> His spirit was gone for to sport aloft
>> In the realms of the good and great.

In the *Century* excerpt, this ingenious example of the doggerel of the day was quietly omitted. Perhaps it too closely resembled the kind of "serious" poetry published in magazines at that time. In fact, we find an example of it in the work of its editor, Richard Watson Gilder. Following the second excerpt from *Huckleberry Finn* in the February 1885 issue, "Jim's Investments, and King Sollermun," Gilder included a sample of his own work, a poem entitled "An Autumn Meditation." It too was of the graveyard genre.

Gilder fancied that there was a parallel between nature and human events, that nature reflected the solemnity of human life and death. It was an idea that Stephen Crane would mock in *The Red Badge of Courage* (1895). As bedraggled troops march away from the field of battle, that same nature ignores human suffering as "a golden ray of sun" shines through heavy rain clouds. In "An Autumn Meditation," the best time to die is evidently in the fall:

> Let me, too, die when Autumn holds the year, —
> Serene, with tender hues and bracing airs, —
> And near me those I love; with no black thoughts
> Nor dread of what may come.

When it comes time for Stephen Dowling Bots to die, his body is treated like a carcass simply to be retrieved and drained of the well water. When Gilder goes, though, he'll do it in "the cool rush" of "northern winds" and "sunset skies."

Then shall I fade
From life to life; pass, on the year's full tide,
Into the swell and vast of life's great sea
Beyond this narrow world.

Twain wasn't simply making fun of bad poetry, he was undercutting its pre-Darwinian philosophy of "life to life." *Adventures of Huckleberry Finn* was a subversive book for its day, an ideological torpedo aimed at the heart of Victorian values. The author himself hardly realized this fact as he extended his Tom Sawyer tale into the sequel that became a classic.

If anybody at the time, Gilder, for example, or even the former editor of the *Atlantic Monthly,* Clemens's friend Howells, had taken this book seriously, had entertained the wild idea that it was more than either a boy's book or perhaps the best of American humor, a genre looked down on by most of the Anglo-American literary establishment, it probably would have never been excerpted in the staid *Century.* Samuel Langhorne Clemens was hiding more than his real name behind "Mark Twain."

The first two chapters of Howells's *The Rise of Silas Lapham* appeared in the November issue of *Century,* just a month before the Grangerford episode from the forthcoming *Adventures of Huckleberry Finn.* In selecting his leading character's last name, Howells suggested that Silas was laughable in his attempts to become a member of Boston's social elite. The nouveau riche businessman is indeed ignorant of the cultural niceties, but this unsophisticated fool is also stubbornly honest.

The Rise of Silas Lapham became the first important novel about the ethics of the American businessman. Before the Civil War this individual, whose primary goal was to make money, had limited his investments generally to the amount of personal capital, but by the 1880s it was becoming clearer that his assets were readily mortgaged to the point of indebtedness that threatened to weaken his moral resolve. Howells may have had his friend Clemens in the back of his mind as he wrote his novel. For Mark Twain, now a trademark as much as a nom de guerre, was fast becoming a businessman with the Webster publishing company, and he was already losing money in other investments, including the Paige Typesetter.

Ever since the days of the California gold rush of 1849, Sam Clemens, who at thirteen saw so many leave Hannibal for the mines, had wanted to become rich. Already rich in 1885, he wanted to become richer, much richer. He made daily calculations in his notebooks as to how many newspapers around the world would have to pay him to use his typesetter (when it was finally perfected, which it never was) and how much they would have to pay him. He would have been the richest of the robber barons. Whereas Clemens was clearly a better artist than businessman, Howells's fictional extension of him was no better in society. The first five chapters of *The Rise of Silas Lapham* were excerpted in the 1884 issues of the *Century*. The society dinner scene, where Silas gets drunk and embarrasses himself and his family, would appear in the April 1885 issue. The following day Silas humbly apologizes to the son of his hosts, a young man who he hopes will marry one of Silas's two daughters.

Eight years earlier, at another dinner party in Boston, Mark Twain had embarrassed himself in the eyes of Howells and others when he entertained the diners at the *Atlantic Monthly* banquet in honor of John Greenleaf Whittier. He told a story of three drunken miners in Nevada who had misrepresented themselves as Ralph Waldo Emerson, Henry Wadsworth Longfellow, and Oliver Wendell Holmes. Not only were these New

England sages held in the highest esteem, but they were also guests at the dinner that evening. Known then mainly as the Wild Humorist of the Pacific Slope, Mark Twain had allegedly dishonored them to their faces. Actually, the speech had been received in its proper spirit of humor on the evening of its delivery, but Howells and Clemens, in the words of one who studied the entire incident in detail, "had churned themselves into a state of mind which bore little relation to external reality," and the press followed suit.[23] At Howells's suggestion, Clemens wrote letters of apology to Emerson, Longfellow, and Holmes.

Like Clemens, whose flamboyant house in Hartford was thought by some to be gaudy, the fictional Silas Lapham and his wife had dubious taste in architecture. "Lapham," Howells wrote in chapter two of his novel, "had not yet reached the picture buying stage of the rich man's development, but they decorated their house with the costliest and most abominable frescoes." There are other parallels between Silas Lapham and Samuel Langhorne Clemens, besides their sharing two initials. Both married women socially above them. Both lost a male child. Both were nouveau riche businessmen who invested recklessly in stocks. In chapter 7 of the novel, Howells even has one of his characters quote a line from Twain's famous sketch, "Jim Smiley and His Jumping Frog." And later on, the family attends a performance of *Colonel Sellers,* adapted from *The Gilded Age.* Twain thought that he saw himself reflected in Bartley Hubbard of Howells's *A Modern Instance* (1882), a character who also appears in the first chapter of *The Rise of Silas Lapham.* "You didn't intend Bartley for me," he told Howells in a letter of July 24, 1882, "but he *is* me. . . . Mrs. Clemens indignantly says he doesn't resemble me."[24] That was because Bartley is a cad, and Clemens was, as far as we know, a faithful husband, but the parallel between Silas Lapham and himself may have been too acute for the same kind of casual observation. We know that Howells and Clemens were best friends and loved each other, but professionally Howells probably considered Mark Twain a humorist more than anything else, not on the same aesthetic level as his other close friend, Henry James.

Howells's descriptive use of period detail in *The Rise of Silas Lapham* brings us as close to day-to-day American life in the 1870s as anything in John Updike's profile of a businessman a hundred years later in *Rabbit Is Rich* (1981). Silas's thoroughbred trotting horse and sleek cutter find their equivalent in Rabbit Angstrom's "1978 Luxury Edition liftback five-door Corona." Both men have become rich by accident in America, where such things are possible. Silas is a successful merchant who advertises his "mineral paint" on natural landscapes, turning beautiful boulders into billboards. "I never saw anything so very sacred about a big rock, along a river or in a pasture, that it wouldn't do to put mineral paint on it in three colors," he tells a newspaper reporter doing a story on him for the "Solid Men of Boston" series. "I say the landscape was made for man, and not man for the landscape." Unfortunately, neither is the polite society of Boston made for this self-made man whose presence there is compared to mineral paint smeared on the delicate art of nature. Combining the social drama of Henry James and the domestic intrigue of Jane Austen, Howells reached the pinnacle of his literary achievement in this story of the time. In doing so, he was the first to introduce into American literature the businessman who, though braggart and bore he might be, still manages to remain above the criminal temptations of the robber barons and their minions. Like Huckleberry Finn, Silas Lapham is the ideal of the incorruptible American — crude, ill-mannered at times, but somebody who refuses to undercut his sense of honesty in order to survive. Howells's novel expresses the hope of the social Darwinists in the 1880s that "natural selection" doesn't always trump human virtue.

* * *

December 1884 found Sam Clemens still away from home, in only the second of the four-month tour with Cable. "Be piously grateful that as yet you are permitted to remain with your household & under the shelter of your delightful home; & do all your praying now," he told the cartoonist Thomas Nast from Syracuse, "for a time is coming when you will have to go railroading & platforming, & then you will find you cannot pray any more because you will have only just time to swear enough." "Been railroading since 4 o'clock this morning," he told Livy when he arrived in Rochester on December 6. Two days later he was jokingly approached in Toronto by "a most gentle-faced attractive girl in black [who] kept looking back as if she were trying to muster pluck enough to speak to me." Finally, she came up to him and "said with a little tremor of fright in her voice, 'Don't you remember me, Mr. Clemens?'" One of the pieces he had just recited at the Toronto performance had come from chapter 25 of *A Tramp Abroad,* where the narrator and his companion bet each other as to the age of an attractive young woman they encounter in a resort in Lucerne. On the pretense of thinking that he has mistaken her for someone back home, the narrator plans to ask the question. But before he can proceed, the young woman, persuaded that they know each other, puts him on the defensive with a battery of questions about folks they should know in common. The narrator finds himself up a stump when the young woman keeps referring to "Darley," who the puzzled narrator guesses "must be some kind of animal, — possibly a dog, maybe an elephant."[25]

The punch line reveals that Darley is a "negro."

Because of the delay in publication due to the mutilated illustration in *Huckleberry Finn,* Mark Twain was reading aloud from a book that had otherwise not yet been published in America. He was doubly outraged, therefore, when he discovered just two days before Christmas that a Boston bookseller was not only advertising *Adventures of Huckleberry Finn* for sale but also offering it at a reduced price. Twain suspected that Estes & Lauriat, the offending bookseller, had no copies to sell and was simply trying to advertise its store. "These vermin [crossed out for "people"] deliberately lied when they made that statement," he told Charley Webster. Estes & Lauriat would become the next candidate for one of the many lawsuits Mark Twain was forced to initiate during his career in order to protect his valuable reputation and copyrights. Of special interest to us today is the way that the bookstore advertised the book. What became a classic for its subversive plot line about a boy and a black slave was described here as "a mine of humor" — the "most humorous book" that "the prince of American humorists" had ever written.[26]

Humor, of course, was Mark Twain's bread and butter. Although in his most lucid considerations of his oeuvre he considered *Huckleberry Finn* his best book, he would never know exactly why. Some at the time called it Huck's autobiography, but in a way it was Sam Clemens's autobiography. Just as Huck lounges through life, Mark Twain lounged on the speaker's platform, now converted for the first time from a rostrum for didactic lectures to a venue for what the *Brooklyn Daily Eagle* called "a new form of popular entertainment," in which the "elocutionary art supplements the printer's." As the tour moved from Detroit to Cleveland on the seventeenth, he noted in his journal that he had not "railroaded any" for fifteen years, ever since his second lecture tour in 1872–73. Usually, such trips took up most of the day. Ever the humorist absorbing material, he noticed a newly married couple across from him on the train. "This morning," he noted, "the usual new bride got aboard the train, & she began as usual her furtive love-pattings & pawings and pettings of her lovey-dove." She had finally said yes after the usual term of courtship and become the man's wife. He noted, however, that the real courting began with the wife *after* the wedding, and that the groom must have wondered "how he could ever have thought *he* knew anything about courting." At last the bride fell asleep with her head on her new husband's shoulder, secure in the thought that only death would do them part. Nothing had changed in such a scene, he thought, until the young beauty began to snore. The funnier part, as this true comedian sensed, was not the snoring but the female courting. The snoring was simply evidence that her sleep "was honest, & not gotten up for effect, as those former sleeps were."[27]

As Christmas approached, Sam Clemens was eager to get home to his wife and three daughters. The tour recessed for nine days beginning on December 19. Not long after he arrived in Hartford, the family had a surprise for him. Livy had adapted *The Prince and the Pauper* into a play in which the children and their playmates in the Nook Farm community took part. Gerhardt pitched in with the theater curtain and helped construct the stage scenery. Sam suspected something, since certain rooms in their spacious home were off limits to him. They had been used to prepare the stage sets, but the performance itself took place in George Warner's home across the way. At the time of the performance, possibly on Christmas Eve, Sam was led across the grounds to the Warner house and given a seat right in front of the stage. His eldest daughter, Susy, played the Prince, and Clara, two years younger at age eleven, the part of Jane Grey. The play became a family tradition, and eventually the author himself played the part of Miles Hendon, who helps the outcast prince regain his kingdom.[28]

That Yuletide holiday may have been the acme of Sam Clemens's happiest days since his boyhood in Hannibal. This stretch of good luck ran from the late sixties, when he met Olivia and published his first travel book, and the early seventies, when his growing family first moved to Hartford, to the early 1890s, when he and his wife and daughters took refuge in Europe from the financial recession that darkened that decade in America. Home in Hartford meant family and friends, all of whom were also at their own personal pinnacles that holiday season. It was doubtless hard to leave home again on December 28, when Clemens took the train to Pittsburgh to rejoin Cable for an appearance the following day. The temperature had risen from below freezing to forty-two degrees in the grimy city, turning the snow into slush in a place where it was often dark at noon because of the pollution from the blast furnaces of Andrew Carnegie's steel mills. Soot darkened most of the city's buildings and church steeples. The only light came from the melting snow that still covered the city at the triangle where the Allegheny and Monongahela Rivers conjoined to form the Ohio, a stream that ultimately emptied into the mighty Mississippi River.

Its recent chronicler was about to publish a more famous history of that river, one that would immortalize both its narrator and his creator. Mark Twain apparently had no idea of its literary greatness. The *Pittsburgh Dispatch* of December 30 reported that he read from the part of the novel that is considered farcical today and out of sync with the great drama of an underclass boy and a runaway slave. "All modern American literature comes from one book by Mark Twain called 'Huckleberry Finn,'" Ernest Hemingway wrote in *The Green Hills of Africa* in 1934. "If you read it you must stop where the Nigger Jim is stolen from the boys. That is the real end. The rest is just cheating."

><><

TWO

Skirting the
Mason-Dixon

><><

The Clemens-Cable tour was in effect an advance publicity
campaign for the *Adventures of Huckleberry Finn*. Twain ultimately introduced into his repertoire as many as fifteen passages
from the forthcoming novel in the winter of 1885. One of them
had already been published in the *Century,* and another ("Jim's
Investments, and King Sollermun") appeared in the January
Century. "Well, mamma, dear," he wrote Livy on December 29,
following their appearance in Pittsburgh. "To-night I read the
new piece, . . . & it's the biggest card I've got." The "King Sollermun" excerpt found its humor in the ignorance of the black
man. It was the era in which some reformers were convinced
that blacks could be taught to read only if words were spelled
as they were colloquially pronounced (e.g., "bin" for "been").[1]
Huck tells the fugitive slave Jim about royalty, but the only king
Jim has ever heard about is the biblical king Solomon, and he
fails to understand the irony of dividing the child between two
disputing parties. "I never see such a nigger," Huck exclaims.

"Whenever we strike a Southern audience they laugh them-
selves all to pieces," he told his wife on New Year's Day from
Kentucky.[2] More than twenty years after the Emancipation
Proclamation, the idea of a free Negro was gaining ground,

enough in the North at least for a lynching in the South to make national news. The *New York Times* of January 1 carried "A Negro's Strange Story." It emanated from "a trustworthy negro" in North Carolina who had barely escaped being hanged, while his companion was hacked "nearly to pieces" before being strung up. As was usually the case, the victims were accused of raping a white woman. The survivor pleaded his innocence and was spared the hangman's noose; instead he was simply tied up and thrown in the river. He miraculously escaped drowning. Even though lynching was considered a crime then, the white majority quietly tolerated it: no one was ever tried and convicted for the act throughout the nineteenth century.

Slavery had ended, but the prejudice against blacks persisted. The "nigger Jim" of *Huckleberry Finn* became "Nigger Jim" in newspaper reports of Twain's readings from his masterpiece, just as Harriet Beecher Stowe's "Uncle Tom" was turned into a racial stereotype in the popular dramatization of *Uncle Tom's Cabin*. Cable and Twain, both Southerners, never dared to take their tour below the Mason-Dixon Line. As they fringed the postwar South in Kentucky, which like Sam's native state of Missouri remained in the Union during the war, blacks in Mississippi strove to hold a state convention to confront the problem of the Jim Crow South: "We the undersigned, members of the colored race, and citizens of the State of Mississippi, after mature deliberation upon the discouraging circumstances surrounding our race, in this State and the South generally, . . . do hereby unite for a general mass convention to convene in the city of Jackson on the ___ day of January, 1885."[3]

On the nine-hour train ride between Indianapolis and Springfield, Illinois, a few days later, a run that stopped every "half a mile" to pick up and discharge locals, Sam described to his wife a small country boy who "discussed a negro woman in her easy hearingdistance, to his 17-year old sister: 'Mighty good clothes for a nigger, *hain't* they? *I* never see a nigger dressed so fine before.'" Twain agreed that the black woman was indeed "thoroughly well & tastefully dressed." He added that she "had more brains & breeding than 7 generations of that boy's family."[4]

Actual slavery was being replaced then with the rewards of the "colonization craze." The Europeans were the most active, but the United States would be involved in its own colonization efforts, beginning with the Spanish-American War of 1898, something Mark Twain supported before it led to the country's occupation of the Philippines and years of fighting insurgents there. The excuse for such expansionism may have been the "White Man's Burden" in Europe, which was merely shorthand for providing colonies for its growing population. In America it would be the freeing of Filipinos from Spain, a ruse to conceal the fact that its expanding naval forces required this important fueling station in the Pacific.

The year that *Huckleberry Finn* finally appeared on its home turf featured business failures and strikes by underpaid workers, mostly immigrants from southern Europe. Andrew Carnegie, who would relentlessly reduce the wages of his employees in the steel industry, proclaimed at the beginning of 1885 that he was a socialist. "Still," a reporter asked in a story entitled "A Million-aire Socialist" in the *New York Times* of January 2, 1885, "you have closed down the Edgar Thomson Works [in Pittsburgh], and some people will wonder how you can hold such principles and throw your employees into idleness." "The workmen are to blame for that," Carnegie responded, because "they allow other Bessemer mills to work at less wages than we pay." Carnegie added that his company could not afford to "make and sell steel rails at $27 a ton" and thus had to close rather than sell rails "at less than cost." Carnegie ultimately gave away most of his money, but not before he stamped his name on local libraries around the country and otherwise enjoyed his wealth and fame.

The country was in perpetual upheaval, it seemed. Camden, New Jersey, brought in the New Year with drunken orgies at Bridge Avenue and Mickle Street, not far from the Delaware River and the working-class neighborhood where Walt Whitman lived in a row house. On Long Island, the police arrested tramps by the hundreds. Those able-bodied among them were put to work at the Kings County penitentiary. Nobody felt sorry for them, including Mark Twain, who had turned away in anger homeless people who came right up to the front door of his Hartford mansion asking for a handout. The hero of the Civil War, General Grant, was dying of cancer; bulletins of his steady demise would continue until summer. The Reverend Henry Beecher, America's most famous minister (despite an earlier scandal involving a female parishioner), was said to be in low spirits, somewhat exhausted perhaps in trying to explain away the conclusions of Mr. Darwin's "theory." Wages around the country were plunging — at the Roxbury Carpet Company near Boston, at the woolen factory in Chester, Pennsylvania, at the Elastic Fabric Mill in Springfield, Massachusetts, and at Carnegie's Homestead Steel Works in Pittsburgh, where the self-described socialist had reduced wages by as much as 10 percent. In Chicago, the socialists were blamed for unrest that would lead in the next year to what became known as the Haymarket Riots.

Back in Boston on January 14, the United States Circuit Court heard the suit that Clemens had filed against Estes & Lauriat. The Boston bookstore was advertising his new book at a price

$0.50 lower than Webster & Company's subscription price of $2.75. "Such an advertisement," he told the sellers back on January 7, "necessarily works me injury. It put a prohibitory obstruction in the path of my canvassers." He had asked for an injunction against the booksellers, but the judge denied the request on February 10, saying that the booksellers had in no way interfered with the jobs of the book agents for Webster & Company.[5] Mark Twain was a businessman as well as a writer, or at least he thought he was a businessman. His quarrels with Charley Webster, the namesake of Charles L. Webster & Company, demonstrate his general ineptitude for business. Half the time neither one of them knew what was going on, leading at one point to an embezzlement of $25,000 by their bookkeeper.

The writer in him, however, always knew the way. Occasionally he would critique stories sent to him by amateur writers. While still on the lecture circuit with Cable, he wrote to a Mrs. Whiteside that her story wasn't a story but "a moral essay." Telling her not to be shocked at his bluntness, he wrote that literature was "an *art,* not an inspiration." It wasn't something that could be picked up, but was to be learned, if at all possible, over a number of years. In anticipation of the way in which he would make fun of James Fenimore Cooper ten years later, he told Mrs. Whiteside: "When *you* shall have served on the stage a while (if you ever should), you will not send another heroine, unacquainted with the histrionic art, to ask a manager for a 'star' part & *succeed* in her errand. And after you yourself shall have tried to descend a rain-water pipe, once, unencumbered, you will always know better, after that, than to let your hero descend one, with a woman in his arms."[6]

* * *

Twain appears in this letter to the unfortunate Mrs. Whiteside to resist the notion of the *born* writer. He himself had been writing since he was a teenager. He had learned to write, indeed had become a budding humorist, while working on his brother Orion's newspaper in Hannibal. Now he was the leading humorist in America.

But to succeed the humorist had to know human nature at its core, and Sam Clemens knew it long before he became Mark Twain. He even knew it before learning the river as a steamboat pilot. In chapter 18 of *Life on the Mississippi* (1883), he had written: "When I find a well-drawn character in fiction or biography I generally take a warm personal interest in him, for the reason that I have known him before — met him on the river." It was on the river as well as off it in the town of Hannibal that Sam as a young man first grasped human nature. Before satirizing the "damned human race" as Mark Twain, Sam Clemens had done it as W. Epaminondas Adrastus Perkins, his first pseudonym.

That was in 1852. Now it was 1885, and his finest depiction of the human comedy was about to be issued on American side of the Atlantic. It would take another generation or two before *Huckleberry Finn* came to be regarded as a classic, but a very few critics — such as Brander Matthews in the London *Saturday Review* of January 31 — immediately noted a "higher level" than that of the popular story it had succeeded, *The Adventures of Tom Sawyer*. Besides Howells's *Silas Lapham* and Grant's *Memoirs,* other notable books published in the year of the American edition of *Huckleberry Finn* included Helen Hunt Jackson's popular *Ramona*. Henry James's *The Bostonians* was being serialized in the *Century* that year, and James also brought out *The Literary Remains* of his father, a friend of Emerson's. To many, *The Literary Remains* of the senior Henry

James was dead on arrival, but Sam, as he told Livy on February 3, also found the junior Henry James's novel *The Bostonians* "unspeakably dreary."[7] A more famous book, written with the optimism of the transcendentalist, was Josiah Royce's *Religious Aspects of Philosophy*. S. Weir Mitchell, today best remembered for encouraging "meddlesome gynecology," published the second edition of *Lectures on the Diseases of the Nervous System, Especially in Women*. There were other notable appearances: Sara Orne Jewett's *A Country Doctor*, which along with *The White Heron* (then in serialization) ushered in the local color movement in America; Theodore Roosevelt's *Hunting Trips of a Ranchman*; Henry M. Stanley's influential *The Congo and the Founding of Its Free State*; Robert Louis Stevenson's *Treasure Island*; Charles Dudley Warner's *My Summer in a Garden*; and Émile Zola's *Germinal*.

Mark Twain had not been on tour since the early 1870s, when he had also despised the long train rides, the invasion of privacy, and the notoriously uncomfortable American hotels. It's not clear why he went out again, even in the company of Cable, whom he much admired in spite of his religious nature (Cable refused to travel on Sundays). Following their performance at the Central Music Hall in Chicago on January 16, the *Chicago Tribune* described "a wide diversity in the manners, methods, and styles of the two men, but a contrast only brings out in stronger relief the merits of both." Mark Twain, the reporter continued, "is funny in every movement, word, and it may be truly said, thought." Cable's humor was of a "deeper quality . . . quiet in demeanor . . . and always dignified, except when delineating some ridiculous character."[8]

Ultimately, Twain stole the show, often with antics that were spontaneous and completely unrehearsed. One evening he accidentally answered an encore for his partner. As Cable told his wife, Twain "was equal to the emergency. He stood still a moment, then said in the drollest way imaginable — 'I'll go back and get him.' . . . Of course I would not go, so he went back and raised another laugh, saying, 'He's sung all he knows' — and went on with 'The Jumping Frog,' which is getting a superb reception."[9] When it was time for his own encore, the *Tribune* report continued, Twain "unwittingly created a great deal of merriment by failing to find the proper exit. . . . He crossed the stage twice, tried every door, and was amazed at the great number of wrong doors he could find." Such a show of befuddlement perhaps went well with his reading that evening, which according to the newspaper came almost exclusively from *The Innocents Abroad.* He did, however, read one excerpt from "the advance sheets" of *Huckleberry Finn.* Like the later Charlie Chaplin, Mark Twain clowned his way to greatness. Huck's story, his autobiography, held a lot of laughs to both obscure and emphasize its pathos.

The audience that night had braved severe snowstorms to see the performance. Chicagoans no doubt welcomed the diversion. Two days later the city's socialists "met and delivered their usual weekly denunciation of the capitalists. . . . One speaker characterized the right of private property as a cancer in the body of mankind. It must be cut out, and dynamite was the instrument to do it with. The Patent Office was denounced as a robber, and sentiments making consumption as free as production and taking the price off necessaries of life were expressed." Other trade organizations denounced the socialist movement, and the newspapers continued to enflame the public as to the dangers of such foreigners.[10]

Word of Zola's *Germinal* in the American magazines was possibly helping to put the middle class in America a little more on edge. (Its first English translation would not become available until 1888.) Its plot focuses on coal miners in northern France. The "germ" or agent of rebirth in the novel was socialism, a doctrine that was already leading to strikes in the United States and abroad. With the robber barons' ostentatious lifestyles, more and more people making only starvation wages looked to violence as a way of redressing the inequity. Assassination societies allegedly existed for the secret murder of political opponents. "Dynamite as a Weapon" read the headline in the *New York Times* for February 2. "Trouble Among the Miners," said the headline two days later, "Reductions Causing Great Discontent in Ohio." In Lowell, Massachusetts, nearly 500 workers at a factory went on strike in the face of a 10 percent reduction in their wages.[11] Labor unrest was also reported in Pennsylvania. "The Striking Weavers in Philadelphia Cause Trouble," read the *New York Times* headline on February 28. The xenophobic press was steadfastly opposed to the cause of labor. "Socialists in Pittsburg," was the headline in the March 10 *New York Times,* "A Nest of Useless People That Ought to Be Broken Up." By 1885 German immigrants had replaced the Irish as the most despised ethnic minority because of their reputation for socialism and anarchy.

In *Germinal* Zola spoke of Charles Darwin as "that apostle of scientific inequality." His theory was good only, he said, for "aristocratic philosophers" — such as the American realists, who were also grappling with the horrid but irrepressible idea of evolution, still trying to demonstrate in their novels that not *everybody* was ruled utterly by heredity and environment. Howells's Silas evidently wasn't. Twain's Huck wasn't either. But Zola's pitiful coal miners were, and practically every literary creation of Twain's in the wake of *Huckleberry Finn* would be as well. There would be no "territory" to "light out" to in the case of Hank Morgan in *A Connecticut Yankee in King Arthur's Court* or the victims of "training" in the posthumously published versions of *The Mysterious Stranger.* There were the masters and slaves in every human cycle. All efforts at reform were doomed. "Supposing the old society were no longer to exist, swept away to the crumbs," Zola wrote in *Germinal,* " . . . was it not to be feared that the new world would grow up again, slowly spoilt by the same injustices, some sick and others flourishing, some skillful and intelligent, fattening on everything, and others imbecile and lazy, becoming slaves again."[12]

In February, the *Century* had published the third and final excerpt from *Huckleberry Finn.* The February issue also contained Grant's essay on the Battle of Shiloh (the first of three essays to be published in the magazine as Grant signed his book contract with Webster & Company) and "The Confederate Side" of the story, "told by the son of Gen. Albert Sidney Johnston." The general himself had perished in the 1862 battle. Back home, young Susy was already reading the advance book version of *Adventures of Huckleberry Finn.*[13] Having only read in most cases the excerpts in the *Century,* the critics were already sharpening their knives. The opinions of the "boy's book" would be decidedly mixed.

"Royalty on the Mississippi: As Chronicled by Huckleberry Finn" was how the February installment in the *Century* introduced the chapters on the "Duke" and the "Dauphin," who board Huck and Jim's raft not long after the Grangerford episode and claim to be descended from English and French royalty. Twain was a voracious reader of history, and the Clemens family had entertained the possibility of aristocratic connections on both sides. While lecturing in England in the early 1870s, Twain had paid close attention to the newspaper coverage of the Tichborne affair, a celebrated trial in which the fraudulent claimant to an aristocrat's fortune was sent to the penitentiary for ten years. A cousin of Twain's mother had pestered him over the years to underwrite a genealogical search of the ancestry going back to the Earl of Durham, but the writer made better use of the material in his fiction.

The excerpt wasn't wholly devoted to the American claimants. It opens with the romance of the river itself and the unlikely alliance of a white boy and a black slave on the run. "Sometimes we'd have that whole river all to ourselves, for the longest time. Yonder was the banks and islands, across the water; and maybe a spark, — which was a candle in a cabin window — and sometimes on the water you could see a spark or two — on a raft or a scow, you know; and may be you could hear a fiddle or a song coming over from one of them crafts. It's lovely to live on a raft."

It was the longest of the three excerpts the *Century* published, a goodly chunk of the story, running from the arrival of the river frauds through the Wilks episode in which the Duke and the Dauphin attempt to bilk the daughters of a dead man out of their money and estate. It is after this section that Huck loses Jim to slave catchers and writes his powerful letter about going to hell to Miss Watson. Twain saved that part for the platform.

* * *

By the time of its American publication on February 18, *Adventures of Huckleberry Finn* had already received a wide exposure. Not only had large portions of it been published in the *Century*, but the novel had appeared in England and Canada on December 10 (the reason for the book's official 1884 publication date). As a result, reviewers were more than prepared to issue their judgments as soon as the book came out in the States. The first ones, from the Boston newspapers that had assailed him back in 1877 for his allegedly demeaning remarks about Emerson, Longfellow, and Holmes, were clearly unfriendly. In fact, the *Herald* of February 1 didn't wait for the book to appear, but attacked it in its third *Century* excerpt. "Royalty on the Mississippi," it warned, "is pitched in but one key, and that is the key of a vulgar and abhorrent life." Three weeks later, on February 20, the *Daily Globe* piled on with a nit-picking insult, saying that the book was "supposed to be [written in] a boy's dialect." "On the very second page, "it continued, "this 'low-down,' uneducated urchin is made to say 'commence.'"

In fact, the worst reviews came out of New England, where the author had resided for fifteen years. Only in Hartford did he get good press. The *Courant* published a long review also on February 20, probably written by Twain's former coauthor Charles Dudley Warner. Warner followed Brander Matthews's lead by pronouncing the "sequel" a very distinct literary advance over *Tom Sawyer*. Still adhering to telling a boy's story on the Mississippi River, Mark Twain, the reviewer continued, "has not before presented it to the imagination so distinctly nor so powerfully." A little later, on March 9, the *Hartford Daily Times* chimed in at the same level of enthusiasm, quoting at length from the Judith Loftus episode, where Huck dresses as a girl to obtain information about the slave catchers from a woman whose husband is one of the slave catchers in search of Jim.

But these were the only relief from the bad reviews in Boston. The *Evening Traveller* of March 5 suggested that Twain's lawsuit against Estes & Lauriat had been a publicity stunt. (It may have been; the *San Francisco Bulletin* of March 14 even suggested that the story of the mutilated illustration had also been a sales tactic). The *Traveller* sneeringly suggested that Twain "will probably have to resort to the law to compel some to sell it by any sort of bribery or corruption. It is doubtful if the edition could be disposed of to people of average intellect at anything short of the point of the bayonet." It closed by criticizing the Gerhardt bust as being as tasteless "as the book itself."

The bust *was* crudely done. One has to wonder just why the famous Mark Twain included it in his masterpiece, and why he didn't get an established artist. Was it something to do with his lingering fondness for Hattie Gerhardt? Now twenty-two, she had returned from Paris after her husband. The couple was still living in Hartford in 1884 when the bust was completed. Twain possibly saw her when he visited Gerhardt, perhaps to view his post-Parisian work, which may have included other busts of Hattie. Or she possibly visited his Hartford mansion with her husband.

Regardless, *Huckleberry Finn* was rejected in New England mainly for having bad manners. No mention was made of its antislavery theme. That attention wouldn't fully emerge until the end of the century, at the height of the lynchings. For now it was the faulty grammar and the slovenly habits of a boy who smoked and skipped school. As a true Victorian, and in contrast to Zola, Twain never crossed the line that separated social life from its sexual appetites. Moreover, his depiction of the details of a slave's life in *Huckleberry Finn* is mild when compared to the description in *Germinal* of the pathetic lives of French miners. Zola was so frank in his novels that he was seen as being as disgraceful as Walt Whitman in America. In the age in which even piano legs were covered, the *Nation* in its issue of April 2 excoriated Zola for his sordid details and sexual allusions. "Neither in England nor in France could there be found a community so depraved, so utterly God-forsaken as that of

M. Zola's miners. A picture of wickedness without a single re-deeming feature is not true art; much less is it true to nature." The shocking realities of Stephen Crane and Theodore Dreiser were right around the corner.

* * *

Mark Twain may have been suspected of boosting his sales through the lawsuit against Estes & Lauriat, but as it turned out he didn't have to do anything on his own to help sales. Sometime in March, the trustees of the Concord Public Library banned the book from its collection on the grounds that it was "flip-pant, irreverent, and trashy." The book, the committee implied, was better suited "to the slums than to intelligent, respectable people."[14] When asked why it purchased the book in the first place, the committee responded that it did so on the basis of the "author's reputation," presumably from *The Innocents Abroad* and *Roughing It.* It later added that the library did not collect fiction anyway, but that response came after the library in the hometown of Ralph Waldo Emerson and Henry David Thoreau had already become something of a laughingstock.

In an open letter to the *Boston Daily Advertiser,* which had applauded the banning on March 23, Clemens thanked Frank A. Nichols of the Free Trade Club of Concord for making him an honorary member. "It does look," he wrote on March 28, "as if Massachusetts were in a fair way to embarrass me with kind-nesses this year." He pointed out that the library banning would immensely increase sales not only in Concord, where the book wouldn't be freely available, but also around the country, where other libraries were allegedly following Concord's example. "You are doubtless aware," he pointed out, "that one book in a public library prevents the sale of a sure ten & a possible hundred of its mates. And secondly it will cause the purchasers of the book to read it, out of curiosity, instead of merely intending to do so, after the usual way of the world."

He also ridiculed the judicial decision that denied his injunction against Estes & Lauriat. The judge, he said, "has just decided, in open court, that a Boston publisher may sell not only his own property in a free & unfettered way, but may also as freely sell property which does not belong to him, but to me — property which he has not bought, & which I have not sold. Under this ruling I am now advertising that judge's homestead for sale; & if I make as good a sum out of it as I expect, I shall go on & sell the rest of his property."[15] It was no longer healthy to tangle with Mark Twain. He had held his tongue back in 1877 when the New England establishment had lynched him in the press over the Whittier birthday speech. This time even Howells, who had urged him back then to apologize to Emerson, Longfellow, and Holmes, helped Twain revise his stinging letter that was sent to the *Advertiser* on April 2. It is not known for sure whether the *Advertiser* actually published Twain's letter, but Warner pitched in and published it in the *Courant* on April 4.

By March, Twain had finished his tour with Cable and could pay more attention to business, not only regarding his book but Grant's *Personal Memoirs* that Webster & Company had contracted to publish. In writing it, the country's greatest war hero faced a Herculean task. "Gen. Grant," the *Chicago Daily Tribune* stated on March 8, "is exerting himself to get his War reminiscences written out before death stops his pen." The General had started by dictating, "but his constitutional lack of fluency was aggravated . . . , and it was soon found that the use of his voice, even in a whisper, brought on inflammation and swelling in his diseased throat." Clearly, while the press and the public revered him as a military genius, they had no idea that he could write what would become an American classic. "He has never practiced at composition for publication," the report said, "and it comes awkward." At this juncture the first volume of the *Memoirs* had been completed and edited. The second volume was only halfway done.

The article noted that at least one of the editors of the *Century* was not pleased that Grant had taken his book to Webster & Company. The magazine had assumed that after publishing several articles with it, Grant would naturally publish his "autobiography" with it as well. Mark Twain was correctly named as the reason that Grant's negotiations with the *Century* failed. Twain, the article continued, "has not been so reckless as a humorist as to share the profits of his fun with anybody. He has mastered the subscription book business." Having profited by having his own book excerpted by the *Century,* he now stole away its other big author. The story made it sound as though Grant had chosen a lowly subscription publisher over an established one simply because he needed the money for his surviving family.

And of course it was true. Grant was not only desperately ill, he was also desperately in need of money. But instead of receiving credit for bailing out the Union general and former president, Twain was viewed as manipulative and exploitative. He was depicted in the press for a brief time as someone who would do anything for money, even subject a dying hero to the grueling task of finishing his memoir. At least the *Century* had paid Grant in advance for his war articles. Favoring the *Century* over Mark Twain, the *Tribune* story headlined "Gen. Grant's Book" painted a dreadful picture of the ailing Grant, whose physical decline it said made him unrecognizable "by anybody guided only by his familiar portraits as he sits writing his book."

The robustness of Ulysses S. Grant had vanished: "He has the limp whiteness of a suffering invalid." His face had changed, and his hair and beard had been allowed to grow much longer than he had previously worn them. This to avoid disturbing his painful throat. Moreover, "he has no teeth, the removal of the few that he had rendering the false ones impracticable."[16]

Hence, the opprobrium cast upon *Huckleberry Finn* may have come from sources other than the high moral ground of critics who objected to Huck's "systematic use of bad grammar."[17] Curiously, that editor at the *Century* who had resented Twain's signing of Grant was not in the majority because the magazine not only published excerpts from *Huckleberry Finn* but also invited the humorist to contribute to its "Battles and Leaders of the Civil War" series. His huge success and popularity couldn't be ignored. The invitation, however, would cause Twain some discomfort since as a contributor who had deserted the war after two weeks he would be writing alongside the greatest generals of the conflict. What would it do to his public image?

Well, literary reputations in most cases were fleeting things anyway. Later, Clemens worried that his name recognition would fade shortly after his death, leaving his wife and daughters without enough money. After his death in 1910, his surviving daughter, Clara, and his official biographer, Albert Bigelow Paine, also feared that his sales would diminish. They did all they could to protect his name, suppressing many of his unpublished pieces, particularly those that satirized biblical truth. Susan Warner, the forgotten author of the once phenomenally popular *Wide, Wide World* (1850), died in March 1885, and an astonished press meditated on the literary fate of this author of a novel that had sold half a million copies in its day — far more than *The Scarlet Letter,* published the same year, prompting its author,

Hawthorne, to condemn his competition as that "damned mob of scribbling women." Had he still lived, Hawthorne might have been gladdened to learn not only that he hadn't been forgotten but that in 1885 nineteen out of twenty "reading people" would "be moved to inquire who Miss Susan Warner was that her death should be made the subject of a press dispatch." Warner had never matched the success of the multivolume *Wide, Wide World*, and so, according to the obituary notice in the *New York Times* of March 19, she had faded from public view.

This lack of name recognition may have resulted from the fact that Warner, like Clemens, had written under a pseudonym (Elizabeth Wetherell). But more than that, she had been forgotten, the obituary suggested, because she had written popular or sentimental fiction, "romances" that had nothing to do with real life. Although it rivaled in sales Harriet Beecher Stowe's great novel, *Wide, Wide World* was "purely artistic, so to speak," a mere "picture of life" rather than a literary contribution to the discussion of a "burning question," such as slavery. There was really no "story" in it. This death notice went on to quote "an astonished M. Taine" that it was only in America "that a three-volume novel is devoted to the moral progress of a girl of thirteen." In fact, Susan Warner had developed the new genre of the domestic novel that would be heralded by feminist critics in the next century the way *Huckleberry Finn* was later hailed as an American classic. Yet in 1885, *Wide, Wide World* was remembered only as sentimental ephemera, and *Huckleberry Finn* was pronounced "trashy."

"Trashy and vicious" wrote Samuel Bowles, editor of the *Springfield Republican* and Emily Dickinson's friend. It was high time "that this influential pseudonym should cease to carry into homes and libraries unworthy productions." The trouble with Mark Twain was that even though he was "a genuine and powerful humorist," he lacked "a reliable sense of propriety. His notorious speech at an *Atlantic* dinner, marshalling Longfellow and Emerson and Whittier in vulgar parodies in a Western miner's cabin, illustrated this, but not in much more relief than the 'Adventures of Tom Sawyer' did, or than these Huckleberry Finn stories do." The *Century* excerpts were enough, Bowles said, "to tell any reader how offensive the whole thing must be." They were no better in tone than the "dime novels" that had flooded the market. Mr. Clemens might be smarter than that competition, but his moral level was low, making his books just as harmful.[18]

* * *

And so it went — good and bad reviews. Actually, this kind of attention was somewhat new to Twain, for subscription books ordinarily didn't get reviewed in the big magazines because subscription publishers didn't advertise in their pages. Controversy overcame this problem. Twain may indeed have sued that one bookseller as a PR trick, the way Walt Whitman, another vernacular writer, had emblazoned a quote from Emerson's letter on the spine of *Leaves of Grass*. Twain in fact suspected that Estes & Lauriat didn't *have* any copies of *Huckleberry Finn* to sell at a reduced price. The Webster & Company edition wasn't available until late February, and it is doubtful that the booksellers could have gotten any copies from England. But would Twain have gone so far as to grossly deface one of his illustrations? Not likely.

American publishing wasn't exactly reduced to "Paris Journalism," a practice depicted in the latest novel in Balzac's *Human Comedy*. The *New York Times* of March 22 spoke of its hero, Lucien de Rubempré, "a young provincial poet with a shrinking, sensitive, and pure soul," who rises in the ranks of "boulevard journalists." In order for an author to get from them a favorable review of his book, he had to bribe these critics with free copies of his book, which they sold to scalpers. Or "if a manager would have these newspaper critics praise the new play he produces, he must first put their minds in a favorable attitude by sending to each of them a dozen tickets, and these they sell also." Twain knew that there was more to succeeding as a writer in America than simply writing the books; one had to scheme a little to get them noticed.

That same month one of Fenimore Cooper's three daughters died suddenly in Cooperstown. "Since the death of her father, in 1851, the deceased lady had lived quietly in Cooperstown with her two sisters."[19] Cooper's daughter may have died, but Cooper's reputation surely hadn't. And with its survival came the survival of the status quo in American writing that still reflected British standards. Chingachgook (the last of his tribe in Cooper's Leatherstocking series) may have been the literary precursor of the fugitive Jim, but he spoke better English. "Mark Twain is having a great deal of trouble with his 'Huckleberry Finn,'" the *New Orleans Daily Picayune* of April 11 observed. "He cannot swim in literature with it, and public libraries are rejecting it as trash that is not worth shelf room."

As ever, Mark Twain wielded the weapon of humor. "The Advertiser & the Republican still go for me daily," he told Charley Webster and suggested that they add a new "Prefatory Remark" to *Huckleberry Finn,* setting it "right after the copyright page in all future editions":

Huckleberry Finn is not an imaginary person. He still lives; or rather, *they* still live; for Huckleberry Finn is two persons in one — namely, the author's two uncles, the present editors of the Boston *Advertiser* & the Springfield *Republican*. In character, language, clothing, education, instinct, & origin, he is the painstakingly & truthfully drawn photograph & counterpart of these two gentlemen as they were in the time of their boyhood, forty years ago. The work has been most carefully & conscientiously done, & is exactly true to the originals, in even the minutest particulars, with but one exception, & that a trifling one: this boy's language has been toned down & softened, here & there, in deference to the taste of a more modern & fastidious day.

This mocking gem was not published in Clemens's lifetime. "Livy forbids the 'Prefatory Remark,'" he told Webster; "therefore, put it in the fire."[20]

Twain had other fish to fry. Before the reality of having to write about his war service became a constant concern, he worried about his financial investments, especially the one into which he had poured the most money. "*Now* the dam type-setter is in lucrative shape at last," he exclaimed to Webster, who was not only his junior partner in Webster & Company but Clemens's business manager as well. Sam was referring to James W. Paige, whom he had met at the Farnham Type-Setting Company in Hartford, where the machinist was perfecting an automatic typesetting machine. Sam had been throwing money at its development since the early 1880s, up to $3,000 a month. The project would tragically come to naught by the early 1890s, leading him to declare bankruptcy for his publishing house. But in 1885 he could still dream that his part ownership in the new invention would make him richer than ever. "Formerly Page [sic] was to sell us only the right to make 1000 machines — now the number is unlimited. Formerly it was estimated that each machine would cost $1600; now only $1000. Formerly it was proposed to sell them at $5000 each; that is still the idea."[21] His excitement was almost palpable. He was thrilled at the idea that selling 400 of the machines would bring in $2 million, 80 percent of it profit. Every newspaper in the country, indeed the world, would have to buy one!

Life for him was riding high in the spring of 1885. He published two bestsellers that year — his own *Huckleberry Finn* and the first volume of Grant's *Memoirs* in December — two of the finest American classics of the postwar period, one fiction and the other nonfiction. He was visiting the ailing author regularly now. "I may go down at 10:30, reaching Gen. Grant's house [Mount McGregor, the Grant cottage in Saratoga Springs, New York] toward 2 p.m.," he told Webster in his usually dictatorial way. "If [there's] anything I ought to know before going there, you or Gerhardt meet me at the R.R. station." He was also copyediting Grant's work. "There will be nothing to do but transfer my marks to his proof when he sends it to you. My marks will not be seriously important, since they concern grammar & punctuation only," wrote the former typesetter. He would be accused of doing more than simple editing, but history has shown the work to be Grant's.[22]

While Grant wrote his memoir in spite of his painful throat, Ferdinand Ward, the "Napoleon of Finance" who had involved Grant and his son in questionable bank dealings, returned to the country and was in jail awaiting trial. James D. Fish, ex-president of one of the banks involved in the scandal, was also on trial for misapplying funds and making false statements with the intent to defraud. Grant was a witness for the prosecution, having made his testimony by deposition. The New York City courtroom was packed to hear what Grant had had to say.

Around 1880 his son had become a partner with Ward, and subsequently the general invested $100,000. When asked what he was led to think he was worth in 1884 just before the scandal broke, Grant responded stoically: "I supposed that I was worth well nigh to a million dollars." He testified that he never knew he was "anything else than a special partner clear to the end" in the Ward-Grant partnership. He had "no suspicion of any rascality" on the part of Mr. Fish. The deposition was long and involved and must have tired the ailing general. "I was out at Gen. Grant's this evening," Sam wrote Livy on April 8. "Col. Fred [Grant] said the General was restful, & very happy, exceedingly pleased, over the inflowing expressions of sympathy from rebel soldiers of all ranks of the South." The oath for the deposition was waived for the former president and national hero.[23]

Grant was still far from getting on his feet financially. Without Twain's intervention with the memoirs, the Civil War general and former president might have died leaving his family penniless. Of all those rich men who had surrounded him in his best days, no one came forth to help him in his moment of greatest need. There was little charity in the air nationally amid the labor strikes and robber baron extravagance. Tramps were regularly made fun of in the press. The homeless held no moral ground in 1885. One tongue-in-cheek article entitled "Watch-Tramps" appeared in the *New York Times* of March 29. If "thoroughly trained," tramps were thought to make good "watch-dogs." They were much preferred to actual watchdogs: "A big dog must be kept in the yard, and he is generally asleep in his kennel while burglars are breaking into the house. The tramp, on the other hand, can be kept in the house, shut up in a comfortable tramp closet, or chained securely in the upper hall."

Mark Twain's name was in the news for more than his book

and lawsuits. On March 27, the Mississippi River steamboat "Mark Twain" exploded near Memphis, killing five men and injuring four. The bodies of the dead "were blown about 500 feet over a tree top into an open field."[24] The Civil War having long ago diminished the river traffic described in *Life on the Mississippi,* the boat was then being used exclusively as a ferryboat. Twenty-seven years earlier, Mark Twain, as he must have been painfully reminded by the news story, had lost his younger brother in an even more horrific steamboat accident, also near the city of Memphis. Young Henry Clemens was the first of a series of painful losses the funnyman suffered during his lifetime. Sam's son, Langdon, had died before the age of three in 1872. Others would depart suddenly and weigh on his heart mightily. Autobiographically, the important death in *Adventures of Huckleberry Finn* is of that of Huck's drunkard father, who was even more distant from his son than Marshall Clemens had been from his own father.

* * *

The Concord Library's announcement of the "death" of *Huckleberry Finn* was clearly as premature as the later announcement of Mark Twain's death around the turn of the century. In "Twain and the Concord Sages," the *New York Sun* of April 6 made fun of the claim that the library had rejected Twain's book purportedly on the grounds that it didn't collect fiction. "It appears," the newspaper wrote, "that the Trustees must have purchased the volume in question under the mistaken idea that they were acquiring a biographical work, and that 'Huckleberry Finn' was a real person. If this was the case, it is easy to understand why the summer philosophers should hasten to get rid of MARK TWAIN's book." Also satirizing the dreamy reputations of the Transcendentalists that had hailed from Concord (Emerson and Thoreau now dead) and the town where now stood Amos Bronson Alcott's so-called Concord School of Philosophy, America's first summer school, the editors asked, "Was it quite candid, though — quite worthy of natures permanently occupied with the True, the Beautiful, and the Good — to attempt to conceal their rather amusing mistake behind a formal process of condemnation and excommunication?" The story closed by asking whether the trustees had mistaken Huck for "a neo-Platonist philosopher."

The idea of Huck as a Transcendentalist was funnier in the 1880s than it perhaps seems today. That American philosophy based on English and German Romanticism said that nature was an emblem of the divine, almost part for part. It was neo-Platonist in that it subscribed to Plato's idea that at the beginning of time everything, which was compacted into the mind of God, split apart with the Fall of man and thus rendered everybody and everything only half of themselves. Ever since, man was unconsciously striving to reconnect, or to become "whole" again. The desire to be "good" was the desire to become whole again. Emerson, as the father of American Transcendentalism, a movement that had receded with the Civil War, had asked in *Nature* (1836) just what nature meant; that is, did its harmony have a higher meaning? A year later in "The American Scholar" address at Harvard, he announced that "nature is the opposite of the soul," or God. Everything in nature was microcosm, all being drawn back to its original source in what he also called the Over-Soul.

The term "Transcendentalism" was originally a pejorative that suggested that Emerson and his disciples foolishly had their heads in the clouds, but it took hold in the decades following Emerson's pronouncements and led to a new American sense of self-reliance. In the field of literature, the spirit of Transcendentalism lay behind the newly envisioned literary effort that did not consider itself inferior to the literature and thoughts of the motherland, England. "We have listened too long to the courtly muses of Europe," Emerson had said in "The American Scholar," and he predicted that America would soon become the beacon of the world. Just the first few years of the 1850s saw the appearance of such American classics as *The Scarlet Letter* (1850), *Moby-Dick* (1851), *Walden* (1854), and *Leaves of Grass* (1855).

The last, by Walt Whitman, was considered in its own time as "trashy" as *Huckleberry Finn*. Both authors were vernacular writers who wrote in the language of the street, what later became the American language, as H. L. Mencken argued in his groundbreaking study in linguistics.[25] Walt Whitman and Mark Twain wrote books that did not stand the literary test of standard English. It wasn't out of ignorance, of course, as both were typesetters as boys and well knew how to parse and spell. They were celebrating the American tongue, as if the only way to get to the heart of a culture was to use its vernacular language. In larger terms, no poem or dialogue can be fully translated from one language to another because its original version is tied linguistically to the spirit of its message.

Neither the persona in *Leaves of Grass* ("I celebrate myself and sing myself") nor the boy in *Huckleberry Finn* would have been considered fit company with the literary giants of Concord, or the Schoolroom Poets of Boston, a group that included such worthies as Whittier, Longfellow, and Holmes. That was the reason the trustees of the Concord Library rejected *Huckleberry Finn*. For along with *Leaves of Grass*, it constituted an attack on the hopes of American literature to stand equally with British literature. It wasn't simply because Huck was a poor role model for the American child; in that case, it could have been as easily dismissed as a similar book published that year, *The Adventures of Jimmy Brown*. But the author of *Adventures of Huckleberry Finn* was an established literary celebrity who had written a number of bestsellers, beginning with *The Innocents Abroad*. Mark Twain, as Samuel Bowles had feared, was "an influential pseudonym [who] should cease to carry into homes and libraries unworthy productions." Whereas Whitman's poor-selling book had been stifled on the grounds that it was immoral and thus unfit for the standards of the evening lamp or the family circle in the nineteenth century, Twain's book was managing to get into almost every household. Genteel American culture was therefore under attack. In the next century, J. D. Salinger would publish its "sequel," *The Catcher in the Rye* (1951), which on one level combined Whitman's "profanity" with Twain's playfully ungrammatical language.

Democracy was an irresistible leveling instrument, which pulled everything down to the average, or the "divine average" as Whitman idealistically put it. In celebration perhaps of the notion that everybody and anybody was welcome to this extension of Old England that was fast becoming a nation of immigrants from all over Europe, the French Frigate *Isère* was about to sail from Rouen with Frédéric Bartholdi's Statue of Liberty.[26] Lady Liberty would be assembled on a pedestal on what was then called Bedloe's Island in New York harbor. Before the year was out, it was celebrated in the city's first ticker-tape parade, presided over by President Cleveland. There would be no statue of Twain's jumping frog in Central Park, as a contemporary writer had lamented, but the image of Huckleberry Finn would be forever after emblazoned in the American literary imagination.[27]

><del></del>><del></del>

THREE

The Greatest General
Who Ever Lived

As a matter of fact, the statue of Mark Twain the "general" that appeared as part of the frontispiece for *Huckleberry Finn* came about almost by accident. Its origin explains to some extent just why Clemens chose the work of an unknown artist to adorn his best book. When Twain sent Karl Gerhardt to Paris in 1881, he had underestimated how much it would take to sustain the artist and his wife (and shortly thereafter their son) in the City of Light. As a result, Gerhardt was forced to return to Hartford in September of 1884 and look for artist's commissions to support himself and his family. Twain had given the Gerhardts $3,000 to cover them for five years, but it ended up costing him twice as much, and Gerhardt didn't even have enough money to bring back his wife and son until the first of the year. (Money was the reason for this separation, though the temporary split could have involved marital unhappiness. Hattie's flirtatious ways in the face of her husband's total preoccupation with his artwork no doubt persisted.) Upon his return, Clemens recalled that "there was nothing for [Gerhardt] to do — so he made a bust of me in the hope that it might bring him work." Times were hard that fall, so after Gerhardt failed to secure any commissions, Twain must have agreed to purchase the bust for his book."[1]

Even at the outset of the Paris years, the Gerhardts had barely enough to live on, especially after the birth of their son in the summer of 1881. In France, Gerhardt studied under François Jouffroy, the former teacher of the now famous Augustus Saint-Gaudens, the American-born sculptor of the Beaux-Arts era. His Civil War monuments would later inspire Gerhardt to sculpt Grant. In addition to the set allowance the Clemenses had promised him, Gerhardt received extra funds from them for live models, evidence perhaps to his benefactors that he was advancing rapidly in his training. Hattie, during and after her pregnancy, no longer served as her husband's live model, but she still sought to keep alive the interests of his patron with ever so slightly affectionate letters over the years. Not long after their arrival in Paris, she wrote Twain: "I wonder & wish so very often if you do love us just a little bit — even aside from the talent and do you know I do not like to have you fond of anyone else but me and truly. . . ."[2] Twain apparently didn't answer this letter, but he continued his support, even through the birth of their second child in 1883, a daughter whom they named Olivia, after Mrs. Clemens.

Gerhardt was simply lucky to have come in contact with Mark Twain at the height of the author's success. Indeed, the sculptor's luck was based mainly on Hattie, his *carte de visite* to the famous author, who in 1885 was enjoying his annus mirabilis, his year of wonders. The writer continued on, even after his tour with Cable, as busy as ever, involving himself in literary events that also helped promote *Adventures of Huckleberry Finn*. Those included a public reading with more mainstream writers in late April.

The road to fame had been a rather rapid journey. He had modeled the character of Tom Sawyer on himself and two of his Hannibal playmates. He claimed that Huckleberry Finn was based on Tom Blankenship, the son of one of the town's two drunks. In his autobiography he described Blankenship as "ignorant, unwashed, insufficiently fed; but he had as good a heart as ever any boy had." This fantasy was probably cut from the same cloth that makes *Adventures of Huckleberry Finn* a romance about a river rat whose lack of a proper upbringing would have in most cases rendered him a scoundrel. Twain claimed to have heard that Blankenship had become a justice of the peace in Montana, "and was a good citizen and greatly respected." Apparently, there was no evidence for this rumor. In fact, Blankenship followed in his father's footsteps. He was repeatedly arrested for stealing food in Hannibal and died of cholera four years after the publication of the story of a boy with a sound heart and a deformed conscience.[3]

Tom Blankenship didn't grow up to become a success, and Sam Clemens could have met the same fate. Although he was more "middle class," like the models for Tom Sawyer (who were told to stay away from the underclass Blankenship boy), he stemmed from failure. His grandfather, Samuel B. Clemens, had perished in a house-raising accident in what is now West Virginia. He died at thirty-five, in 1805. He may have been intoxicated at the time of this death. His father, John Marshall Clemens, clung to the myth of his father's Virginia aristocracy, much in the way the trinomial southern gentlemen hilariously do in *Pudd'nhead Wilson* (1894). That family connection was just about the only thing he brought with him when he migrated to Missouri, and eventually Hannibal. Named for the famous Supreme Court jurist John Marshall, he became a lowly paid justice of the peace after failing as a shopkeeper. He died before the age of fifty in 1847, when the future Mark Twain was but thirteen. It was in or about this year in which the adventures of Tom Sawyer and Huckleberry Finn were set. Marshall Clemens left behind him a wife and four children, two in their twenties. The eldest, Orion Clemens, was twenty-two at the time and working as a printer in St. Louis. After his father died, he returned home to run a local newspaper that ultimately failed. With the exception of a brief stint out west as the secretary to the territorial governor of Nevada, Orion failed, too, in everything he tried.

It was a legacy to run away from. Sam Clemens had left Hannibal before the age of eighteen, returning regularly in his fiction, but personally and ever so briefly only two or three times. Having apprenticed there as a printer, he set out for St. Louis to look for work. His sole surviving sister, Pamela, was married and living in the city. His stay was short. He set out again, this time for New York City. For the next year he worked alternately in New York City and Philadelphia before returning to St. Louis and other port cities in Missouri and Iowa as well as Cincinnati before embarking on his career in 1858 as a steamboat pilot. It was the job he said he liked best, but he was forced out of it by the war and almost forced into working for the Union army as a pilot. He had already served briefly in the Confederate army or what the Missouri state militia would have become had the state not opted to remain in the Union. When it did, he lit out for the Nevada territory with Orion, who had received his post as territorial secretary of Nevada through his St. Louis connections and his antislavery views.

It is difficult to say just where Sam stood on slavery in 1861. Initially, he may have been a copperhead in Virginia City, Nevada, where many pro-secessionists were sitting out the war. He voted the proslavery ticket in the 1860 presidential election. And for at least the first two years of the war, he was probably pulling for the South. It may have been the influence of journalists out there from the North, but whatever it was, he emerged from the war a Union man. He voted Republican, the party that had opposed slavery, until the 1880s, and he went on, as we know, to write one of the most profound condemnations of slavery in *Huckleberry Finn.* When the war had begun, however, he was no doubt like Huck Finn himself — proslavery until it came down to friends like Jim who were slaves. Growing up, Sam had known "friends" like that — for example, Uncle Daniel, one of his uncle's slaves, became a model for the "nigger Jim." In the story of the boy and the slave and the river, Huck is never against slavery. He simply comes to like Jim better than his owner, Miss Watson. By the time in 1863 that Sam Clemens became Mark Twain, the name he took when he started writing as a humorist for the *Virginia City Territorial Enterprise,* slavery had become "personal."

After the war, his antislavery position was considerably strengthened when he met the Yankee daughter of the wealthy Jervis Langdon, a former supporter of the Underground Railroad. From Nevada in 1863, he had gone first to San Francisco, then to the Hawaiian Islands, and finally to the East Coast, where he booked passage in 1867 on the *Quaker City,* the prototype of the American cruise ship, bound for Europe and the Holy Land. Owing to his success both as a lecturer and a reporter in California and Hawaii, he was commissioned by the *Sacramento Union* to provide a series of travel letters. Initially, the cruise, organized by Henry Ward Beecher's Plymouth Church in Brooklyn, was to include not only America's most famous preacher but also its next-to-most famous Civil War general, William Tecumseh Sherman. As it turned out, both withdrew — Beecher possibly because of his involvement in the extramarital affair that ultimately led to his infamous adultery trial in 1870, and Sherman, who had been Grant's right hand in the war, to kill Indians in the West.

While on the *Quaker City* cruise, Sam met Charles Langdon, the son of Jervis and the brother of Olivia, the woman he first encountered in New York City during the last week of 1867 and married three years later. By the time of his marriage in 1870, Mark Twain was famous for *The Celebrated Jumping Frog of Calaveras County and Other Stories* (1867) and *The Innocents Abroad* (1869), the latter a best seller that approached the success of *Uncle Tom's Cabin* and made him rich enough to wed the girl for whom he always maintained he wasn't worthy. He was crowned as America's leading humorist after the nearly equally successful *Roughing It* in 1872. One book followed another: *The Gilded Age,* written with Charles Dudley Warner, appeared in 1873, followed the next year by a sell-out play based on Twain's part of the book, *Colonel Sellers.* A year later he rediscovered his river-piloting days with "Old Times on the Mississippi," a series of sketches in the *Atlantic Monthly* that became the beginning of *Life on the Mississippi* in 1883. These essays stirred him further to publish his first boy's book, *The Adventures of Tom Sawyer* in 1876, another success. *A Tramp Abroad* and *The Prince and the Pauper* came out in 1880 and 1881. The first was another travel book (a very popular genre in America then), and in the other one he traveled back to the England of Henry VIII to write one of his first stories involving twins. Edward VI and his lookalike, a street urchin, accidentally switch places. *The Prince and the Pauper* was a departure for the humorist who wrote in the American vernacular. There was hardly a laugh in this narrative written in the King's English of Nathaniel Hawthorne and Henry James, two writers Clemens couldn't abide, yet whose kingdom he sought to enter and escape the label of humorist, partly to please his Gilded Age wife and their New England children. In 1885 his daughter began a biography of her father. She wrote that *The Prince and the Pauper* was "unquestionably the best book he has ever written." Its language, the thirteen-year-old added, "is *perfect*." When a fan of *Huckleberry Finn* wrote to say that he was pleased to see that Twain had returned to "his old style," Susy wrote: "That enoyed [*sic*] me greatly."[4]

Mark Twain and Samuel Langhorne Clemens were often at odds with each other on the matter of literature. Twain wrote for money, while the latter sought the prestige enjoyed not only by James but also Sam's closest literary friend, William Dean Howells. Sam's success as Mark Twain was at the root of the condemnation of his masterpiece, *Adventures of Huckleberry Finn*. Moreover, because he was also in demand as America's first stand-up comic, as his tour with Cable demonstrated, he was, as already noted, viewed as a threat to the country's morals and manners. One problem with remaining a humorist was that you were soon forgotten after death. As is the case with comedians today, they often disappear with yesterday's headlines and issues. Near the end of his life while leafing through an anthology of American humorists, he wrote: "In this mortuary volume I find [Petroleum] Nasby, Artemus Ward, Yawcob Strauss, [George Horatio] Derby, . . . [who] are now heard of no more and are no longer mentioned."[5] Names on the lips of everybody during their prime were now forgotten. Nor were their copyrights worth much, with the possible exception of Mark Twain's. At least this humorist made that assumption in 1885 and supported the movement for an international copyright agreement. (*Tom Sawyer* had been rapidly pirated by a Canadian publisher in 1876.) On April 8, 1885, the *Hartford Daily*

Courant quoted the *New York Sun*'s announcement of a public reading in support of the copyright at Madison Square Theatre on April 28. There Mark Twain the humorist would join the ranks of the elite or more upscale writers such as Howells, Julian Hawthorne, Edward Eggleston, and Oliver Wendell Holmes.

* * *

Grant, dying of throat cancer, went decidedly downhill in April. The newspapers were filled with headlines about his imminent demise. "Gen. Grant Much Worse — Another Severe Attack Yesterday Morning — The End Thought to Be at Hand, But He Rallies Again — His Condition Hopeless" (April 2); "Gen. Grant's Sufferings — Strength Gained After Passing Very Low — Sad Scenes of the Night and Early Morning, When the Family Were Twice Called to His Side" (April 3); "Gen Grant Feels Better — His Improvement a Surprise to All — Resting Quietly Through the Day without any Bad Symptoms — No Immediate Apprehensions" (April 9); "Gen. Grant Not So Well — His Throat Honeycombed with Cancer Cells" (April 26). Amazingly, the General was still putting finishing touches on volume two of his memoir. By May 1 Webster & Company had already received orders for 60,000 sets. Yet the rumor that the book was ghostwritten persisted and threatened to stifle interest. The following day Grant rose to rebut the claim in the *New York Times*.

Although Twain had also been accused of ghosting the memoirs, the most he said he ever did was to correct punctuation and grammar. Indeed, he had complete faith in Grant's writing ability and had tried to get the general to write his memoirs as early as 1881. "What a pity he did not write them then," he told an old friend; "& yet it does not seem possible that he could have done the work better at any time of his life than he has done it now while waiting, under a sentence of death. His book ought to take very high rank as literature; and I am sure it will. I am thinking it must take rank with the best purely narrative literature in the language."[6]

Grant dedicated his book to the soldiers of the Mexican and the Civil War. The tribute included those who had fought for the South. "The men of the South," he told a reporter from Philadelphia, "were fighting for a principle which they thought was right and which we did not, but I always looked upon them as citizens of our common country. . . . I never liked to think of them as prisoners of war, and preferred to encourage them to go home under parole."[7] Actually, toward the end of the war Grant had delayed a general prisoner exchange for fear that the South would get back well-fed and healthy soldiers in exchange for Union prisoners who had been near starvation because of the lack of food in the South.

In early May, Twain started the first dictations for his own memoir, known today as the *Autobiography*. He had already made several false starts on his own earlier, and this would be another stab at it as he returned to this autobiographical project again and again for the rest of his life, adopting formal dictations in 1906. His "secretary" in 1885 was James Redpath, the fiery abolitionist who had become "respectable" after the Emancipation and the war and who later founded a speakers' forum. That agency had sponsored Mark Twain's first lecture tour during the 1869–70 season. The first dictations were to begin at the Union Hotel on Asylum Street in New York. "All right, old man. I'm coming down to New York tomorrow," he wrote Redpath from Hartford. "I think we can make this thing blamed enjoyable."[8] The autobiographer and his stenographer began their sessions around May 11 or 12, but the project was short-lived, and unfortunately none of the manuscripts for that period survive. The autobiographical impulse is usually an author's attempt to preempt the inevitable biographer, at least about the formative years when no one else is paying attention to the future famous person. An autobiography also helps to see that the author is not forgotten. Mark Twain worried for the sake of his children and their dependence on future royalties as much as he did about the possibility of lasting fame.

The desire for immortality may have been influenced at this time by the latest effort to restore the good name of Edgar Allan Poe, who had died in 1849. (In an 1876 ceremony unattended by all noted literary persons except Walt Whitman, Poe had been reburied in front of a church in Baltimore.[9]) The effort in 1885 was quickly labeled "too soon" in New York. It was absurd, a sarcastic story in the *New York Times* of May 5, 1885, argued, to suppose "that a man's character is known only to the generation which has never seen him." "Those who were personally acquainted with Poe," the article continued, "believed that he was dissolute, untruthful, and a generally disreputable person. . . . [Poe's admirers] can then not only prove that he was a modern Sir Galahad, but they can also rehabilitate Jefferson Davis, and show that he was passionately devoted to the Union and spared no effort to crush the rebellion headed by Lincoln and Grant." Mark Twain was another "Southerner" whose work did not excite the Northern literati.

That May, James R. Osgood & Company of Boston failed. It may have been due to the notoriety from its publication of *Leaves of Grass,* which in the winter of 1882 became the first book to be officially "banned in Boston." A year later Osgood had published *Life on the Mississippi.* Although it is synonymous with Mark Twain's fame today, it did not do well in the marketplace. Earlier, the firm had published *The Prince and the Pauper,* but in that arrangement Osgood & Company had been merely a distributor, with Twain reaping most of the profits. "Osgood's busted, at last," Sam told Charley Webster on May 5. "It was sure to come."[10] Such, too, would be the fate of Charles L. Webster & Company in a few short years, but in 1885 its prospects were high and profits were soaring, not only from the demand for Grant's memoir but also from the mounting sales of *Huckleberry Finn.*

The same week the first prominent Union general of the Civil War — still called the War of the Rebellion in the North — died. Irvin McDowell, best known for botching the battles at Bull Run, both Confederate victories, died in San Francisco, where he had retired from the army in 1882 to become park commissioner. Mostly remembered for his indecisiveness on the battlefield, he would precede the most decisive general of the war in death by less than three months. The headline on Grant for May 20 said that he had passed the previous night and day "free from pain." His former military comrades, however, were already giving the press stories about the general's bravery in expectation of his demise. Grant, one of his former staff officers told the *Boston Traveller,* had "no fear of anything." Much later, in the wake of World War I, whose devastation diminished the "glory" of war (further eroded by such classics as *All Quiet on the Western Front* and *A Farewell to Arms*), the memory of Grant became tarnished and sullied with jokes about who is buried in "Grant's tomb." But twenty years after the Civil War, he stood as tall as Lincoln and had the mythic status of the twentieth century's John J. "Black Jack" Pershing or George Patton.

The admiring staff officer recalled that on the morning Grant captured Petersburg in 1864, he "stopped to [dictate] a dispatch, leaning against one of the few fences left standing, near a house, the upper part of which had been abandoned by women and children." The civilians had taken refuge in the cellar of the structure that was still being riddled by Confederate artillery. "The writer stood near the General, thinking between shots that it was no place for him, but not seeing how he could leave while the Lieutenant-General remained. When Grant finished his dispatch, looking round and apparently appreciating for the first time what a hot place he was in, he quietly said: 'I see no use in staying here,' and moved off, very closely followed by his staff. . . ." In Chicago, he was already being eulogized. The speaker, a former general in the Army of the Tennessee and current postmaster-general, wondered aloud how he could recall in one speech the multitudinous achievements of "our first commander, the illustrious General whose fame has grown to fill the world!"[11]

Grant was dying, but where was his counterpoint in history, Robert. E. Lee? He had succumbed to heart failure and, no doubt, a broken heart, in 1870. Lee had died at the age of sixty-three; in 1885, Grant would die at the age of sixty-four. Following Appomattox, there had been a call to hang Lee as the ultimate traitor, but Grant sternly opposed it. They had fought together in the Mexican War, the training ground for the generals of both sides in the Civil War. In 1885 Grant was a hero, and Lee still a villain. Yet as the years went by and melted into the twentieth century, lofty memorials of Lee would become pervasive in the South, while Grant's tomb, a memorial at the intersection of Riverside Drive and 122nd Street in Manhattan, faded as a tourist site because of urban decay. Lee no doubt benefited from the fact that interest in remembering the war waned in the North, while it grew in the South, where defeat was being reinscribed as the "Lost Cause." There was even a movement in the early twentieth century to dedicate a monument to Lee in Washington, D.C. Even in the twenty-first century, when Grant's unflattering image as president is being repaired, the National Park Service's website warns potential visitors that "due to its original construction, the inside of Grant's Tomb is not air conditioned and is drafty in the winter" — not much of a teaser. Lee went into history as an officer and a gentleman, whose military genius had been overwhelmed by the industrial North rather than outdone by Grant's strategies. When the Reverend Henry Ward Beecher was preparing his eulogy for Grant, he wondered how much the general had abused alcohol. Like Poe, who drank and had also attended West Point, Grant would pay — as he had in life — for his intemperate ways.

* * *

In 1885 America was just getting over the nightmare of the Civil War. It was the first time that a Democrat occupied the White House since the troubled 1850s when that party had stood for slavery. For those of Anglican background in society's upper and middle classes, it was a time of clarity in terms of the makeup of the universe, where everything still flowed from the center, or the Logos. It was the age of the robber barons, who saw themselves as the ultimate achievement of Western culture. The architecture of their mansions swam in its glory with rooms decked out in the period styles of Louis XIV, Louis XV, and the Italian Renaissance. To visit, for example, the Vanderbilt home in Newport or the Flagler home in Palm Beach today is to walk through their dreamworld. When Henry Flagler, cofounder with Rockefeller of Standard Oil, sat in his garden, he would ask himself how anything in the next world could be as beautiful. Like the fictional Silas Lapham, whose character is perhaps a satire on the robber baron, Flagler believed in an ordered universe. Carved out of the ideals of literary realism and social Darwinism, William Dean Howells's Lapham — like Flagler — believed that certain individuals could always prevail. They would not be pawns of the forces of heredity and environment.

Meanwhile, that privileged fly on the wall in the period between the Civil War and 1900, Henry Adams, the novelist and historian who descended from two U.S. presidents, had acquired another kind of "education" in which the universe had become a "multiverse." "The child born in 1900," Adams wrote in *The Education,* "would . . . be born into a new world which would not be a unity but a multiple. . . . He found himself in a land where . . . order was an accidental relation." What Adams had learned frightened him into wondering whether too many more generations after his would survive. The Virgin had been overtaken by the Dynamo, as essentialism faded into relativism. The cold efficiency of science and technology now overwhelmed the beautiful fecundity of art. As Darwin's precept of natural selection became more and more evident, Adams struggled to resolve the contradiction between the advances in scientific reason and the persistence of social chaos, "especially the persistently fiendish treatment of man by man."[12] This, too, was Mark Twain's dilemma after he finished writing *Adventures of Huckleberry Finn.* Huck, the petty thief with a conscience, had nowhere to go after the slave Jim was "freed" but west to the territories. And increasingly, as he continued to write, Mark Twain had nowhere to go either.

A Connecticut Yankee in King Arthur's Court (1889), which began as a satirical celebration of the uses of technology, ends in a blood bath. *Pudd'nhead Wilson* (1894) essentially reverses the racial progress of *Huckleberry Finn*, when the female protagonist, Twain's first realistic depiction of a woman, is "sold down the river" not once, but twice, first by her son and then by the author, who discards her at the end of his story. One version of the posthumously published *Mysterious Stranger* ends in chaos when the cosmic joke is finally revealed — that we live in a world created by "a God who could make good children as easily as bad, yet preferred to make bad ones; who could have made every one of them happy, yet never made a single happy one." The devil in the form of one last trickster, one last Tom Sawyer performance, declares: "There is no God, no universe, no human race, no earthly life, no heaven, no hell. It is all a Dream, a grotesque and foolish dream. Nothing exists but You. And You are but a *Thought* — a vagrant Thought, a useless Thought, a homeless Thought, wandering forlorn among the empty eternities!"[13]

In a letter dated June 1, 1885, to Charles Warren Stoddard, who had acted as Twain's private secretary during the fall of 1873 when he was lecturing in London, Clemens defended his growing skepticism: "You must not make the mistake of supposing that absolute peace of mind is obtainable only through some form of religious belief; no, on the contrary, I have found that as perfect a peace is to be found in absolute unbelief." He concluded by saying that he looked back with "shuddering horror upon the days when I believed I believed. . . ."[14] That same day Beecher was in the newspaper for a sermon he had given on evolution. The clergy of the day were charged with explaining away Darwin's doctrine without looking antiscientific. "That the whole world and the universe was created by God," he told his congregation, "is the testimony of the entire Bible. But how this was done, whether by the direct force of the creative will, or indirectly through gradual changes, the Scripture does not declare. The grand truth is that this work did not come into being by chance, but was the product of an intelligent being and that the divine will is expressed by what we call natural laws."[15]

No, in this age of evolutionary theism it would never be "by chance." Unity was still its shibboleth. Twain did not dare speak candidly if he spoke publicly. Even his magnum opus had been a romance that upheld the unity of goodness in the world. Huck does the right thing, regardless of whether he thinks so. The slave Jim is avuncular and kind, not bitter and angry at being treated by most people as property. Even Whitman, nearly on his deathbed five years later, could envision the same intelligence that Beecher insisted upon. Sitting in his sickroom on the second floor of his shabby row house in Camden in the heat of summer and amid the noise from the street below, the Good Gray Poet clearly sensed "something again unseen." A faint breeze at sunset delivers him to the divine source of life:

> Thou, messenger-magical strange bringer to body and spirit of me,
> (Distances balk'd — occult medicines penetrating me from head
>   to foot,)
> I feel the sky, the prairies vast — I feel the mighty northern lakes,
> I feel the ocean and the forest — somehow I feel the globe itself
>   swift-swimming space;
> Thou blown from lips so loved, now gone — haply from endless
>   store, God-sent.[16]

In early June Mark Twain gave a reading from *Huckleberry Finn* and his other books in Unity Hall in Hartford. He had tried to get Howells to join him, but the reigning "dean" of American literature wasn't about to go on stage with America's most popular platform performer, even though the two had read together in support of an international copyright law back in April. He begged off with obvious flattery, saying that he would never dare to "read within a hundred miles of *you*" if he could help it. Twain loved to hear Howells read from his work. He was then enjoying the latest installment of *The Rise of Silas Lapham* in the June *Century*. In chapters 19–21, the nouveau riche businessman faces a double crisis, one domestic and the other financial. First, the supposed suitor of one of his two daughters turns out to prefer her sister. Should the second daughter, who is attracted to the suitor, be miserable and deny the relationship, thus making all three miserable? Howells's solution, as articulated through the advice of a Boston clergyman, is to fall back on the principle of the "economy of pain." Why not reduce the suffering to one since she would eventually survive the slight?

Silas is at sea on this issue and leaves the problem mainly to his wife. He is too busy with matters at the office where his ex-partner, Milton K. Rogers, has involved him in a land deal that will ultimately threaten to compromise him ethically. Rogers is one of the "new," postbellum businessmen who recklessly invest in get-rich schemes. "He's been dabbling in every sort of fool thing you can lay your tongue to," Silas tells his wife, who had shamed her husband into renewing his relations with Rogers because he had slighted him in the dissolution of their former partnership, "wild-cat stocks, patent-rights, land speculations, oil claims, — till he's run through about everything." As Sam Clemens read his friend's narrative, he failed to see himself in the picture. He was at the time increasingly investing in the doomed Paige Typesetter and allowing Webster & Company to agree, on the basis of the success of his book and Grant's, to other book contracts that would lead the firm to bankruptcy.

Livy was reading Howells's latest novel, too. After finishing the July segment, she confided to her diary that the story "showed more the moral struggles of mortals than any thing Mr. Howells has ever done before."[17] In chapters 22–25, the penultimate section of *The Rise of Silas Lapham* to appear in the *Century,* the domestic crisis slackens into a solution in which the other sister will eventually marry a cousin. But Silas reveals to his wife that he too (like Sam Clemens) has also been dabbling in stocks and has suffered heavy losses. Howells dramatizes the "evil" of speculation in the age of the robber baron. This novel — about the declining ethics of the American business-man — created a new literary genre that would culminate at the beginning of the twentieth century with Theodore Dreiser's *The Financier* (1912) and *The Titan* (1914). Silas saves the day, if only temporarily, for what a later U.S. president would call the "business" of America, by refusing to play along with Rogers's scheme in the shady land deal and ultimately by going into bankruptcy himself. In 1894 Mark Twain would also face bankruptcy, and — with the same ethical resolve — would pay back all his creditors 100 percent on the dollar.

Howells's focus on the "moral struggles of mortals" in *Silas* hadn't extended to the civil rights of freedmen, a campaign that had a long way to go in 1885. But at least the movement now had a pulse. The state senate of Illinois passed its first civil rights bill on June 4. It gave "colored people" the same rights as whites in hotels, restaurants, and theaters. To discriminate finally became a crime, though a misdemeanor with a fine of not less that $25 and not more than $500 as well as a possible prison term of not more than one year.[18] One wonders how and if it was enforced in 1885. The usual excuse middle-class whites gave for discriminating against blacks was that it was done not to abuse their statures as human beings but merely because of the demands of the marketplace: other whites would boycott their businesses. The North had yet to be populated with the grand exodus of blacks from the South that would occur in the first decades of the twentieth century, and their excuse for segregation in the 1880s did not rely wholly on the argument of racial inferiority, still heard in the South.

Democracy was on the move in America, at least symbolically. The Statue of Liberty was ready for erection in New York harbor. The problem, however, was a lack of funds to build the pedestal. To assist the fund raising in a campaign initiated by Joseph Pulitzer, owner of the *New York World,* the American Committee of the Statue of Liberty sold miniatures of the statue for a dollar apiece at Macy's.[19] Otherwise, the fund-raising consisted of nickels and dimes from hundreds of thousands of Americans. The statue wasn't formally dedicated until October 28, 1886.

* * *

Despite all the financial help Twain had provided, Gerhardt continued to depend on his patron for commissions. Through the connection with Webster & Company, he was able to befriend the Grant family and sculpt the ailing General. "I shook hands with the Genl yesterday, and he remembered me," Gerhardt excitedly told Clemens on June 26. "You can't help making a noble statue of the General, even if you only catch glimpses of him & get no regular sittings," Twain responded the same day, "for the inspiration will do the rest." The humorist later testified that Gerhardt's bust was regarded "as the most nearly correct likeness of Grant."[20] Always the businessman, Twain got the general's family to approve a scheme of selling terra-cotta miniatures of the bust for $5 apiece ($50 for bronze) as part of the campaign to sell the memoirs. These did not sell nearly as well, however, as the two-volume memoir. In fact, they proved to be yet another of Mark Twain's failed investments. The bust that Gerhardt had cast had a "worn look," in the words of Munich sculptor Rupert Schmid, whom the *World* reported had also been commissioned by the Grants to do a sculpture. "I shall remove that," he told the newspaper, "and I feel confident that I will, after one more sitting, be able to present a faithful likeness of Gen. Grant as he appeared before he was prostrated by the cancer." Twain strongly disagreed with the choice of Schmid, committing to his journal emphatically the statement (in German): "It should not be done by a foreigner."[21]

This seemingly xenophobic comment was not unusual for Americans in the wake of the Civil War, when foreign powers had so openly pondered whether or not to recognize the Confederacy. As private secretary to his father, the American ambassador to England during the war, Henry Adams became disgusted with the hypocrisy of the British prime minister. Until the war turned around largely as a result of Grant's victories in the West, Adams wrote: "The Governments and society of Europe . . . regarded the Washington Government as dead."[22] Grant's tour of the world in 1879 had symbolically consolidated the image of the United States as a world power following its victory over the South. Already, as the time of the hero's death approached, the relics and trophies from his victory lap were being shipped from the Grant residence to Washington. In June Colonel R. N. Bachelder was sent from the War Department to oversee the transfer of "rare furniture and bric-a-brac." The treasures included a Mexican onyx cabinet presented to the general by the people of Pueblo, Mexico; bronze vases from Japan; porcelain jars from China; gold cigar cases from the celestial and second kings of Siam, and so on.[23] The ex-president was clearly being celebrated for his military career. By June Grant had reportedly finished the second volume of his memoir. The cancer was now spreading rapidly and he could barely talk.

At the beginning of July, Sam headed off for Mount Mc-Gregor, New York, the general's last residence, to pay his final respects. Gerhardt was still there, this time sculpting Grant's granddaughter — anything to stay connected with the fame that might yet ignite his career as a sculptor. Hattie had joined him there, ingratiating herself with the Grant family the way she had with the Clemenses. Sam told Livy about the bust of Jesse Grant's daughter, and he described the general as stoic in the face of imminent death. "The General is as placid, serene, & self-possessed as ever," he wrote on July 1. "Manifestly, dying is nothing to a really great & brave man." Indeed, Mark Twain was, as Justin Kaplan has noted, "Grant-intoxicated." Clemens told Gerhardt, as the amateur sculptor completed his work at the family cottage: "There is limitless inspiration in the thought that the features which you are modeling are those of a man whose name will still be familiar in the mouths of men in a future so remote that the very constellations in the skies of to-day will have visibly changed their places."[24]

Here was somebody who had fled the war, after two weeks of Tom Sawyer antics in 1861, to become, years later, part of the inner circle of the great general, whose legacy many thought nearly beyond comprehension. Sometime in 1885, perhaps in the months leading up to Grant's death, the *Century* editors approached Mark Twain for a war memoir of his own — what would become "The Private History of a Campaign That Failed." It was to appear under the general heading of their "Century War Series," with the main purpose of interesting "veterans in their own memories and of instructing the generation which has grown up since the War for the Union."[25] Conceived in 1883, the series began in November of the following year with the first of what turned out to be three of Grant's essays before he decided to take the book that sprang from them to Webster & Company. The series had to begin with him, for without exception the others, as Twain recorded in his autobiography, "refused to write a line unless the leading actor of the war should also write."[26] We can only speculate as to why the editors also asked Mark Twain to write and why he accepted. It was possibly because of his connection with Grant through Webster & Company. Everyone in the publishing business knew that *he* was Webster & Company.

"Mark Twain," wrote the *San Francisco Chronicle* on June 15, "is almost, if not quite, the busiest man in town. He has on hand the project of publishing General Grant's book about the war." Twain was a "notable exception to the rule," continued the *Chronicle,* "that literary fellows have no heads for money-making. His enterprises, from the first issue of 'The Innocents Abroad' to the manufacture of his patent scrap-book, have not yet yielded a failure, and the present venture will, he confidently thinks, enrich him immensely." The article went on to recount that Twain had hurried the general through a preliminary sketch of the second volume, for fear that if he died before finishing the work it would lose considerable value at the marketplace. Even though its completion had been announced, it noted that "much remains to be interpolated in case the dying hero lingers long enough to do it."

Twain's joining the "dying hero" and others in the *Century* series that December, matching the general's *Personal Memoirs* with his "Private History," no matter how paltry they were in comparison to Grant's, may have been an effort to soften his image in the eyes of the press from appearing to take mercenary advantage of the fading general. At least he had *tried* to serve in uniform and so wasn't altogether another greedy businessman. The publicity he received on the matter of publishing Grant's memoir had not been altogether positive. The *Chronicle* report not only presented the writer in the context of a Gilded Age entrepreneur but also went into almost personal detail on the matter of Twain's finances, noting not only that he had made thus far $200,000 on his books, $100,000 lecturing, and another $50,000 on his self-pasting scrapbook, but also disclosing that his "wife's fortune" was worth $75,000. Described as "a common figure in upper Broadway," the paper noted that he was always "careful to get into print correctly," especially with regard to the forthcoming Grant book. Something of a confidence man, perhaps — indeed, one of the first public personalities in America — Mark Twain, it said, did not particularly mix in any of the literary circles, but preferred the life of the businessman. Nearly omnipresent on the lecture circuit, "he does not look as well on the street as on the platform. His stature seems less, his clothes are not so carefully donned, and his manner devoid of the drollery which helps his delivery of humor. He is not a joker in private life."[27]

On July 6 he wrote to the *Boston Herald,* asking for "fair play, nothing more. I can't reply when the newspapers make misstatements about me. It wouldn't do — the public would quickly tire of it." Ever watchful of his public image, Twain continued: "And so I would like to ask you to let me have a look at things like 'The New Book — a Good Story' — (dated New York June 20) before you print them. I will correct them, & at the same time will leave untouched all statements about me which are *true,* howsoever damaging they may be." He pointed out that he made this request of the *Herald* because the paper had never mistreated him, as far as he knew. That wasn't, he said, the case with the *Boston Advertiser,* which had savaged *Huckleberry Finn* back in March. Actually, the *Herald* had piled on, saying on February 1 that the third installment of the novel in *Century* ("Royalty on the Mississippi") was "pitched in but one key, and that is the key of a vulgar and abhorrent life."

He found the statements in the *Herald* story of June 20 personally offensive "to my character, if I have one — & I like to think I have." If not, the attack "damages the character of a man who certainly has one — General Grant." He went on to defend himself against charges that he had stolen Grant away from *Century.* Grant had not broken an agreement with the magazine to publish a book-length memoir because he never had such an agreement. Furthermore, Twain continued, he didn't make an offer "which no regular publisher felt like competing with." He merely offered the general twice as much as the Century Company had offered. This offer, he argued, was surpassed by several other publishers, but he got Grant's book because Webster & Company had the best facilities for selling the most copies — that is, through subscription publishing, in which potential purchasers were sought out for prepaid orders for the volume. He complained that the faulty press stories had foisted upon him the reputation "of being a pushing, pitiless, underhanded sharper — but I don't quite deserve it." Twain told a slightly different story in his autobiography, stating that he offered Grant a 70 percent royalty figure.[28] Whatever the case, the book became a best seller, and Grant's widow and heirs escaped the disgrace of becoming impoverished. Essentially, Clemens bailed out Grant. Both were poor businessmen, though, and it would be simply a matter of time before somebody would have to bail out Mark Twain.

To complicate the Grant relationship even further, Gerhardt got into trouble with the Grant family over his creation of the general's death mask; it led to a controversy that would preoccupy the newspapers for the rest of the year. It concerned a photograph that Gerhardt had made as well as a death mask, which he later refused to hand over to the Grants. It all started around the middle of July when Gerhardt wrote his wife from Saratoga Springs that there had been something of a falling out between himself and the family. Evidently, Mrs. Grant became upset when she heard that Gerhardt was waiting around to make the death mask. Hattie sent the letter over to Twain, who in turn scolded her husband. "You are in danger of wearing out your welcome up there," he wrote from Elmira. "Now *don't* let that happen." At this point Twain was still hoping that the statuettes would be a success. "The General sick all these months, the family distressed, worried — a stranger present whose projects are of a sort to get into print & add to the worry — don't you see, it is a most easy thing for you to become a burden & one too many."[29] He urged him to pack up his things and depart at once. As it turned out, Gerhardt didn't have to leave. Hattie went up there with her baby and charmed the Grant family back into their hands. Gerhardt told Twain that his wife "will be the means of my getting a commission here."[30] His patron might have remembered that it had been essentially Hattie who had convinced him to send her husband to study his craft at the École des Beaux-Arts in Paris.

* * *

U. S. Grant died at 8:06 on the morning of July 23, 1885. Sam had come to believe that anybody who died was lucky not to have to endure the human condition any longer. He would say so about every family member who departed. Grant now could live on through his book. "The second volume was finished last week, to the last detail; & was formally delivered to Charley Webster at Mt. McGregor last Saturday," he told Livy from New York City. "General Grant having not another interest in this world to live for, died. He would have died three months ago if his book had been completed. I am satisfied of that."[31] *Harper's Weekly* had commissioned a poem from Walt Whitman and planned to publish it in April, but as the general held on, the editors delayed publication until May 16, after asking the poet to add one more stanza to acknowledge that Grant still lived:

> And still shall be: resume again, thou hero heart!
> Strengthen to firmest day, O rosy dawn of hope!
> Thou dirge I started first, to joyful shout reverse!
> > and thou, O grave,
> Wait long and long!

The poem, ultimately called "The Death of General Grant," emphasized that an era had passed with his death. "As one by one withdraw the lofty actors / From that great play on history's stage eterne, / . . . Victor's and vanquish'd — Lincoln's and Lee's — now thou with them, / Man of the mighty days — and equal to the days!" It was fortunate that the poet wrote before Grant's death because the next day it was reported that Whitman himself had collapsed in front of his Camden house from a heat stroke — yet another of those "lofty actors" preparing to pass through.[32]

The preface to the *Personal Memoirs* opened with the proverb, "Man proposes and God disposes." It reflected Grant's stoicism as a witness to history. "I have entered upon the task," he wrote, "with the sincere desire to avoid doing injustice to any one whether on the National or Confederate side." He told his reader that he had finished the first volume and "a portion of the second" before he came under his death sentence. He died as he lived, focused on the present moment. His final service to the nation had been to complete his memoirs. "Concealing from Mrs. Grant at first, and for as long a time as possible, the nature of his disease," the *New York Times* reported on July 27, as funeral plans were being completed, "he showed through his whole illness the same earnest desire to spare others from sharing his misery. Day after day, with patient and cheerful fortitude, the silent man — never more grandly silent — bore the ceaseless torture and waited calmly for the end."

Following her husband's cue, Julia Grant asked President Cleveland to include Confederate generals as pallbearers at the funeral. Generals Sherman, Sheridan, and three former Union flag rank officers joined Simon B. Buckner and Joseph E. Johnston in the procession, along with five other prominent Americans.[33] Grant had defeated General Buckner at the battle of Fort Donelson in 1862, where the late commander's first two initials, suggestive up to this point of the "United States," ever afterward stood for "Unconditional Surrender." He had encountered General Johnston during the siege of Vicksburg a year later. Grant might have defeated Sam Clemens during the Missouri campaign of 1861, but the future humorist had already left for Nevada with his brother Orion after having made a virtue of retreat on the field of battle. Interestingly, that episode in the war marked Grant's victory over fear itself. He had been ordered to attack the troops of Colonel Harris, whose army was encamped in Florida, Missouri — Mark Twain's birthplace. Grant wrote in his memoirs that he would have given anything to be safely back in Illinois until it occurred to him that Harris had been as much afraid of him as he had been of Harris. "This was a view of the question I had never taken before," he wrote, "but it was one I never forgot afterwards. From that event to the close of the war, I never experienced trepidation upon confronting the enemy."[34]

Grant's funeral was a weeklong affair, beginning on August 4. First a private funeral was held in Saratoga Springs. Then the body was taken to Albany, the state capital, where it lay in state until the next day when it was taken aboard a steamer for New York City, where it lay in state again at City Hall. There had been some discussion as to just where Grant ought to be buried. Washington had been buried at his home at Mount Vernon, and Lincoln's body had been taken back to Illinois. Some thought Washington, the nation's capital, would be the most appropriate place, but this idea was generally derided out of a supposition that Washington might not remain the capital once the United States had finished its western expansion. "Some day," wrote Mark Twain to the *New York Sun* of July 27, "the West will be numerically strong enough to move the seat of Government. . . . Then the city of Washington will lose its consequence, & pass out of the public view & the public talk." New York was the fitting place for Grant's tomb, he opined. "Twenty centuries from now New York will still be New York, still a vast city, & the most notable object in it will still be the tomb & monument of Gen. Grant." It was fitting, the consensus said, that Grant's grave should be with "the largest community of his countrymen."[35] Grant in Central Park, where life was buoyant, first came to mind, but the Grants finally decided on at what was then the end of Riverside Drive in Morningside Heights. It was somewhat deserted, but Mayor William Russell Grace argued that the erection of such a colossal monument ought to be constructed in "isolated grandeur."[36]

The general had passed.

>✕<

FOUR

March of the
White Man

>✕<

The runaway slave is called a "nigger" more than two hundred times in *Adventures of Huckleberry Finn*, but naturally no objection was made at the time; the trouble was with the description of the *white* boy, who proved to be a slovenly role model for the American boy, so loved and written about in the nineteenth century. The "N-word," as it is called today, was a historically accurate term for Southerners or Southwesterners to use in antebellum America. It was not quite synonymous with "slave" in the sense that it was used for blacks whether they were enslaved or freed. This American minority went by a number of terms in the nineteenth century, including "blacks." One, used in Whitman's "Song of Myself, is "cuff," originating from the act of cuffing, or hitting a slave with the back on your hand or wrist. "Kanuck, Tuckahoe, Congressman, Cuff, I give them the same, I receive them the same," the poet of democracy in *Leaves of Grass* proclaims. Blacks were sometimes addressed as "Cuffy." But "nigger" prevailed into the twentieth century. It is important, however, to remember that the phrase "Nigger Jim," as the name of the black character, is featured in criticism throughout the twentieth century, never exactly appears in the novel as two connected words of address. It is always the lowercase "nigger Jim," as in "the nigger Jim." The word also underscores the great irony in *Huckleberry Finn,* for Huck is no abolitionist. He doesn't disapprove of slavery in general. He objects to it only in the case of "the nigger Jim" whom he has befriended on the Mississippi River. He befriends a "nigger" and is ashamed of it.

Twain's friend Cable meanwhile was busy defending the rights of freedmen in the South. He had published "The Freedman's Case in Equity" in the January number of the *Century* (the same issue that contained the second installment of *Huckleberry Finn*), and he received a great deal of criticism, most of it emanating from the South, from which he had fled in 1884. His rejoinder, it was announced in the *New York Times* of July 13, would appear in the September issue of the *Century* under the title of "The Silent South." "Mr. Cable's delicate satires on the Creoles" in *Old Creole Days,* the *Times* continued, had implied "to that thin-skinned section of Americans the idea of a taint of African blood." As a consequence, it made it "almost impossible" for him to continue living in New Orleans. "He has not helped himself," it concluded, "by his outspokenness in regard to the negro in his present social phase. Mr. Cable is a reformer who readily adopts the instructive tone, and his Southern fellow-countrymen do not relish his lectures and reproofs."

The torrent of abuse aimed at "The Freedman's Case in Equity" had shocked this twice-wounded veteran of the Fourth Mississippi Cavalry. Not long after he and Twain had parted on March 2, at the close of their lecture tour, Cable had made a visit to his hometown of New Orleans, only to find himself scorned by practically everyone he knew there. He was regarded there as a traitor trying to please Northern readers. Southern newspaper editors revised their interpretations of his writings.

Not only the Creole issue came up for reconsideration; they now saw the recently published *Dr. Sevier* as subversive, especially where one of the characters exclaims of antislavery that "your cause was right." The *New Orleans Times-Democrat* of February 2 counted and quoted nine Southern newspapers that had attacked Cable for "The Freedman's Case in Equity," asserting that his views would lead to social chaos, including miscegenation and racial warfare.[1]

"The late Southern slave," Cable declared at the outset of the essay, "has within two decades risen from slavery to freedom, from freedom to citizenship, passed on into political ascendency, and fallen again from that eminence." Curiously, Mark Twain reflects on the same problem at the end of *Huckleberry Finn,* where Huck asks Tom what he had intended to do if their escape plan — "to set a nigger free that was already free" — had worked. Cable was ahead of the curve on advocating equity for the former slave, but then so too was Twain, though indirectly and certainly not politically. "The Twins of Genius," as they were billed on their lecture tour, were in their different ways both on the side of the future. Yet as progressive as they were on the "race issue," they wouldn't measure up to the standards of today's idea of racial progress.

In "The Freedman's Case in Equity," Cable had gotten himself into a bit of a bind in arguing for civil equity for the Negro. Even though slavery had become a thing of the past, the question of civil equity had "withered away" since the end of the war. As a result, the nation stood at another watershed. The country had adopted six million blacks as citizens, and it was now time to give them full access to public institutions. This included mass transit, and here Cable cited an example that anticipated Rosa Parks's refusal to move to the back of the bus in the twentieth century. In the case of a "negro minister" who tried to assert his legal rights on the East Tennessee, Virginia & Georgia Railway, white passengers "gave him a sound flogging and forced him to a seat among his own color and equals." This example of civil inequality, however, was undercut by Cable's inadvertent suggestion that miscegenation was a desired outcome of social equity. "The occasional mingling of [the Negro's] blood with that of the white man," Cable wrote, wrought no change in the white attitude toward the black: "two, four, eight, multiplied upon or divided into zero, still gave zero for the result."

Interestingly, Cable's observation would be echoed in Mark Twain's description of its main character Roxy in *Pudd'nhead Wilson,* who "was as white as anybody, but the one sixteenth of her which was black outvoted the other fifteen parts and made her a negro," and — it must be added in this antebellum tale — a slave. We might even say "farce," as Twain had published just before *Pudd'nhead* a farce entitled *The American Claimant* (1892). What begins in *Pudd'nhead Wilson* as an ironic denunciation of slavery concludes with a chortle that characterized the white view of the freedman in the 1890s. As with the ending of *Huckleberry Finn,* this novel about slavery inevitably ended as a farce.

"The Freedman's Case in Equity" was attacked on all sides, but Cable's rebuttal that September in the *Century* responded mostly to Henry W. Grady's "In Plain Black and White," which appeared in the magazine's April issue. Though polite in its disagreement, Grady's essay hinted that Cable, though a New Orleans native and a Confederate veteran, was of New England heritage and thus had never truly understood Southern culture. And while the editor of the *Atlanta Constitution* agreed that freedmen should have equal opportunities in the public sphere, they had to remain apart socially and be subject to white supremacy in matters of intelligence and character. Under the title of "The Silent South," Cable wrote a long essay, more than four times the length of his January essay, in which he laid out the case for the freedman and also defended himself against any charge of "negrophilia." The problem, he said, stemmed from "our persistent mistaking [the black's] civil rights for social claims." He had not argued for social equality, merely civil equity — that is to say, while Cable considered the blacks clearly inferior to whites, they nevertheless deserved equal rights to education, transportation, and so on. Civil rights, he insisted, did not mean social equality. "Social equality," he stressed, "is a fool's dream. The present writer wants quite as little of it as the most fervent traditionist [*sic*] of the South. . . . Social equality can never exist where a community, numerous enough to assert itself, is actuated, as every civilized community is, by an intellectual and moral ambition."

With the perspective of more than a century, we can perhaps better understand not only how progressive the "twins of genius" were on race, but also how they were not dedicated to accepting blacks as full equals. Recently, an edition of "Huck Light" (i.e., without the N-word) has eliminated Twain's use of that word to describe black people. Essentially abandoning the argument that its use is historically accurate and must be included, it has replaced it with "slave."[2] Twain himself would have changed the word if he had thought it would hurt sales then, but instead it *helped* sales because it casually expressed the superior attitude of most whites toward blacks in 1885. The black man was no longer a slave, but he was still considered genetically inferior and unfit for social equality. Huck knows this, and when Aunt Sally asks him whether anybody was hurt in the steamboat accident he lied about, he replies, "No'm. Killed a nigger."

* * *

As Cable smoldered under the criticism that winter and planned his response in "The Silent South," he may have discussed the matter with Twain, since they were together every day for two months following the publication of "The Freedman's Case in Equity." These two Southerners, whose lecture circuit carefully skirted the South, could hardly have ignored the question in their daily conversations. Twenty years after the end of the Civil War, both of them were authors of writings that centered on the "Negro problem." Mark Twain, however, had not begun as a "Southern" writer. He had made his early marks with *The Innocents Abroad* and *Roughing It,* which were about Europe and the American West rather than the South. Indeed, his earliest start came exclusively in the West, where he wrote more than one hundred stories and sketches for newspapers and San Francisco magazines, work culminating in the national success of "Jim Smiley and His Jumping Frog" in 1865. The "South" came back to him as a source of fiction in the 1870s when he was asked to recall for the *Atlantic Monthly* his experiences as a steamboat pilot on the Mississippi. Those recollections led to his "Southern" fiction in *Tom Sawyer, Huckleberry Finn,* and *Pudd'nhead Wilson.* If Twain did discuss "The Freedman's Case in Equity" with Cable in the winter of 1885, it is curious that he never wrote about it to anyone in his extant correspondence. More than likely, he did not want to risk his popularity with Southern readers by joining Cable in his political assaults on the status quo, the way he would over American imperialism at the end of the century.

The newspapers' abuse of Cable that winter extended to the North and to gossip about him as Twain's lecture partner, innuendos about his Sunday practices (refusing to travel on the Sabbath) and even a story that Cable had resented Twain's stealing the show during their performances. In May, Cable complained bitterly to the offending newspapers and also wrote to Twain, implying that he too might respond to "slanderous and libelous" statements about them. Indeed, Cable may have wanted Mark Twain to assert his support of his friend publicly in the wake of the blistering abuse he had received for his defense of the freedman's civil rights, but if so he was disappointed. "My dear boy," Twain wrote him, "don't give yourself any discomfort about the slanders of a professional newspaper liar [this from the same man who had complained to the press about the stories claiming that he was taking advantage of Grant] — we can*not* escape such things. . . . To take notice of it in print is a thing which would never have occurred to me. Why, my dear friend, flirt it out of your mind — straight off."[3]

Sam had had his minor differences with Cable during their tour, even thinking that *Cable* was hogging the stage. He complained frequently to his wife, but he ultimately told her that he held George Washington Cable in the highest esteem. At the time of his letter to Cable, he may have been slightly annoyed when his touring partner had failed to join the authors' reading for the American Copyright League on April 28 and 29. Cable's refusal, he told Howells, "was eminently characteristic — to this effect: If they want me to read, let them pay my price."[4] Actually, this assumption was unfair, for Cable had not only been distracted by the scandalmongering in the press, but he was also preoccupied with his wife's current illness. When the *Boston Herald* had criticized him for not joining the other authors, he replied on May 14 that it was false that he had "rudely declined" the invitation. It was also a lie, he added, that he was not a victim of the lack of an international copyright law, which would not come about until 1891.

Twain protected his literary name, while Cable risked his for a good cause, one that persisted well into the twentieth century. "A Colored Man Lynched," announced the *New York Times*. Datelined July 25, 1885, from Atlanta, the murder took place in Douglasville, west of the capital city ("New Growth. Old Charm. Always Home" is the same town's website motto today). One Peter Stamps was lynched by a mob of 500 men for an "alleged assault" on Ida Abercrombie, the daughter of a well-to-do farmer. The local sheriff was taking Stamps out of the county when the mob intervened. A day later a lynching took place in Mound City, Illinois, but this victim was a white man. It is sometimes forgotten that blacks were not the sole victims of such vigilante actions. This lynching victim had killed a man who, divorced from his first wife only the day before, married the murderer's daughter without asking his permission. The story in the *New York Times* of July 27 never explains why the mob lynched him, other than saying that the condemned man had committed "an exceedingly cruel and cowardly murder."

No writer in America had yet turned to the lynching phenomenon in America as a basis for his or her art. In 1885 the ideal of realism still prevailed. Following the Civil War there was a call for more realistic plots in fiction. No longer could the psychological novel such as Hawthorne's *The Scarlet Letter* (1850) depend on the moonlight of romance where the facts of broad daylight are obscured. Yet realism, while it paid attention to everyday details, also subscribed to the myth of the individual. There is no moonlight in Henry James's *The Portrait of a Lady* (1881), but the protagonist there maintains her dignity in spite of social failure, something Edith Wharton's Lily Bart of *The House of Mirth* (1905) would not be able to do in the next age. James brought the psychological novel to a new level, but it was too much for Mark Twain. "You are really my only author," he told Howells, whose books did not probe so deeply the inner sanctum of his characters. "I wouldn't give a damn for the rest. I bored through Middlemarch during the past week, with its labored & tedious analyses of feelings & motives, its paltry & tiresome people, its unexciting & uninteresting story. . . . I can't stand George Eliot, & Hawthorne & those people; I see what they are at, a hundred years before they get to it, & they just tire me to death. And as for *The Bostonians* [then being serialized in the *Century*], I would rather be damned to John Bunyan's heaven than read that."[5]

Bunyan's heaven was akin to being in church, where all earthly enjoyments were abjured. The heavens of Henry James, in Twain's view, repudiated the same enjoyments, trading them for the life of the mind. As unfair as this attitude might strike lovers of literature today, it is true that Mark Twain survived such assaults as Van Wyck Brooks's *The Ordeal of Mark Twain* (1920) and continues to be widely read, while Henry James has been preserved almost exclusively by academic attention. Indeed, it is curious that *Adventures of Huckleberry Finn* succeeds today as collegiate literature as well as popular fiction. In its own day, Twain's magnum opus was considered to be a prime example of inferior art. Although it is not mentioned specifically because the particular focus was on graphic art, *Blackwood's Magazine* that summer declared that art had sunk "lower in standard in proportion as it is more widely diffused." "Artists no longer paint up to cultured connoisseurs, but down to the common people; and this democracy among patrons and painters has vulgarized art." The magazine complained that art no longer dealt with imagination and reason but had grown "naturalistic and real; something to be measured and weighed, as any other commercial commodity."[6]

Mark Twain thought that he wrote for money and that his literary productions were in fact likened to commercial commodities. As he told Howells a couple of years later, "Yes, high & fine literature is wine, & mine is only water; but everybody likes water." He had never "in even one single instance," he told another literary acquaintance, tried to "cultivate the cultivated classes. I was not equipped for it, either by native gifts or training . . . always hunted for bigger game — the masses."[7] Perhaps, but that was not the opinion of his daughter Susy or his wife, Livy. And it wasn't truly his conclusion. Unlike *Tom Sawyer, Huckleberry Finn* had a point, a moral, a theme (despite Twain's prefatory warning that anyone seeking such a thing in the book would be shot). They crept into that boyhood story almost on their own, just as happens in all great literature. And it isn't simply slavery that the theme of *Huckleberry Finn* is concerned with. If that were the case, how would it have been relevant when it was published, more than twenty years after the Emancipation Proclamation, when even the shame of slavery was becoming lost in the theatrical melodramas of *Uncle Tom's Cabin?* True, there remained the slavery of discrimination in the 1880s and well beyond. Besides the distraction of the N-word, where indeed is its controversy or true message today? It is to be had in its profound depiction of human nature — how it is hypocritical and undependable, yet ever so predictable. This novel, as opposed to *Tom Sawyer*, is about conscience, and the plight of the freedman isn't far away. It's not about Tom Sawyer's puppy love and grave robbers, but an underclass boy in a much more serious dilemma.

That dilemma had led to the Civil War and Reconstruction. Reconstruction ended just around the time that Twain began writing *Huckleberry Finn*. In 1877 the scheme to end discrimination had failed, had fizzled after much corruption on the part of the very people, the victorious Yankees, who had enacted it. The experiment left the South embittered and in no mood to extend its hand in friendship to its ex-slaves. Yet even if Reconstruction had been fair, it wouldn't have erased the master-slave relationship between whites and blacks in the South. As Cable conceded in "The Silent South," "it has been carefully demonstrated that, not from Emancipation or Enfranchisement, or anything else in or of the later war, or of Reconstruction, but from our earlier relation to the colored man as his master, results our view of him as naturally and irrevocably servile." In such a shadow, whites could hardly do other than to equate the freedman's civil rights with his social rights. We find the same confusion in *Huckleberry Finn*: Jim might be free, but he is still enslaved by tradition.

Discrimination against the black was in no way confined to the South in 1885. Northerners concerned with the failure of Reconstruction worried that the freedman might relocate north of the Mason-Dixon Line. They mainly feared the younger generation, which had grown up outside the "peculiar institution" of slavery. The *Hartford Times* of July 28 published the account of a resident of the town, a Republican, who had recently toured the South and sounded an alarm: "The fact is, in a few words, that the negro of to-day who has just arrived at manhood is the most worthless of God's creatures. He only works when he cannot steal to live, and, with enough in his pocket to subsist for three days he is rich. . . . The females are as bad, if not worse, than the men. Virtue is almost unknown among these young women." The anonymous writer, perhaps a neighbor of Mark Twain's in Nook Farm, pointedly excluded from his condemnation former slaves like the Clemens butler George Griffin. That sort were "generally sober" and industrious. But the others, those between the ages of twenty and twenty-five, presented a grave problem to "to the wisest men of that section." He hastened to add that the white feeling in the South toward the North consisted of "but one sentiment — perfect kindness."

* * *

Huckleberry Finn may have been water, but it was holy water. One of the most impressive aspects of that book is its point of view. Its subversive condemnation of slavery is delivered through the eyes of a thirteen- or fourteen-year-old boy who doesn't realize the importance of what he describes. Using the first person, Mark Twain gives us a two-tiered narrative. When Huck describes, for example, the Grangerford household, which impresses him so ("There warn't no bed in the parlor"), the desire of middle-class America comes firmly into view. The family has decorated its home with souvenirs from Philadelphia and the East, the same way New Englanders, whose towns with narrow streets resembled villages in England, had borrowed their displays of taste from "our old home." Twain would make much of American envy of the British in the book with the two river frauds, the Duke and the Dauphin.

He shows conflicting sides of the American character, particularly along the river that divides east and west. When Huck responds to Aunt Sally's question as to whether anyone was hurt in the blowout of the cylinder head, she answers: "Well, it's lucky; because sometimes people do get hurt. Two years ago last Christmas, your uncle Silas was coming up from Newrleans on the old Lally Rook, and she blowed out a cylinder-head and crippled a man. And I think he died, afterwards." After being informed that nobody had been killed in the accident that Huck reports on, she goes off into another story quite unconnected with the topic at hand. "He was a Babtist. Your uncle Silas knowed a family in Baton Rouge that knowed his people quite well. Yes, I remember now, he *did* die. Mortification set in, and they had to amputate him." Here Twain fell back on his tricks as a humorist — with the pointless digression and a malapropism. But there is a deep structure to his humor. Buried in the digression and the humor is the pathos of how easily and invisibly white America could absorb another death of a black man. It explores the same depths of the human condition as those books Twain told Howells he hated — Hawthorne's *The Scarlet Letter* or Henry James's *The Portrait of a Lady*. The serious writer in Mark Twain, however, remained incognito, ever in the garb of the humorist. In the scene just described, the author cloaks one of his most moving scenes in humor. Despite his family's wish — indeed, his own partly conscious desire — to be highbrow like James or Howells (he had already tried with *The Prince and the Pauper* and would try again with *Personal Recollections of Joan of Arc*), it is as if Mark Twain wrote best under a self-imposed form of censorship. The public expected it. And he never missed a chance to reinforce that role because he saw it as his bread and butter.

>✦✦✦<

FIVE

"The Private History
of a Campaign That Failed"

>✦✦✦<

When a Samuel Clements of Elma, New York, applied for a state pension, the letter of congratulation was sent to Samuel Clemens of Elmira, New York. "I have not applied for a pension," Twain wrote Commissioner John C. Black on July 8, 1885. "I have often wanted a pension — often ever so often I may say; but inasmuch as the only military service I ever performed during the war was in the Confederate army, I have always felt a delicacy about asking you for it."

No doubt the essay promised to the *Century* on his brief soldiering days was on his mind as he responded. Later that month when reminded by the magazine that he still owed it his contribution to their "Battles and Leaders" series, he told its editor, Robert Underwood Johnson, that he was trying again to work on the essay, adding, "Don't you wait for me — just jam in the other Generals."[1] Indeed, his mock refusal of the military pension may be its prelude, one of the first times he ever talked publicly, or at least in print, about his brief military service. Since a pension had been offered to Clements, he wrote in the July 8 letter to Black, which appeared in the *St. Louis Dispatch* of July 27, that he "felt strengthened" to consider it. "I haven't any pensionable diseases myself, but I can furnish a substitute, a man who is just simply a chaos, a museum of all the different kinds of aches and pains, . . . a man who would regard 'rheumatism and sore eyes' as mere recreation and refreshment after the serious occupation of war."

This letter appeared in the press only four days after Grant's death, when the nation was getting ready to observe the passing of the greatest participant in that "serious occupation of war." Delicacy and keen balance were the order of the day in writing anything funny about the war. Mark Twain would have to observe it, too, in "The Private History of a Campaign That Failed." He asked that if the pension were indeed granted, "please hand it to Gen. Hawley, United States Senator [and former governor of Connecticut] — I mean hand him the certificate, not the money. The letter was signed "S. L. Clemens/ Known to the police as 'Mark Twain.'"[2]

Mark Twain had yet to reveal his service as a Civil War deserter. He was working on that admission, and by August he had completed a draft of "The Private History of a Campaign That Failed." Apparently his wife Livy disapproved of the first full version of the essay that Sam intended to send to Robert Underwood Johnson. In a letter to the *Century* editor on August 15, he wrote: "I have been grinding away at my war article, & have only finished it this moment." He added, "Mrs. Clemens will edit it to-night." Two days later in a postscript, he informed Johnson that Livy had vetoed the essay "in its present shape." She may have objected to Sam's initial mention of an old man, probably Colonel Ralls, "reading his Bible and praying." Whatever he had written was a revision of an off-the-cuff response to a toast at a dinner hosted by the Putnam Phalanx, the oldest military organization in the United States (the account from the *New York Times* is reprinted in the prelude).

"I wouldn't have missed being here for a good deal," Clemens told the assembled veterans that evening. He insisted, he said, on his right "to be escorted to this place as one of the military guests. For I too am a soldier. I am inured to war. I have a military history." There was no mention of the Marion Rangers, just an account of how he joined up with a ragtag state militia in Ralls County. Its purpose, he said, was "to repel invasion." This led to confusion in Missouri, because it wasn't made clear whether the militiamen were defending the state from the North or from the South. "We couldn't really tell which side we were on." The state's governor favored the South, but Missouri ultimately remained in the Union, though it became the scene of guerilla warfare throughout the conflict.

Ben Tupper, who in the recently published *Tom Sawyer* was but a boy imitating a steamboat, is now "19 years old, 6 feet high, 3 feet wide" in "The Private History." "He was town-bred and did not seem to have any correct idea of military discipline. If I commanded him to shut up, he would say, 'Who was your nigger last year?'" Most regiments in the Civil War were homegrown, with all their members coming from the same small town, all having grown up together. Whoever organized the unit usually became its "colonel." In the case of Clemens's band, it was Tom Harris, whom everybody had known as that "darned telegraph operator" in Hannibal. Traditional military discipline was lacking from the start. The unit had not spent any time in "basic training." Moreover, unlike Henry Fleming's fear in *The Red Badge of Courage* that he would appear as a coward in front of the men of his village, these militiamen mainly "felt insulted" at the inconveniences they faced in the field. "They complained that there was an insufficiency of umbrellas." In his speech that evening in 1877, hardly a decade after the war's end, Clemens treated the whole episode as a comedy of errors, a Tom Sawyer escapade gone bad. "So there and then, on the spot, my brigade disbanded itself and tramped off home, with me in the tail of it. . . . We were the first men that went out of it anywhere, . . . and this is the first time that the deeds of those warriors have been brought officially to the notice of humanity."

"What did you do in the war, Daddy?" None of Clemens's daughters was old enough to ask that question in 1877; in fact, one was not yet born. Still, the question must have been pervasive in the decades following the bloodiest conflict in American history. Well over 600,000 Americans from the North and South perished. Their memory and deeds were kept alive by the hundreds of thousands who had rather miraculously survived the war. Walt Whitman's younger brother George survived both a wounding and imprisonment in two Confederate prisons. He enlisted as a private and left the army in 1865 as a brevetted lieutenant colonel, ever after, like so many other soldiers who had reached the commissioned ranks, to be addressed as "Colonel." Two sons of John Quarles, Sam Clemens's favorite uncle, whose Missouri farm he "moved" down river to Arkansas in *Huckleberry Finn,* served as commissioned officers in the Confederate army. Sam was in his twenties when the war broke out and could have easily taken part in the war. Indeed, he almost did participate when a Union colonel sought to draft him into service as a steamboat pilot for the North. Instead, he went out west to the Nevada Territory with his older brother Orion and became first a gold and silver miner and then — in 1863 — a reporter for the *Virginia City Enterprise* under the pseudonym "Mark Twain."

He came east from Hawaii and San Francisco in 1865 with the national success of "Jim Smiley and his Jumping Frog." He went east as a comedian, an American humorist, that "writer of the left hand" who hid his past behind the façade of humor. Twelve years later, in 1877, after the successes of *The Innocents Abroad, Roughing It,* and *The Adventures of Tom Sawyer,* he felt it was safe — at least locally, in Hartford — to reveal his military history, hiding behind the same guise of humor that had brought him to his national fame in 1865. He could confess it as long as he made it funny, laying no claim to the heroism of the war's dead and living. But now, in 1885, with his heavy involvement with Grant's memoir, indeed with his close association to the general who was barely cold in his tomb, he dared to end his funny wartime story with something tragically serious, the death of a mysterious stranger. He even went so far as to initially entitle his contribution to the *Century*'s prestigious Civil War series "My Campaign Against Grant."

Even in jest, Mark Twain wouldn't have dared to use such a title if Grant still lived. The general was dead, of course, but he hadn't yet been fully laid to rest. In the ensuing years between his funeral and the construction of Grant's tomb, the general would continue as a presence in the minds of a grateful nation. The executive committee of the newly formed Grant Monument Association had collected only $83,028.19, as of October 2, 1885, according to the *New York Times* of that date. Ultimately, $600,000 was raised for the memorial. The general's remains initially resided in a vault in Riverside Park. Sentries guarded the "temporary" sarcophagus around the clock. It would take another twelve years for the final monument to be completed and dedicated, on what would have been Grant's seventy-fifth birthday. The tomb, consisting of more than 8,000 tons of granite, soon afterward became the most popular tourist site in New York City. Over 600,000 people visited the mausoleum in 1906, far exceeding the number of visitors to the Statue of Liberty until the First World War. When, however, the palatial monument was turned over to the National Park Service in 1959, its glory began to fade quickly. By the time of the Vietnam War in the stormy antiwar 1960s and 1970s, its walls were covered with graffiti. The tomb then served as a public bathroom and a shelter for the homeless. The military hero and former two-term president of the United States, whose five-hour funeral march from City Hall to Riverside Park in 1885 had been attended by more than one million spectators, was now host to drug addicts and prostitutes. It wouldn't be until 1997, on the centennial of its erection, that Grant's tomb would be restored to its original dignity.

THE PRIVATE HISTORY OF A CAMPAIGN THAT FAILED

BY MARK TWAIN   (*Century Magazine,* December 1885)

You have heard from a great many people who did something in the war; is it not fair and right that you listen a little moment to one who started out to do something in it, but didn't? Thousands entered the war, got just a taste of it, and then stepped out again, permanently. These, by their very numbers, are respectable, and are therefore entitled to a sort of voice, — not a loud one, but a modest one; not a boastful one, but an apologetic one. They ought not to be allowed much space among better people — people who did something — I grant that; but they ought at least to be allowed to state why they didn't do anything, and also to explain the process by which they didn't do anything. Surely this kind of light must have a sort of value.

Out West there was a good deal of confusion in men's minds

during the first months of the great trouble — a good deal of unsettledness, of leaning first this way, then that, then the other way. It was hard for us to get our bearings. I call to mind an instance of this. I was piloting on the Mississippi when the news came that South Carolina had gone out of the Union on the 20th of December, 1860. My pilot-mate was a New Yorker. He was strong for the Union; so was I. But he would not listen to me with any patience; my loyalty was smirched, to his eye, because my father had owned slaves. I said, in palliation of this dark fact, that I had heard my father say, some years before he died, that slavery was a great wrong, and that he would free the solitary negro he then owned if he could think it right to give away the property of the family when he was so straitened in means. My mate retorted that a mere impulse was nothing — anybody could pretend to a good impulse; and went on decrying my Unionism and libeling my ancestry. A month later the secession atmosphere had considerably thickened on the Lower Mississippi, and I became a rebel; so did he. We were together in New Orleans, the 26th of January, when Louisiana went out of the Union. He did his full share of the rebel shouting, but was bitterly opposed to letting me do mine. He said I came of bad stock — of a father who had been willing to set slaves free. In the following summer he was piloting a Federal gun-boat and shouting for the Union again, and I was in the Confederate army. I held his note for some borrowed money. He was one of the most upright men I ever knew; but he repudiated that note without hesitation, because I was a rebel, and the son of a man who owned slaves.

In that summer — of 1861 — the first wash of the wave of war broke upon the shores of Missouri. Our State was invaded by the Union forces. They took possession of St. Louis, Jefferson Barracks, and some other points. The Governor, Claib Jackson, issued his proclamation calling out fifty thousand militia to repel the invader.

I was visiting in the small town where my boyhood had been spent — Hannibal, Marion County. Several of us got together in a secret place by night and formed ourselves into a military company. One Tom Lyman, a young fellow of a good deal of spirit but of no military experience, was made captain; I was made second lieutenant. We had no first lieutenant; I do not know why; it was long ago. There were fifteen of us. By the advice of an innocent connected with the organization, we called ourselves the Marion Rangers. I do not remember that any one found fault with the name. I did not; I thought it sounded quite well. The young fellow who proposed this title was perhaps a fair sample of the kind of stuff we were made of. He was young, ignorant, good-natured, well-meaning, trivial, full of romance, and given to reading chivalric novels and singing forlorn love-ditties. He had some pathetic little nickel-plated aristocratic instincts, and detested his name, which was Dunlap; detested it, partly because it was nearly as common in that region as Smith, but mainly because it had a plebeian sound to his ear. So he tried to ennoble it by writing it in this way: *d'Unlap.* That contented his eye, but left his ear unsatisfied, for people gave the new name the same old pronunciation — emphasis on the front end of it. He then did the bravest thing that can be imagined, — a thing to make one shiver when one remembers how the world is given to resenting shams and affectations; he began to write his name so: *d'Un Lap.* And he waited patiently through the long storm of mud that was flung at this work of art, and he had his reward at last; for he lived to see that name accepted, and the emphasis put where he wanted it, by people who had known him all his life, and to whom the tribe of Dunlaps had been as familiar as the rain and the sunshine for forty years. So sure of victory at last is the courage that can wait. He said he had found, by consulting some ancient French chronicles, that the name was rightly and originally written d'Un Lap and said that if it were translated into English it would mean Peterson: *Lap,* Latin or Greek, he said, for stone or rock, same as the French *pierre,* that is to say, Peter; *d,*' of or from; *un,* a or one; hence, d'Un Lap of or from a stone or a Peter; that is to say, one who is the son of a stone, the son of a Peter — Peterson. Our militia company were not learned and the explanation confused them; so they called him Peterson Dunlap. He proved useful to us in his way; he named our camps for us, and he generally struck a name that was "no slouch," as the boys said.

That is one sample of us. Another was Ed Stevens, son of the town jeweler, — trim-built, handsome, graceful, neat as a cat; bright, educated, but given over entirely to fun. There was nothing serious in life to him. As far as he was concerned, this military expedition of ours was simply a holiday. I should say that about half of us looked upon it in the same way; not consciously, perhaps, but unconsciously. We did not think; we were not capable of it. As for myself, I was full of unreasoning joy to be done with turning out of bed at midnight and four in the morning, for a while; grateful to have a change, new scenes, new occupations, a new interest. In my thoughts that was as far as I went; I did not go into the details; as a rule one doesn't at twenty-four.

Another sample was Smith, the blacksmith's apprentice. This vast donkey had some pluck, of a slow and sluggish nature, but a soft heart; at one time he would knock a horse down for some impropriety, and at another he would get homesick and cry. However, he had one ultimate credit to his account which some of us hadn't: he stuck to the war, and was killed in battle at last.

Jo Bowers, another sample, was a huge, good-natured, flax-headed lubber; lazy, sentimental, full of harmless brag, a grumbler by nature; an experienced, industrious, ambitious, and often quite picturesque liar, and yet not a successful one, for he had had no intelligent training, but was allowed to come up just any way. This life was serious enough to him, and seldom satisfactory. But he was a good fellow anyway, and the boys all liked him. He was made orderly sergeant; Stevens was made corporal.

These samples will answer — and they are quite fair ones. Well, this herd of cattle started for the war. What could you expect of them? They did as well as they knew how, but really what was justly to be expected of them? Nothing, I should say. That is what they did.

We waited for a dark night, for caution and secrecy were necessary; then, toward midnight, we stole in couples and from various directions to the Griffith place, beyond the town; from that point we set out together on foot. Hannibal lies at the extreme southeastern corner of Marion County, on the Mississippi River; our objective point was the hamlet of New London, ten miles away, in Ralls County.

The first hour was all fun, all idle nonsense and laughter. But that could not be kept up. The steady trudging came to be like work; the play had somehow oozed out of it; the stillness of the woods and the somberness of the night began to throw a depressing influence over the spirits of the boys, and presently the talking died out and each person shut himself up in his own thoughts. During the last half of the second hour nobody said a word.

Now we approached a log farm-house where, according to report, there was a guard of five Union soldiers. Lyman called a halt; and there, in the deep gloom of the overhanging branches, he began to whisper a plan of assault upon that house, which made the gloom more depressing than it was before. It was a crucial moment; we realized, with a cold suddenness, that here was no jest — we were standing face to face with actual war. We were equal to the occasion. In our response there was no hesitation, no indecision: we said that if Lyman wanted to meddle with those soldiers, he could go ahead and do it; but if he waited for us to follow him, he would wait a long time.

Lyman urged, pleaded, tried to shame us, but it had no effect. Our course was plain, our minds were made up: we would flank the farm-house — go out around. And that is what we did.

We struck into the woods and entered upon a rough time, stumbling over roots, getting tangled in vines, and torn by briers. At last we reached an open place in a safe region, and sat down, blown and hot, to cool off and nurse our scratches and bruises. Lyman was annoyed, but the rest of us were cheerful; we had flanked the farm-house, we had made our first military movement, and it was a success; we had nothing to fret about, we were feeling just the other way. Horse-play and laughing began again; the expedition was become a holiday frolic once more.

Then we had two more hours of dull trudging and ultimate silence and depression; then, about dawn, we straggled into New London, soiled, heel-blistered, fagged with our little march, and all of us except Stevens in a sour and raspy humor and privately down on the war. We stacked our shabby old shot-guns in Colonel Ralls's barn, and then went in a body and breakfasted with that veteran of the Mexican war. Afterwards he took us to a distant meadow, and there in the shade of a tree we listened to an old-fashioned speech from him, full of gunpowder and glory, full of that adjective-piling, mixed metaphor, and windy declamation which was regarded as eloquence in that ancient time and that remote region; and then he swore us on the Bible to be faithful to the State of Missouri and drive all invaders from her soil, no matter whence they might come or under what flag they might march. This mixed us considerably, and we could not make out just what service we were embarked in; but Colonel Ralls, the practiced politician and phrase-juggler, was not similarly in doubt; he knew quite clearly that he had invested us in the cause of the Southern Confederacy. He closed the solemnities by belting around me the sword which his neighbor, Colonel Brown, had worn at Buena Vista and Molino del Rey; and he accompanied this act with another impressive blast.

Then we formed in line of battle and marched four miles to a shady and pleasant piece of woods on the border of the far-reaching expanses of a flowery prairie. It was an enchanting region for war — our kind of war.

We pierced the forest about half a mile, and took up a strong position, with some low, rocky, and wooded hills behind us, and a purling, limpid creek in front. Straightway, half the command were in swimming, and the other half fishing. The ass with the French name gave this position a romantic title, but it was too long, so the boys shortened and simplified it to Camp Ralls.

We occupied an old maple-sugar camp, whose half-rotted troughs were still propped against the trees. A long corn-crib served for sleeping quarters for the battalion. On our left, half a mile away, was Mason's farm and house; and he was a friend to the cause. Shortly after noon the farmers began to arrive from several directions, with mules and horses for our use, and these they lent us for as long as the war might last, which they judged would be about three months. The animals were of all sizes, all colors, and all breeds. They were mainly young and frisky, and nobody in the command could stay on them long at a time; for we were town boys, and ignorant of horsemanship. The creature that fell to my share was a very small mule, and yet so quick and active that it could throw me without difficulty; and it did this whenever I got on it. Then it would bray — stretching its neck out, laying its ears back, and spreading its jaws till you could see down to its works. It was a disagreeable animal, in every way. If I took it by the bridle and tried to lead it off the grounds, it would sit down and brace back, and no one could budge it. However, I was not entirely destitute of military resources, and I did presently manage to spoil this game; for I had seen many a steamboat aground in my time, and knew a trick or two which even a grounded mule would be obliged to respect. There was a well by the corn-crib; so I substituted thirty fathom of rope for the bridle, and fetched him home with the windlass.

I will anticipate here sufficiently to say that we did learn to ride, after some days' practice, but never well. We could not learn to like our animals; they were not choice ones, and most of them had annoying peculiarities of one kind or another. Stevens's horse would carry him, when he was not noticing, under the huge excrescences which form on the trunks of oak-trees, and wipe him out of the saddle; in this way Stevens got several bad hurts. Sergeant Bowers's horse was very large and tall, with slim, long legs, and looked like a railroad bridge. His size enabled him to reach all about, and as far as he wanted to, with his head; so he was always biting Bowers's legs. On the march, in the sun, Bowers slept a good deal; and as soon as the horse recognized that he was asleep he would reach around and bite him on the leg. His legs were black and blue with bites. This was the only thing that could ever make him swear, but this always did; whenever the horse bit him he always swore, and of course Stevens, who laughed at everything, laughed at this, and would even get into such convulsions over it as to lose his balance and fall off his horse; and then Bowers, already irritated by the pain of the horse-bite, would resent the laughter with hard language, and there would be a quarrel; so that horse made no end of trouble and bad blood in the command.

However, I will get back to where I was — our first afternoon in the sugar-camp. The sugar-troughs came very handy as horse-troughs, and we had plenty of corn to fill them with. I ordered Sergeant Bowers to feed my mules; but he said that if I reckoned he went to war to be dry-nurse to a mule, it wouldn't take me very long to find out my mistake. I believed that this was insubordination, but I was full of uncertainties about everything military, and so I let the thing pass, and went and ordered Smith, the blacksmith's apprentice, to feed the mule; but he merely gave me a large, cold, sarcastic grin, such as an ostensibly seven-year-old horse gives you when you lift his lip and find he is fourteen, and turned his back on me. I then went to the captain, and asked if it was not right and proper and military for me to have an orderly. He said it was, but as there was only one orderly in the corps, it was but right that he himself should have Bowers on his staff. Bowers said he wouldn't serve on anybody's staff; and if anybody thought he could make him, let him try it. So, of course, the thing had to be dropped; there was no other way.

Next, nobody would cook; it was considered a degradation; so we had no dinner. We lazied the rest of the pleasant afternoon away, some dozing under the trees, some smoking cob-pips and talking sweethearts and war, some playing games. By late suppertime all hands were famished; and to meet the difficulty all hands turned to, on an equal footing, and gathered wood, built fires, and cooked the meal. Afterward, everything was smooth for a while; then trouble broke out between the corporal and the sergeant, each claiming to rank the other. Nobody knew which was the higher office; so Lyman had to settle the matter by making the rank of both officers equal. The commander of an ignorant crew like that has many troubles and vexations which probably do not occur in the regular army at all. However, with the song-singing and yarn-spinning around the camp-fire, everything presently became serene again; and by and by we raked the corn down level in one end of the crib, and all went to bed on it, tying a horse to the door, so that he would neigh if any one tried to get in.*

We had some horsemanship drill every forenoon; then, afternoons, we rode off here and there in squads a few miles, and visited the farmers' girls, and had a youthful good time, and got an honest good dinner or supper, and then home again to camp, happy and content.

For a time, life was idly delicious, it was perfect; there was nothing to mar it. Then came some farmers with an alarm one day. They said it was rumored that the enemy were advancing in our direction, from over Hyde's prairie. The result was a sharp stir among us, and general consternation. It was a rude awakening from our pleasant trance. The rumor was but a rumor — nothing definite about it; so, in the confusion, we did not know which way to retreat. Lyman was for not retreating at all,

---

*It was always my impression that that was what the horse was there for, and I know that it was also the impression of at least one other of the command, for we talked about it at the time, and admired the military ingenuity of the device; but when I was out West three years ago I was told by Mr. A. G. Fuqua, a member of our company, that the horse was his, that the leaving him tied at the door was a matter of mere forgetfulness, and that to attribute it to intelligent invention was to give him quite too much credit. In support of his position, he called my attention to the suggestive fact that the artifice was not employed again. I had not thought of that before.

in these uncertain circumstances; but he found that if he tried to maintain that attitude he would fare badly for the command were in no humor to put up with insubordination. So he yielded the point and called a council of war — to consist of himself and the three other officers; but the privates made such a fuss about being left out, that we had to allow them to be present. I mean we had to allow them to remain, for they were already present, and doing the most of the talking too. The question was, which way to retreat; but all were so flurried that nobody seemed to have even a guess to offer. Except Lyman. He explained in a few calm words, that inasmuch as the enemy were approaching from over Hyde's prairie, our course was simple: all we had to do was not to retreat *toward* him; any other direction would answer our needs perfectly. Everybody saw in a moment how true this was, and how wise; so Lyman got a great many compliments. It was now decided that we should fall back on Mason's farm.

It was after dark by this time, and as we could not know how soon the enemy might arrive, it did not seem best to try to take the horses and things with us; so we only took the guns and ammunition, and started at once. The route was very rough and hilly and rocky, and presently the night grew very black and rain began to fall; so we had a troublesome time of it, struggling and stumbling along in the dark; and soon some person slipped and fell, and then the next person behind stumbled over him and fell, and so did the rest, one after the other; and then Bowers came with the keg of powder in his arms, whilst the command were all mixed together, arms and legs, on the muddy slope; and so he fell, of course, with the keg, and this started the whole detachment down the hill in a body, and they landed in the brook at the bottom in a pile, and each that was undermost pulling the hair and scratching and biting those that were on top of him; and those that were being scratched and bitten scratching and biting the rest in their turn, and all saying they would die before they would ever go to war again if they ever got out of this brook this time, and the invader might rot for all they cared, and the country along with him — and all such talk as that, which was dismal to hear and take part in, in such smothered, low voices, and such a grisly dark place and so wet, and the enemy may be coming any moment.

The keg of powder was lost, and the guns too; so the growling and complaining continued straight along whilst the brigade pawed around the pasty hillside and slopped around in the brook hunting for these things; consequently we lost considerable time at this; and then we heard a sound, and held our breath and listened, and it seemed to be the enemy coming, though it could have been a cow, for it had a cough like a cow; but we did not wait, but left a couple of guns behind and struck out for Mason's again as briskly as we could scramble along in the dark. But we got lost presently among the rugged little ravines, and wasted a deal of time finding the way again, so it was after nine when we reached Mason's stile at last; and then before we could open our mouths to give the countersign, several dogs came bounding over the fence, with great riot and noise, and each of them took a soldier by the slack of his trousers and began to back away with him. We could not shoot the dogs without endangering the persons they were attached to; so we had to look on, helpless, at what was perhaps the most mortifying spectacle of the civil war. There was light enough, and to spare, for the Masons had now run out on the porch with candles in their hands. The old man and his son came and undid the dogs without difficulty, all but Bowers's; but they couldn't undo his dog, they didn't know his combination; he was of the bull kind, and seemed to be set with a Yale time-lock; but they got him loose at last with some scalding water, of which Bowers got his share and returned thanks. Peterson Dunlap afterwards made up a fine name for this engagement, and also for the night march which preceded it, but both have long ago faded out of my memory.

We now went into the house, and they began to ask us a world of questions, whereby it presently came out that we did not know anything concerning who or what we were running from; so the old gentleman made himself very frank, and said we were a curious breed of soldiers, and guessed we could be depended on to end up the war in time, because no government could stand the expense of the shoe-leather we should cost it trying to follow us around. "Marion *Rangers!* Good name, b'gosh!" said he. And wanted to know why we hadn't had a picket-guard at the place where the road entered the prairie, and why we hadn't sent out a scouting party to spy out the enemy and bring us an account of his strength, and so on, before jumping up and stampeding out of a strong position upon a mere vague rumor — and so on and so forth, till he made us all feel shabbier than the dogs had done, not half so enthusiastically welcome. So we went to bed shamed and low-spirited; except Stevens. Soon Stevens began to devise a garment for Bowers which could be made to automatically display his battle-scars to the grateful, or conceal them from the envious, according to his occasions; but Bowers was in no humor for this, so there was a fight, and when it was over Stevens had some battle-scars of his own to think about.

Then we got a little sleep. But after all we had gone through, our activities were not over for the night; for about two o'clock in the morning we heard a shout of warning from down the lane, accompanied by a chorus from all the dogs, and in a moment everybody was up and flying around to find out what the alarm was about. The alarmist was a horseman who gave notice that a detachment of Union soldiers was on its way from Hannibal with orders to capture and hang any bands like ours which it could find, and said we had no time to lose. Farmer Mason was in a flurry this time, himself. He hurried us out of the house with all haste, and sent one of his negroes with us to show us where to hide ourselves and our tell-tale guns among the ravines half a mile away. It was raining heavily.

We struck down the lane, then across some rocky pasture-land which offered good advantages for stumbling; consequently we were down in the mud most of the time, and every time a man went down he blackguarded the war, and the people that started it, and everybody connected with it, and gave himself the master dose of all for being so foolish as to go into it. At last we reached the wooded mouth of a ravine, and there we huddled ourselves under the streaming trees, and sent the negro back home. It was a dismal and heart-breaking time. We were like to be drowned with the rain, deafened with the howling wind and the booming thunder, and blinded by the lightning. It was indeed a wild night. The drenching we were getting was misery enough, but a deeper misery still was the reflection that the halter might end us before we were a day older. A death of this shameful sort had not occurred to us as being among the possibilities of war. It took the romance all out of the campaign, and turned our dreams of glory into a repulsive nightmare. As for doubting that so barbarous an order had been given, not one of us did that.

The long night wore itself out at last, and then the negro came to us with the news that the alarm had manifestly been a false one, and that breakfast would soon be ready. Straightway we were lighted-hearted again, and the world was bright, and life as full of hope and promise as ever — for we were young then. How long ago that was! Twenty-four years later.

The mongrel child of philology named the night's refuge Camp Devastation, and no soul objected. The Masons gave us a Missouri country breakfast, in Missourian abundance, and we needed it: hot biscuits; hot "wheat bread" prettily criss-crossed in a lattice pattern on top; hot corn pone; fried chicken; bacon, coffee, eggs, milk, buttermilk, etc.; — and the world may be confidently challenged to furnish the equal to such a breakfast, as it is cooked in the South.

We staid several days at Mason's; and after all these years the memory of the dullness, the stillness and lifelessness of that slumberous farm-house still oppresses my spirit as with a sense of the presence of death and mourning. There was nothing to do, nothing to think about; there was no interest in life. The male part of the household were away in the fields all day, the women were busy and out of our sight; there was no sound but the plaintive wailing of a spinning-wheel, forever moaning out from some distant room, — the most lonesome sound in nature, a sound steeped and sodden with homesickness and the emptiness of life. The family went to bed about dark every night, and as we were not invited to intrude any new customs, we naturally followed theirs. Those nights were a hundred years long to youths accustomed to being up till twelve. We lay awake and miserable till that hour every time, and grew old and decrepit waiting through the still eternities for the clock-strikes. This was no place for town boys. So at last it was with something very like joy that we received news that the enemy were on our track again. With new birth of the old warrior spirit, we sprang to our places in line of battle and fell back on Camp Ralls.

Captain Lyman had taken a hint from Mason's talk, and he

now gave orders that our camp should be guarded against surprise by the posting of pickets. I was ordered to place a picket at the forks of the road in Hyde's prairie. Night shut down black and threatening. I told Sergeant Bowers to go out to that place and stay till midnight; and, just as I was expecting, he said he wouldn't do it. I tried to get others to go, but all refused. Some excused themselves on account of the weather; but the rest were frank enough to say they wouldn't go in any kind of weather. This kind of thing sounds odd now, and impossible, but there was no surprise in it at the time. On the contrary, it seemed a perfectly natural thing to do. There were scores of little camps scattered over Missouri where the same thing was happening. These camps were composed of young men who had been born and reared to a sturdy independence, and who did not know what it meant to be ordered around by Tom, Dick, and Harry, whom they had known familiarly all their lives, in the village or on the farm. It is quite within the probabilities that this same thing was happening all over the South. James Redpath recognized the justice of this assumption, and furnished the following instance in support of it. During a short stay in East Tennessee he was in a citizen colonel's tent one day, talking, when a big private appeared at the door, and without salute or other circumlocution, said to the colonel:

"Say, Jim, I'm a-goin' home for a few days."

"What for?"

"Well, I hain't b'en there for a right smart while, and I'd like to see how things is comin' on."

"How long are you going to be gone?"

"'Bout two weeks."

"Well, don't be gone longer than that; and get back sooner if you can."

That was all, and the citizen officer resumed his conversation where the private had broken it off. This was in the first months of the war, of course. The camps in our part of Missouri were under Brigadier-General Thomas H. Harris. He was a townsman of ours, a first-rate fellow, and well liked; but we had all familiarly known him as the sole and modest-salaried operator in our telegraph office, where he had to send about one dispatch a week in ordinary times, and two when there was a rush of business; consequently, when he appeared in our midst one day, on the wing, and delivered a military command of some sort, in a large military fashion, nobody was surprised at the response which he got from the assembled soldiery:

"Oh, now, what'll you take to *don't*, Tom Harris!"

It was quite the natural thing. One might justly imagine that we were hopeless material for war. And so we seemed, in our ignorant state; but there were those among us who afterward learned the grim trade; learned to obey like machines; became valuable soldiers; fought all through the war, and came out at the end with excellent records. One of the very boys who refused to go out on picket duty that night, and called me an ass for thinking he would expose himself to danger in such a foolhardy way, had become distinguished for intrepidity before he was a year older.

I did secure my picket that night — not by authority, but by diplomacy. I got Bowers to go, by agreeing to exchange ranks with him for the time being, and go along and stand the watch with him as his subordinate. We staid out there a couple of dreary hours in the pitchy darkness and the rain, with nothing to modify the dreariness but Bowers's monotonous growling at the war and the weather; then we began to nod, and presently found it next to impossible to stay in the saddle; so we gave up the tedious job, and went back to the camp without waiting for the relief guard. We rode into camp without interruption or objection from anybody, and the enemy could have done the same, for there were no sentries. Everybody was asleep; at midnight there was nobody to send out another picket, so none was sent. We never tried to establish a watch at night again, as far as I remember, but we generally kept a picket out in the daytime.

In that camp the whole command slept on the corn in the big corn-crib; and there was usually a general row before morning, for the place was full of rats, and they would scramble over the boys' bodies and faces, annoying and irritating everybody; and now and then they would bite some one's toe, and the person who owned the toe would start up and magnify his English and begin to throw corn in the dark. The ears were half as heavy as bricks, and when they struck they hurt. The persons struck would respond, and inside of five minutes every man would be locked in a death-grip with his neighbor. There was a grievous deal of blood shed in the corn-crib, but this was all that was spilt while I was in the war. No, that is not quite true. But for one circumstance it would have been all. I will come to that now.

Our scares were frequent. Every few days rumors would come that the enemy were approaching. In these cases we always fell back on some other camp of ours; we never staid where we were. But the rumors always turned out to be false; so at last even we began to grow indifferent to them. One night a negro was sent do our corn-crib with the same old warning: the enemy was hovering in our neighborhood. We all said let him hover. We resolved to stay still and be comfortable. It was a fine warlike resolution, and no doubt we all felt the stir of it in our veins — for a moment. We had been having a very jolly time, that was full of horse-play and school-boy hilarity; but that cooled down now, and presently the fast-waning fire of forced jokes and forced laughs died out altogether, and the company became silent. Silent and nervous. And soon uneasy — worried — apprehensive. We had said we would stay, and we were committed. We could have been persuaded to go, but there was nobody brave enough to suggest it. An almost noiseless movement presently began in the dark, by a general but unvoiced impulse. When the movement was completed, each man knew that he was not the only person who had crept to the front wall and had his eye at a crack between the logs. No, we were all there; all there with our hearts in our throats, and staring out toward the sugar-troughs where the forest foot-path came through. It was late, and there was a deep woodsy stillness everywhere. There was a veiled moonlight, which was only just strong enough to enable us to mark the general shape of objects. Presently a muffled sound caught our ears, and we recognized it as the hoof-beats of a horse or horses. And right away a figure appeared in the forest path; it could have been made of smoke, its mass had so little sharpness of outline. It was a man on horseback; and it seemed to me that there were others behind him. I got hold of a gun in the dark, and pushed it through a crack between the logs, hardly knowing what I was doing, I was so dazed with fright. Somebody said "Fire!" I pulled the trigger. I seemed to see a hundred flashes and hear a hundred reports, then I saw the man fall down out of the saddle. My first feeling was of surprised gratification; my first impulse was an apprentice-sportsman's impulse to run and pick up his game. Somebody said, hardly audibly, "Good — we've got him! — wait for the rest." But the rest did not come. We waited — listened — still no more came. There was not a sound, not the whisper of a leaf; just perfect stillness; an uncanny kind of stillness, which was all the more uncanny on account of the damp, earthy late-night smells now rising and pervading it. Then, wondering, we crept stealthily out, and approached the man. When we got to him the moon revealed him distinctly. He was lying on his back, with his arms abroad; his mouth was open and his chest heaving with long gasps, and his white shirt-front was all splashed with blood. The thought shot through me that I was a murderer; that I had killed a man — a man who had never done me any harm. That was the coldest sensation that ever went through my marrow. I was down by him in a moment, helplessly stroking his forehead; and I would have given anything then — my own life freely — to make him again what he had been five minutes before. And all the boys seemed to be feeling in the same way; they hung over him, fully of pitying interest, and tried all they could to help him, and said all sorts of regretful things. They had forgotten all about the enemy; they thought only of this one forlorn unit of the foe. Once my imagination persuaded me that the dying man gave me a reproachful look out of his shadowy eyes, and it seemed to me that I could rather he had stabbed me than done that. He muttered and mumbled like a dreamer in his sleep, about his wife and his child; and I thought with a new despair, "This thing that I have done does not end with him; it falls upon *them* too, and they never did me any harm, any more than he."

In a little while the man was dead. He was killed in war; killed in fair and legitimate war; killed in battle, as you may say; and yet he was as sincerely mourned by the opposing force as if he had been their brother. The boys stood there a half hour sorrowing over him, and recalling the details of the tragedy, and wondering who he might be, and if he were a spy, and saying that if it were to do over again they would not hurt him unless he attacked them first. It soon came out that mine was not the only shot fired; there were five others, — a division of the guilt which was a grateful relief to me, since it in some degree lightened and diminished the burden I was carrying. There were six shots fired at once; but I was not in my right mind at the time, and my heated imagination had magnified my one shot into a volley. The man was not in uniform, and was not armed. He was a stranger in the country; that was all we ever found out about him. The thought of him got to preying upon me every night; I could not get rid of it. I could not drive it away, the taking of that unoffending life seemed such a wanton thing. And it seemed an epitome of war; that all war must be just that — the killing of strangers against whom you feel no personal animosity; strangers whom, in other circumstances, you would help if you found them in trouble, and who would help you if you needed it. My campaign was spoiled. It seemed to me that I was not rightly equipped for this awful business; that war was intended for men, and I for a child's nurse. I resolved to retire from this avocation of sham soldiership while I could save some remnant of my self-respect. These morbid thoughts clung to me against reason; for at bottom I did not believe I had touched that man. The law of probabilities decreed me guiltless of his blood; for in all my small experience with guns I had never hit anything I had tried to hit, and I knew I had done my best to hit him. Yet there was no solace in the thought. Against a diseased imagination, demonstration goes for nothing.

The rest of my war experience was of a piece with what I have already told of it. We kept monotonously falling back upon one camp or another, and eating up the country. I marvel now at the patience of the farmers and their families. They ought to have shot us; on the contrary, they were as hospitably kind and courteous to us as if we had deserved it. In one of these camps we found Ab Grimes, an Upper Mississippi pilot, who afterwards became famous as a dare-devil rebel spy, whose career bristled with desperate adventures. The look and style of his comrades suggested that they had not come into the war to play, and their deeds made good the conjecture later. They were fine horsemen and good revolver-shots; but their favorite arm was the lasso. Each had one at his pommel, and could snatch a man out of the saddle with it every time, on a full gallop, at any reasonable distance.

In another camp the chief was a fierce and profane old blacksmith of sixty, and he had furnished his twenty recruits with gigantic home-made bowie-knives, to be swung with the two hands, like the *machetes* of the Isthmus. It was a grisly spectacle to see that earnest band practicing under the eye of that remorseless old fanatic.

The last camp which we fell back upon was in a hollow near the village of Florida, where I was born — in Monroe County. Here we were warned, one day, that a Union colonel was sweeping down on us with a whole regiment at his heels. This looked decidedly serious. Our boys went apart and consulted; then we went back and told the other companies present that the war was a disappointment to us and we were going to disband. They were getting ready, themselves, to fall back on some place or other, and were only waiting for General Tom Harris, who was expected to arrive at any moment; so they tried to persuade us to wait a little while, but the majority of us said no, we were accustomed to falling back, and didn't need any of Tom Harris's help; we could get along perfectly well without him — and save time too. So about half of our fifteen, including myself, mounted and left on the instant; the others yielded to persuasion and staid — staid through the war.

An hour later we met General Harris on the road, with two or three people in his company — his staff, probably, but we could not tell; none of them were in uniform; uniforms had not come into vogue among us yet. Harris ordered us back; but we told him there was a Union colonel coming with a whole regiment in his wake, and it looked as if there was going to be disturbance; so we had concluded to go home. He raged a little, but it was of no use; our minds were made up. We had done our share; had killed one man, exterminated one army, such as it was; let him go and kill the rest, and that would end the war. I did not see that brisk young general again until last year; then he was wearing white hair and whiskers.

In time I came to know that Union colonel whose coming frightened me out of the war and crippled the Southern cause to that extent — General Grant. I came within a few hours of seeing him when he was as unknown as I was myself; at a time when anybody could have said, "Grant? — Ulysses S. Grant? I do not remember hearing the name before." It seems difficult to realize that there was once a time when such a remark could be rationally made; but there *was,* and I was within a few miles of the place and the occasion too, though proceeding in the other direction.

The thoughtful will not throw this war-paper of mine lightly aside as being valueless. It has this value: it is a not unfair picture of what went on in many and many a militia camp in the first months of the rebellion, when the green recruits were without discipline, without the steadying and heartening influence of trained leaders; when all their circumstances were new and strange, and charged with exaggerated terrors, and before the invaluable experience of actual collision in the field had turned them from rabbits into soldiers. If this side of the picture of that early day has not before been put into history, then history has been to that degree incomplete, for it had and has its rightful place there. There was more Bull Run material scattered through the early camps of this country than exhibited itself at Bull Run. And yet it learned its trade presently, and helped to fight the great battles later. I could have become a soldier myself, if I had waited. I had got part of it learned; I knew more about retreating than the man that invented retreating.

* Mark Twain *

SIX

>†××†<

The "Private" History
and the
"Personal" Memoir

>†××†<

While vacationing in Dublin, New Hampshire, in the summer of 1905, Mark Twain started a work called "3000 Years Among the Microbes." His narrator astoundingly wakes up as a microbe in the body of a drunkard. "Our world [or the body of the tramp]," the microbe tell us, "is as large and grand and awe-compelling to us microscopic creatures as is man's world to man. Our tramp is mountainous, there are vast oceans in him, and lakes that are sea-like for size, there are many rivers (veins and arteries) which are fifteen miles across, and of a length so stupendous as to make the Mississippi and the Amazon trifling little Rhode Island brooks by comparison. As for our minor rivers, they are multitudinous, and the dutiable commerce of disease which they carry is rich beyond the dreams of the American custom-house."[1] In other words, man's relationship to God is as distant as that of a microbe to the human body — in this case, a town drunk like Pap Finn. Twain had come a long way since twenty years before, when he had published the hopeful picture of an underclass boy who chose "right" over "wrong" and was prepared to "go to hell" for it. Twenty years after *Huckle-*

berry Finn he was lost in the twentieth century, far from social Darwinism and the morality of Silas Lapham.

Seventy years down the road, in 1975, Annie Dillard would ask: "What if God has the same affectionate disregard for us that we have for barnacles?" In her masterpiece, *Pilgrim at Tinker Creek,* the "tramp" is — in a reworking of nineteenth-century evolutionary theism — evolution itself. Late in Twain's century, God revealed himself not through the Bible but through evolution, leading to the concept of social Darwinism, in which certain results of "natural selection" were more favorable than others. In Dillard's century, evolution "loves death more than it loves you or me." We were moral beings in an amoral universe. "We have not yet encountered any god who is as merciful as a man who flicks a beetle over on its feet"[2] So it went in the twentieth century, the age of relativism over essentialism. Mark Twain must have known that this train had left the station. Yet as he stepped into the twentieth century, he longed for the nineteenth: "I took 65 years of it, just on risk, but if I had known as much about it as I know now I would have taken the whole of it."[3]

In the October 1885 issue of *Harper's,* George Parsons Lathrop published "Mark Twain's Home." He dutifully described the Nook Farm neighborhood and the darkened wood walls "under a paneled ceiling, and full of easy-chairs, rugs, cushions, and carved furniture" that adorned Mark Twain's home. "No, my house has not got a name," the owner of 351 Farmington Avenue was quoted as saying. "It has a number, but I have never been able to remember what it is." The reading public, Lathrop noted, expected the subject to be funny, even "when talking to a serious point, or narrating some experience not especially ludicrous in itself." There was always the "lingering suspicion of humorous possibilities in his manner, which, assisted by the slow, emphatic, natural drawl of his speech, leads one to accept actual facts of a prosaic kind as delicious absurdities."

There was more than drollery to Mark Twain. "Those who see much of this author in private," wrote the son-in-law of the late Nathaniel Hawthorne, "discover in him a fund of serious reflection and keen observation."[4] Twain realized more and more that, as *Adventures of Huckleberry Finn* went down into literary history, he was indeed a moral animal living in an amoral world. That September the newspapers continued to report amorality on the human level. In the Rock Spring Massacre, a mob of white men murdered a number of Chinese laborers in Wyoming "because they received the same wages" as the whites, mainly Irish and Swedes. "The ringleader was a laborer who had been earning $4 a day." No charges were ever filed against the killers.[5]

In North Carolina, four blacks — including one woman — falsely accused of murder were taken from their prison cells and hanged. "The negroes were tied, hands and feet, and made to stand upon their horses. They were given five minutes to make any confessions and to pray. They protested their innocence to the last, and as they prayed their horses were driven from under them. At noon to-day [September 29] the bodies were still hanging, and looked upon by thousands." The victims had "belonged" before the war to the white family they had been accused of murdering. Hardly more than twenty years after the Emancipation Proclamation, lynching began on a grand scale in America. Black rights would assuredly have to wait awhile. Frederick Douglass felt betrayed when in the spirit of national reconciliation the reputation of Robert E. Lee began to be restored. George Washington Cable wrote to Thomas Wentworth Higginson that he had never seen an argument against giving the vote to women (Sam Clemens had to be converted) that was anything but flimsy: "If our mothers are not fit to vote they ought to stop bearing sons."[6]

In 1885 the Clemens family was rounding out its annual summer in Elmira, where Sam did all of his serious writing. It was only there, in an octagon-shaped study in the woods about fifty yards from his sister-in-law's spacious home, that he could find enough uninterrupted time to develop or finish anything. Usually, he read aloud in the evening what he had written that day to the family seated on the cottage's broad front steps. At the time he was probably already at work on the early part of *A Connecticut Yankee in King Arthur's Court.* Cable had reintroduced him to the chivalry of Malory's *Morte d'Arthur* during their tour together the previous lecture season. Doubtless encouraged in his current work by the continuing sales of *Huckleberry Finn,* which had sold more than 60,000 copies by September 1885, he was disappointed to learn that the English edition wasn't doing that well. "It is true that Huck Finn has not treated you kindly," he told Chatto & Windus, the firm that had published his other books in England, "but it must be because the English people do not understand the dialect." While disappointed in the English sales of his book thus far, he was utterly astonished to learn that the same firm had decided not to publish Grant's memoirs. Chatto & Windus refused to give the Grants the same generous royalty terms as had Webster & Company. "The Grant contract made Webster & Company's duty plain," he told Charley Webster, "he must get the best terms, & accept none other — but we had hopes, anyway [in offering the same terms to Chatto & Windus], & stuck to them."[7]

The orders for the Grant volumes in America kept piling up. Their total would attest to the general's nearly cosmic fame. All the while, Sam had kept at his draft of his own comparatively pathetic war memoir. Livy had been unsatisfied with it. They both must have felt the pressure. His wife had grown up in Elmira, New York, only a mile from the harshest prisoner-of-war camp in the North ("Helmira"), second only to the South's Andersonville in Georgia. Her father had strongly supported the antislavery cause that led to the war. Should Sam have gone so public with his scanty war experience — all in the shadow of Grant's, not to mention those essays depicting the experiences of the other generals, both North and South, which were part of the "Battles and Leaders" series? He had looked for a way out. "How would it answer," he asked the *Century* editor of the series, Robert Underwood Johnson, "to put it into the book, and leave it out of the magazine?" He had even offered in that case to sell his article to the *Century* for a nominal two dollars ("and if you crowd me I will take less"). If it went only into the book, he would hope that "its defects might be lost in the smoke and thunder of the big guns all around it . . . ; but in the narrower and peacefuller field of the magazine I think myself it will look like mighty poor weak stuff."[8] As it turned out, "The Private History" never got into the four-volume book that became *Battles and Leaders of the Civil War* in 1887. Its humor only carried it through the magazine phase of its planned publication, but more serious heads wisely found it lacking the dignity of the other essays, which described "campaigns" on which the epic war had turned.

* * *

On the day of Grant's funeral, in July, Clemens had sat with General Sherman and several other flag officers over whiskey and cigars.[9] The same Confederate who had fled in 1861 at the remote possibility of an approaching enemy spent over an hour in the company of a Civil War general after whom a giant redwood tree in California had been named by a naturalist who had fought in Sherman's army. It still stands today at 275 feet, thought to be older than the last millennium. As famous as Mark Twain was as well, it must have been daunting to share the company of such a military hero. Several of the members of the Marion Rangers had subsequently been killed in the war in honorable service. They hadn't skedaddled, they hadn't run from the enemy. As it happened, of course, by lighting out for the Nevada Territory with his brother Orion, Sam Clemens had run from what turned out to be defeat and possibly death. Stephen Crane's boy soldier in *The Red Badge of Courage* retreats "like a blind man" from a battle in which "there was a singular absence of heroic poses." He runs from what turns out to be success, making his cowardice all the more embarrassing. Sam Clemens may have consoled himself with the fact that he had withdrawn from what ultimately became the losing side.

Henry Ward Beecher, America's most famous clergyman, was still polishing his eulogy on Grant for delivery at the Tremont Temple in Boston on October 22. As noted, he had asked Clemens earlier about the general's drinking. Sam had learned from the other generals, perhaps indirectly from the subject himself as he wrote his memoirs, that inebriation probably ceased to be a problem after Grant was promoted to lieutenant general and made commander of the Union army. Indeed, even while drinking, he had been winning the war in the West, beginning with the victories at Fort Henry and Fort Donelson and culminating with the siege of Vicksburg. "It was while Grant was still in the West," Clemens told Beecher in September 1885, "that Mr. Lincoln said he wished he could find out what brand of whisky that fellow used, so he could furnish it to some of the other generals." "He fights," Lincoln added emphatically on another occasion. During the composition of the the *Personal Memoirs,* Clemens had urged Grant to "put the drunkenness in" along with "the repentance & reform" and trust the people. There was no hint of it in the book. Grant "was sore, there," he told Beecher. To further assist the clergyman with his planned speech, Clemens enclosed "some scraps from my Autobiography — scraps about Gen. Grant."[10]

Beecher had heard the story of Grant's tumbling off his horse in New Orleans while reviewing troops, of his frequent "spreeing" in camp — in time of war. When Grant had first felt a sharp pain in his throat in June 1884, his doctors quickly diagnosed the problem as cancer and recommended that he restrict his cigar smoking to once a day. He did so and soon didn't miss even that one. "I could understand that feeling," Clemens wrote Beecher. "He had set out to conquer not the *habit* but the *inclination* — the *desire.*" Ignoring the fact that the cancer, not the patient, had "conquered" the desire, Clemens insisted that it had been the "only true way." He told Beecher that he spoke from experience, no doubt referring to the first year of his marriage when in order to be "worthy" of his new wife he had (temporarily) given up both spirits and tobacco.

"How I do hate those enemies of the human race who go around enslaving God's free people with PLEDGES — to quit drinking, instead of to quit *wanting* to drink," the former member of the youthful Hannibal Cadets of Temperance added. Beecher, described as "the first man to take the sting out of the early theories of Evolution, and who found in science a real aid to religion," so appreciated Clemens's information, its celebration of free will, that he took it straight into his lecture on Grant. In speaking of Grant's "clouded period" of intemperance,

Beecher declared: "At length he struck at the root of the matter. Others agree not to drink, which is good; Grant overcame the *wish* to drink — which is better."[11]

After 1885 American novelists began to abandon the ideal of a moral middle class that Howells had enshrined in *Silas Lapham*. Crane led the way, even while trying to uphold the special place given to Americans of either English or western European backgrounds by making his losers to heredity and environment be Irish in *Maggie Girl of the Streets* (1893). Frank Norris followed in *McTeague: A Story of San Francisco* (1899), exploiting not merely the Irish immigrant, but also expanding his list of Darwinian victims to the stingy German, the crazy Mexican, the dirty Jew — and other such stereotypes designated as inferiors in Herbert Spencer's world of the "survival of the fittest" (his coinage, of course, not Darwin's). Howells approved of their race distinctions, but when Theodore Dreiser, a second-generation German immigrant, depicted his victims of heredity and environment in *Sister Carrie* as typical Americans, Howells strongly disapproved. (Later, he is alleged to have told the young novelist straight to his face that he didn't like *Sister Carrie*). While Howells's main characters are helplessly moral (often leading to their particular dilemmas), Dreiser's Carrie Meeber and George Hurstwood are hopelessly amoral in their pursuit of creature comforts. Simian in their sexual appetites, they violate every last principle of the genteel tradition, which underlay Howells's social universe.

The whole matter of personal morality weighed heavily on the thinking of social leaders near the end of the nineteenth century. In the South, a sense of Malory's chivalry still prevailed. Without it, Confederate forces might not have followed Lee's command to surrender en masse but instead have adopted

Jefferson Davis's plan of scattering into years of guerilla resistance. Northerners were still basking in their victory in the war, perhaps even beginning to believe that their soldiers had originally taken up arms to free the slaves. We know why Southern boys took up arms. They fought to preserve a way of life that included slavery, on which their agrarian economy depended. They fought for "states' rights," and once the war got underway, there was no backing out. Confederate deserters became fugitives in their own land with a price on their heads. One of them, Sam Clemens, got out of the war completely by going beyond the reach of an invading Yankee colonel who had tried to draft him into the Union effort by serving the army as a steamboat pilot. To be safe from the war, Sam had had to go "outside" the United States, to Nevada, then one of its territories, where he joined a large number of other copperheads.

The reason why men from the North dropped what they were doing is less clear. In what had come to be called his recruiting poem, Walt Whitman described the New York scene after the firing on Fort Sumter:

Beat! beat! drums! — blow! bugles! blow!
Through the windows — through doors — burst like a ruthless
    force,
Into the solemn church, and scatter the congregation,
Into the school where the scholar is studying,
Leave not the bridegroom quiet — no happiness must he have
    now with his bride,
Nor the peaceful farmer any peace, ploughing his field or
    gathering his grain,
So fierce you whirr and pound you drums — so shrill you
    bugles blow.

Everybody dropped everything, Whitman romanticized, to sign up for the three months all thought it would take to defeat the South. Every Union soldier fought no doubt to preserve the Union, or *its* way of life as a nation emerging on the world stage. As for slavery, even Lincoln was at least flexible. When challenged by Horace Greeley, the powerful editor of the *New York Tribune,* to make the war formally against slavery by freeing the slaves, Lincoln responded on August 22, 1862: "My paramount object in this struggle is to save the Union, and is not either to save or to destroy slavery. If I could save the Union without freeing any slave I would do it, and if I could save it by freeing all the slaves I would do it; and if I could save it by freeing some and leaving others alone I would also do that."

What his personal feelings about slavery were was another matter, Lincoln insisted, but in fact before he issued the Emancipation Proclamation, effective January 1, 1863, he first offered the South a "Preliminary Proclamation," in which it could keep its slaves until 1900 if it lay down its arms. Whitman's soldier-brother George, after surviving the Battle of Antietam, expressed an opinion that undoubtedly characterized the attitude of Union troops in general, certainly those from New York, where the antislavery feeling was considered "soft." "I see by the papers," Captain Whitman of the Fifty-First Regiment of New York Volunteers told his mother back in Brooklyn, "that Uncle Abe has issued a proclamation declaring the slaves free in all the States that are in rebellion. . . ." He went on to say that it would be better to convince the Southern leaders to "keep their slaves, than to get licked and lose them."[12]

Just what you did in the war did matter in 1885, the question of slavery aside. And Sam Clemens had no right to be called a colonel or even a veteran, as George Whitman and hundreds of thousands of others did. This veteran didn't even have the excuse of Crane's skedaddler who comes back to fight in *The Red Badge of Courage*. Stephen Crane grew up with the Civil War stories. In "The Veteran" (1896), he brings back his protagonist as an old man who reminisces about his experiences in battle. "Could you see the whites of their eyes?" one of the younger members of his audience excitedly asks. His "deferential voice" expressed the veteran's tremendous "social weight." Crane captured how deeply America embraced this war, its memory. When old Fleming finally admits that he initially ran from battle, his grandson is aghast: "his eyes were wide with astonishment at this terrible scandal, his most magnificent grandfather telling such a thing." In the fall of 1885, Sam Clemens, alias Mark Twain, had yet to tell such a thing.

* * *

Preoccupied with putting the finishing touches on his Civil War essay and other distractions, Sam was likely oblivious to the somewhat fragile state of the economy in the fall of 1885. The economic success following the Civil War had been flattened by the Panic of 1873, and ever since business on Wall Street had suffered frequent ups and downs. The headline in the *New York Times* of October 3 announced "Shock to Wall-Street," reporting the failure of the "famous bear leader Henry N. Smith, Jay Gould's old partner and Jay Gould's old dupe in more than one big stock-rigging operation." Losses on Wall Street were "widely distributed." Sam himself may have been one of the losers, what with his many investments. The times otherwise boded no economic ills for the writer who was at the top of his game both as an artist and a businessman, but these ticks in the market were signs of the "great depression" to come, the Panic of 1893, which would see the bankruptcy of Charles L. Webster & Company and the near bankruptcy of Samuel L. Clemens.

Clemens's daily journal of late had been full of business matters, not literary ones. It was no "savings bank," as Emerson had called his literary notebooks from which he would construct his famous essays about self-reliance, but increasingly full of numerical figures and sales strategies. Central among his hopes of joining the ranks of the Andrew Carnegies and the Cornelius Vanderbilts were his high expectations for the Paige Typesetter, an investment that was draining his bank account at the rate of $3,000 a month. "This machine will set the whole alphabet," he wrote, noting that its competitors could not — thus far. "There are 11,000 [news]papers & periodicals in America" — in other words, an inexhaustible market. "The type-setter does not get drunk," the former printer added. "He does not join the Printers' union," the future labor supporter noted. He does not distribute a dirty case, he does not set a dirty proof."[13]

Josh Billings died that October. The humorist whose real name was Henry Wheeler Shaw succumbed to a stroke at the age of sixty-five. If remembered today, it is as the "second most famous humorist" of the nineteenth century. He was one of Mark Twain's models that paved the way for him to become the "most famous humorist" of the nineteenth century. This incredible success was already a fact in 1885, but Twain took little satisfaction in it. If he couldn't become filthy rich, at least he could achieve fame higher than that of a humorist, or the notoriety of a Civil War deserter. In the *New York Times* obituary of October 15, it was pointed out that Josh Billings' *Farmers' Almanac* had sold hundreds of thousands of copies since its initial publication in 1873. "Mr. Shaw's humor," the announcement hedged, "was hidden in, and did not consist of mere phonetic spelling, and underneath the bad spelling of his proverbs and aphorisms there is at times a depth of wisdom and philosophy which entitled him to a higher place in the world of letters than that of a simple humorist."

It was pointed out in the *Washington Post* of October 18 that Josh Billings had rivaled Mark Twain "in turning his putput into cash." They had both turned their "put-puts" into wealth, their small combustible engines into something truly valued by the world, something akin to "literature." It wasn't the Great American Novel, of course. The *Pall Mall Gazette* that month reserved that achievement in America for William Dean Howells. "Slowly and by gradual tentative stages even we Philistine English people," its editors said, "are beginning with grudging reluctance to perceive" that Howells "is beyond distinction a great artist." Twain, however, was on the rise, according to Andrew Lang, who in the 1890s would become the first important critic to recognize *Huckleberry Finn* as an American classic. In 1885, when *Huckleberry Finn* was still being assailed as "trash," he placed Mark Twain on the level of Edgar Allan Poe, whose personal reputation had yet to be fully restored. "Had you lived a generation later," Lang wrote, addressing the dead poet, "honor, wealth, applause, success in Europe and at home would have been yours. . . . It is impossible to estimate the rewards which would have fallen to Edgar Poe, had chance made him the contemporary of Mark Twain."[14]

While Clemens was drinking whiskey with General Sherman at Grant's funeral, the general, knowing that Twain had advised Grant on his memoirs, apparently asked if Twain would read a manuscript of his own. As it turned out, the only book of Sherman's that Webster & Company ever published was a reprint of the general's 1875 *Personal Memoirs,* in 1888. Evidently, the new manuscript was a travel book of sorts, one that Twain frankly told Sherman lacked substance. "It must have the meat on it, & muscle, & the beating heart, & the blood in the veins before it can march," Twain wrote, applying military imagery. He told the general to leave the manuscript unpublished, "for the use of your biographer." He praised instead the already published memoirs and promised that a Webster reprint "could sell a large edition." Sam Clemens may have been awed in the company of such military giants as Grant and Sherman, but he knew he could outgeneral them both when it came to literary instead of military campaigns. Since Sherman had given him "permission to advise," he said, "I regard the permission as a command . . . & [he added significantly] as I have been a soldier myself," it came to him naturally "to obey. My distinct & well-considered advice is, *do not publish it.*"[15] Noting that he would turn fifty in November, he based his advice on thirty-seven years as "a journalist, in more or less active service" and the author and publisher of books for eighteen years.

Now he had told General Sherman that he had been a military man. One wonders whether he ever said the same to Grant. As it turned out, "The Private History of a Campaign That Failed" became possibly the very first antiwar statement in the annals of American literature, preceding Crane's *The Red Badge of Courage* by ten years. Twain's earlier version of 1877 had been merely humorous, but the 1885 essay in the December *Century* introduced the concept of the "unknown soldier," thus anticipating a tradition that would become prominent after World War I. In their stumbling about, the untrained Marion Rangers, Twain wrote in his December essay, mistakenly killed a stranger. "The man was not in uniform, and was not armed," he wrote. "He was a stranger in the country; that was all we ever found out about him. The thought of him got to preying upon me every night; I could not get rid of it."[16] It suggested in its anguish that war was ultimately senseless, legitimized murder. Even Whitman, the Good Gray Poet who during the war had made by his own account more than 600 visits to wounded and dying soldiers in the Washington hospitals, maintained that the war had been worth the enormous sacrifice because it had kept the "Nationality of The States from being strangled."[17]

It would take World War I to challenge this exalted view of war — and then mainly in its literary treatments. It took that long for America to, at the very least, modify its monuments to war, to exchange Grant's tomb for the Tomb of the Unknown Soldier at the Arlington National Cemetery. Congress established the latter in 1921. There are, of course, monuments to the "known" soldiers and sailors of World War II, Korea, and Vietnam. The Vietnam Veterans Memorial, however, is ironically also a monument to the unknowns in that war. Its names of the dead only, almost 60,000, are still "unknown" in effect because they died in the first war the United States ever lost. The latest to be added to the National Mall is the World War II Memorial, which is full of animation. The Vietnam Wall still has the feeling of a church or a funeral, while the Korean War Monument with its statues of soldiers eternally on the move reflects the fact that its campaign ended in a stalemate. In front of both monuments sits Abraham Lincoln, who had a killer named Grant to finish *his* war.

Grant had been criticized for the large number of troops he lost in battle, especially during the Wilderness campaign in Virginia in 1864, as his army moved inexorably toward Richmond, the Confederate capital. His campaign took him over old ground, where the Battle of Chancellorsville (on which, incidentally, *The Red Badge of Courage* would be based) had been fought a year earlier, and Grant's forces were not any more successful than the Union army of Joseph Hooker had been. The difference, however, between the Battle of Chancellorsville and of the Battle of the Wilderness was, in the words of Grant biographer William S. McFeely, "that after Chancellorsville, Hooker cut his losses and, defeated, retreated back across the Rapidan. Grant ignored the losses and — if not victorious, at least undaunted — kept going." Captain George Whitman had his canteen shot completely from his side. His brother Walt wrote their mother: "I steadily believe Grant is going to succeed, & that we shall have Richmond — but O what a price to pay for it."[18]

Apparently, Sam Clemens had not been willing to pay the price, but why did so many others risk and lose their lives for the cause of their side? This was the question Sam had to ask himself as he worked away on "The Private History of a Campaign That Failed." All such speculation concerning human behavior, however, would soon be moot, according to the Reverend Henry Ward Beecher. He told the *New York Times* of the vision he had regarding reforms he expected to see before his death. "Love is gradually gaining in the contest with hate," he piously offered. Roman Catholics and Protestants will even agree. "I expect to see, before I die, all the Indian tribes disbanded and the members of them settled as citizens, holding their private property; all reservations abolished, and an end of all this bloody, guilty Indian question."[19] He made no mention of the legacy of slavery. The dissolution of the "Mormon difficulty" was already under way, as was the bitterness between North and South. Even the European nations were seemingly on the road to reconciliation.

It was an age in which many believed that civilization, or at least American civilization, was on the cusp of perfection, or at least in the process of ongoing amelioration. Even in *Sister Carrie*, the bleakest of deterministic novels, Dreiser wrote in chapter 8: "Our civilization is still in a middle stage, scarcely beast, in that it is no longer wholly guided by instinct; scarcely human, in that it is not yet wholly guided by reason." The huge size of Grant's funeral and the ambitious plans for his tomb were of a piece with the age of the great man in this era of wonder. When the Reverend John McCloskey, archbishop of New York and the first American cardinal, died in October 1885, mourners passed by his coffin in Saint Patrick's Cathedral for twelve hours "at the rate of 70 per minute, or over 4,000 each hour" — in perfect silence![20]

* * *

For the most part, Catholics, immigrants, or the sons and daughters of immigrants, were not included in this Age of the Great Man. They were his pawns, his laborers. One of the industries in the late nineteenth century to emerge was that of the streetcar in American cities, later dramatized by Dreiser in *The Financier* and *The Titan*. In St. Louis strikers literally tore the cars to pieces as they pummeled scabs and attacked the horses with car hooks. In the words of one policeman who had shot dead one of the strikers: "a crowd of about 50 people, divided evenly on both sides of the road, suddenly closed in on the car. They at once began cutting the harnesses. . . . They paid no attention to what we said, though we repeated it, but attacked us with clubs and rocks. I was struck on the arm with a rock and quite badly hurt. We fought the crowd with our sticks, but they were too much for us, and one of the men came behind [Officer] Griffith and knocked him down. He had Griffith face downward and was beating him when I fired, killing the man. Griffith had, just before the man attacked him, fired a shot at a retreating man. I fired only the one shot. When the crowd saw that the man was killed it had the effect of quieting them for a short time."[21]

Blacks were assaulted and lynched in Louisiana and Texas in the month of October 1885. Masked men carried out the assaults near New Orleans. In Mount Pleasant, Texas, east of Dallas, a lynch mob identified as "CITIZENS . . . TO THE NUMBER OF SIXTY-EIGHT left a note pinned to their victim justifying their deed: "This negro was not hanged for the highway robbery he committed [the victim and another black had stolen $1.65 from a sleeping white man] . . . but for the slanderous talk he has had about a certain white family in Mt. Pleasant, which we deem a scandal to the white race. The family is as innocent and pure as the angels in heaven, and we feel that we have not committed a sin in the sight of God, and furthermore, we feel that we have done a great and noble act for our country as gentlemen."[22]

Yes, it was the Age of Chivalry in which gangs of men of honor killed on principle, no matter how flawed that principle was. You were "honorable" if you did what you threatened to do, were consistent. Never mind that Yankee Emerson's advice about a foolish consistency being "the hobgoblin of little minds." Mark Twain blamed Southern chivalry for the outbreak of the Civil War. Cross this line and we fight! I stand by my word. You could commit the crime of lynching an innocent person or tear up a streetcar as long as those affected weren't "gentlemen," code word in this context for white — not black or "foreign" like all those Irish and German immigrants who were also thought to be communists in 1885. Such gentlemen had read or been influenced by too many romances, from *Morte d'Arthur* to the tales of Sir Walter Scott. In *Huckleberry Finn* the steamboat that runs aground is appropriately named the *Walter Scott*. Tom

Sawyer, Huck's sidekick at the end of *Huckleberry Finn,* is full of romantic notions. It is why he fails to tell Huck that Jim is already free when they go through all those antics to liberate him in the chapters Hemingway told us not to read.

In "A Novel Duel," reported in the *New York Times* of October 27, a Texan challenged a Choctaw Indian to a gunfight after he refused to accept a drink in a saloon. "Nothing would satisfy the wounded honor of Chalmers [the white] but blood, and so the other white men and Indians fixed up a fight on the following terms." They were each to stand back to back in the middle of the floor" and run to opposite ends of the saloon and start shooting. "Three rounds were fired in quick succession. Then the Indian began to stagger, and, running toward Chalmers with a drawn knife, plunged it into the Texan's breast just as the latter fired his last bullet, which penetrated the Indian's heart." This was the west that young gentlemen from the east visited for a year or more in search of their fortunes, young men like Tom Corey of *The Rise of Silas Lapham,* whose parents, out of kilter with the work ethic of democratic America, are living on the last generation of family money. Before the Civil War, such destinations included South America, where Sam Clemens had once hoped to get rich on coca (the narcotic dangers of cocaine wouldn't be realized until the turn of the century); instead, after taking a steamboat down the Mississippi to board a transport to the Amazon, he fell in love with steamboating, and the rest is history.

Actually, he had long before fallen in love with the Mississippi. "When a boy," he wrote in chapter 4 of *Life on the Mississippi,* "there was but one permanent ambition among my comrades in our village on the west bank of the Mississippi River. That was, to be a steamboatman. We had transient ambitions of other sorts, but they were only transient. When a circus came and went, it left us all burning to become clowns; the first negro minstrel show that ever came to our section left us all suffering to try that kind of life; now and then we had a hope that, if we lived and were good, God would permit us to be pirates. These ambitions faded out, each in its turn; but the ambition to be a steamboatman always remained." Sam and at least two of his boyhood friends became riverboat pilots, a job that until the Civil War paid the same wages as that of the vice president of the United States.

Sam had yet to focus on Negro lynching. He wouldn't until the end of the century. As we have seen from Cable's balancing act in "The Freedman's Case in Equity" and "The Silent South," the social status of blacks in the United States after the war was complex, to say the least. With the abandonment of Reconstruction in 1877, another form of slavery — the sharecropper system — had emerged, along with the formation of the Ku Klux Klan. These "night riders" enforced a new form of subjugation, whose ultimate weapon was the rope. In 1901 Mark Twain proposed to the American Publishing Company to write a book on the subject after reading about a lynching in his home state of Missouri. He even wrote the first chapter, which was published posthumously in 1923 as "The United States of Lyncherdom." After his publisher Frank Bliss talked him out of the idea, suggesting that it would threaten his book sales in the South ("I shouldn't have even half a friend left, down there, after it issued from the press"), Sam told him in a letter of September 8 that "the lynching-book" still haunted him.[23] He wanted to talk further about its possibilities, but nothing beyond this essay ever materialized. "And so Missouri has fallen," he wrote in the essay. "That great state! Certain of her children have joined the lynchers, and the smirch is upon the rest of us. That handful of her children have given us a character and labeled us with a name, and to the dwellers in the four quarters of the earth we are 'lynchers,' now, and ever shall be."

A white woman had been found murdered in a southern corner of the state. Three blacks, two of them of advanced age, were lynched for the crime. Additionally, Twain wrote, the vigilantes "burned out five negro households, and drove thirty negro families into the woods." Clemens did not dispute the question of guilt, saying that the people of Pierce City "had bitter provocation." No matter. The problem, as he saw it, was that "they took the law into their own hands, when by the terms of their statutes their victim would certainly hang if the law had been allowed to take its course." While not declaring the lynched blacks victims of injustice, he did recognize that they would have been hanged regardless of their guilt or innocence because "there are but few negroes in that region and they are without authority and without influence in over-awing juries."[24]

Living in the North in 1885, in New England where the abolitionist movement had been born, Mark Twain was sensitive about his Southern roots. While this uneasiness shows in his essay about the Missouri lynching, it had first surfaced fully in *Huckleberry Finn*. Huck's guilt haunts the story as much as Sam's guilt had informed his postbellum attitude toward slavery. Ironically, it is Huck's guilt in *opposing* slavery (if only in Jim's case) that haunts the book, for it reflects Sam Clemens's own position as a boy in the South. It is important to remember not only that Twain had relocated to the North after the war but also that he had married the daughter of an abolitionist, an Elmira millionaire who had befriended Frederick Douglass. *Huckleberry Finn* was simply "funny" in 1885, but its lasting humor is mostly based upon a critique of white hypocrisy.

Twain made fun of the master class, but he also sought to defend the Southerner as somebody who tried to do good as long as it didn't involve blacks, in this antebellum novel of *enslaved* blacks. When slave catchers in chapter 16 decide to search the raft and Huck suggests to them that they will find only his father sick with smallpox, they are quickly deterred. With the thought of a fugitive slave on the raft vanished from their minds, they assuage their pity for the boy by floating over on a paddle two gold pieces worth forty dollars. As they go on their way, one of them helpfully tells Huck: "If you see any runaway niggers, you get help and nab them, and you can make some money by it."

* * *

On the last day of October in 1885, Ferdinand Ward was sentenced to ten years at hard labor for grand larceny. He was convicted of swindling the Marine Bank of New York of $71,800. The subheading to the story in the *Times* read: "The Rascal Accepts His Fate Stoically and Has No Words of Regret for his Misdeeds." This was the "rascal" who had caused Grant to lose $100,000 in the spring of 1884, about the time the general learned he had cancer. One of Grant's sons had been in partnership with Ward on Wall Street; the ex-president was assured that the loan of money to fend off bankruptcy would be returned to him within a week. As it turned out, the firm of Grant & Ward needed much more money in order to survive. Grant had acted to help his son Buck (Ulysses S. Grant, Jr.). After initially fleeing from New York, Ward returned to face multiple charges. "He slept last night — if he slept at all — within the walls of Sing Sing Prison," the newspaper story of November 1 continued. Ward, it said, "looked wan, haggard, and nervous." With Grant's funeral barely in the past, the judge who sentenced Ward went out of his way to insist that the financier who had bilked the late Ulysses S. Grant had not been "convicted by reason of any popular clamor against you." Ward served six years and six months of his sentence. Widowed while in prison, he married a second wealthy woman, Belle Storer of Staten Island, in 1894. The bride's father did not attend the wedding, claiming "a business engagement."[25] Ward lived out the rest of his days in Geneseo, New York, where he was reunited with his ten-year-old son.

As Ward went to prison, talk continued as to how to preserve the memory of the man whom he had cheated. The monument fund for Grant's tomb grew and grew, but there was a simultaneous movement to preserve for posterity the very cottage at Mount McGregor in which the great man had finally died. "Cottage" was something of an understatement. In making it available to the Grant family for the months of June and July, when the general had gone there to spend his last days in the cool mountain air of Saratoga Springs, the Philadelphia philanthropist Joseph W. Drexel provided the following description. It was, he said, "of the Queen Anne style of architecture, two stories high, and contains about a dozen rooms. A wide piazza extends around three sides of the house." The ailing Grant's personal quarters were located in a corner of the house facing the wraparound porch. Here atop Mount McGregor he had put the finishing touches on the *Personal Memoirs.*[26]

The plan was to deed the house to the government, as Drexel's gift to the nation that Grant had saved. Drexel announced that the house would "never again be occupied by any family or persons." Since some may have suspected that Drexel, who had been developing his nearby Balmoral Hotel as a resort, was trying to capitalize on Grant's death and lasting fame, he told a reporter from the *New York Herald:* "I hope the public won't regard this cottage idea of mine as an advertisement or show. There is no money in it, I assure you." Perhaps not, but Drexel and his Mount McGregor planners also envisioned a nearby monument that anticipated aspects of Mount Rushmore: they hoped to carve into the granite face of the hill by the cottage "a colossal profile of the General finishing his book." This "lasting memorial" never came to fruition. In fact, the cottage went through a number of uses once its designation as a Grant "memorial" had been exhausted, including becoming an annex to the New York State School for the Mentally Retarded.[27]

Aside from the revitalized tomb in New York, the most enduring memorial to the general is the fifty-dollar bill. The first one classified as today's Federal Reserve note appeared in 1914 with a picture of Thomas Jefferson. Grant replaced him in 1928. He himself was nearly replaced by Ronald Reagan in 2005, but the proposal never got out of congressional committee. Grant, of course, had been a member of the leftist leaning Republican Party of the nineteenth century. Those "radical Republicans," who ruled after the war until the Democrat Cleveland came into office in 1885, had pushed for abolition before the Civil War. As much as Republicans are alleged to love Reagan, they were not about to abandon Grant. The fifty-dollar bill was his last refuge.

Before that he had appeared on three U.S. postage stamps — in 1890, 1902, and 1923. The last image was used on the fifty-dollar bill, often referred to as "a Grant." The image here is of the ex-general and former president around age sixty — broad-shouldered, presidential (out of military uniform), and robust, before his fall to cancer a couple of years later. In 2011 Mark Twain appeared on the "forever" postage stamp. He too is looking hearty and healthy, though as in Grant's case his heavy cigar smoking took its toll in the last decade of his life, when he suffered from what he called "permanent bronchitis."

Sam Grant probably did the same. Yes, Grant's familiar first name was also "Sam," short for his middle name, "Simpson" — but Ulysses Simpson Grant would be known after the war as simply U. S. Grant, with the initials standing for both "United States" and "Unconditional Surrender." Time was now approaching for Sam Clemens's "unconditional surrender." As late as October 1885, he had yet to finish completely his "Private History."

Twain first met Grant during a White House visit in 1870, but his rapt admiration for the general had solidified during a reunion of the Grand Army of the Republic in Chicago in 1879, when he sat on a stage beside Grant and his generals, Sherman, Sheridan, Logan, Pope, and Schofield. The occasion was to welcome Grant home following his world tour, one in which he had used *The Innocents Abroad* as one of his guidebooks. "I think I never sat elbow-to-elbow with so many historic names before," Twain told his wife Livy. "What an iron man Grant is! . . . he never moved a muscle of his body for a single instant, during 30 minutes!" The audience consisted of hundreds of military veterans of the Army of the Tennessee, dining on oysters, filet mignon, and buffalo steaks, along with champagne, punch, whiskey, and six hours of speeches. "Perhaps he never *would* have moved," Twain continued, "but at last a speaker made such a particularly ripping & blood-stirring remark about him that the audience rose & roared & yelled & stamped & clapped an entire minute — Grant sitting as serene as ever — when Gen. Sherman stepped to him, laid his hand affectionately on his shoulder, bent respectfully down & whispered in his ear. Then Grant got up & bowed, & the storm of applause swelled into a hurricane."[28]

Now Grant was dead, and Mark Twain was at the height his fame. Ironically, just as Grant's fame would fade in the twentieth century, Twain's fate during his last twenty-five years would change in the wake of the general's passing. Ahead lay the bitter visions in *A Connecticut Yankee, Puddn'head Wilson,* and *The Mysterious Stranger*. Down his rocky road awaited the bankruptcy of his publishing company, the death of his daughter Susy, then Livy, and finally — on Christmas Eve in 1909 — the accidental death of his other daughter, Jean. As he pushed ahead with his own "Private History," he choked up at the memory of that night in Chicago with Grant and his courageous soldiers, reminding him of the courage he himself had lacked back in 1861. "Imagine what it was like," he told Howells, who had also avoided the war by serving as consul in Venice as reward for writing a campaign biography of Lincoln, "to see a bullet-shredded old battle flag reverently unfolded to the gaze of a thousand middle-aged soldiers most of whom hadn't seen it since they saw it advancing over victorious fields when they were in their prime." Imagine, he said, what it was like when their hero Grant stepped into view. "If I live a hundred years," he told Howells, "I shan't ever forget these things — nor be able to talk about them."[29]

* * *

But now he had to talk about himself in the war. "I was a *soldier* two weeks once in the beginning of the war, and was hunted like a rat the whole time," he told an unidentified fan of his writings. "My splendid Kipling himself hasn't a more burnt-in, hard-baked, and unforgettable familiarity with that death-on-the-pale-horse-with-hell-following-after, which is a raw soldier's first fortnight in the field — and which, without any doubt, is the most tremendous fortnight and the vividest he is ever going to see."[30]

No doubt, this was the way he wanted to open his essay on himself and the war, with something matching the high drama of a Grant and his soldiers. There is something deeply seductive about most war stories. They are almost always exaggerations, full of goose bumps and cheap romance. Only Grant and perhaps his generals with essays in the "Battles and Leaders" series could afford to tell the factual truth. They had no other choice since they spoke not solely for themselves but for hundreds of thousands of brave men still alive, like those that night in Chicago. But Mark Twain, or Sammy Clemens of Hannibal, spoke mainly for himself. As noted, several of the former Marion Rangers had gone on to serve (and die) in the war. A couple of others who had become steamboat pilots before the war continued to live on and from the river after it; they had kept in touch. These boyhood friends would never betray him.

Yet he couldn't make up something out of whole cloth. Even fiction, as he once told his brother Orion, was based on fact. And as a humorist, he couldn't present himself in the fashion in which he had addressed that unidentified reader. Twain's task was to document his two weeks in the war as a Tom Sawyer escapade, keeping his story in character with what the reading public expected. When he spoke at the dramatic GAR meeting in Chicago, he had drawn the contrasting and hilarious picture of the great Grant as once a baby trying to get his big toe into his mouth. The story rocked the house and even made the stone-faced general laugh. "When I lit in with the fifteenth & last [speech of the evening]," he told Howells, "his time was come! I shook him up like dynamite & he sat there fifteen minutes & laughed & cried like the mortalest of mortals." He had known he could "lick" Grant — "this unconquerable conqueror." "He told me he had shaken hands with 15,000 people that day & come out of it without an ache or pain, but that my truths had racked all the bones of his body apart."[31]

Mark Twain's greatest weapon was humor. "Against the assault of laughter, nothing can stand," says the antagonist in the posthumously published "Chronicle of Young Satan." Even Grant's great stature that evening in Chicago could be taken down. Fortunately, Clemens had given no offense then. He still worried about the evening two years earlier, in 1877, when he had been castigated in the press for making the fateful Whittier birthday-dinner speech in which he had ridiculously characterized the equally famous Emerson, Holmes, and Longfellow as three drunks in the Nevada mining region. He mustn't make that type of mistake in his "Private History."

"You have heard from a great many people who did something in the war," he opened the final version of his essay. "Is it not fair and right that you listen a little moment to one who started out to do something in it, but didn't?" Now it was time to hear from one who had stepped into the war, got a taste of it, and promptly stepped out. There were thousands of such veterans, he suggested. "These, by their very numbers, are respectable, and are therefore entitled to a sort of a voice, — not a loud one, but a modest one; not a boastful one, but an apologetic one."[32] The essay is at once an apology and a plea to be allowed to explain just why he and others hadn't participated meaningfully in the war. Against the example of all those veterans of the Army of the Tennessee he set the stories of people like himself who — like Crane's soldier — had tried to make a virtue of retreat.

Meanwhile, the South was still fighting the racial aspects of the war. In Vienna, Georgia, the *Times* of November 2 reported, a lynch mob seized an offending Negro, "took him to the woods, and flogged him to death." Southern chivalry had kept the peace with Lee's surrender at Appomattox, but it had not yet extended it to the freedman whom Cable had tried to assist in establishing civil if not social equality. While Cable spoke out publicly, Twain quietly assisted black college students, remembering, no doubt, that as a former resident of Hannibal, he had once upon a time been proslavery. The fact that he had fought on the side of the South highlighted that ancient history. It was nevertheless to be of little consequence, because whites on both sides of the Mason-Dixon Line, in an effort to forgive and forget, had embraced the principle of national reconciliation. What lingered on, well into the twentieth century, was the undecided fate of blacks for whom the war had supposedly been fought; particularly, those second and subsequent generations of freedmen, whose existence now — in 1885 — was tellingly perceived as the "Negro problem."

꙳

SEVEN

The Killing
of Strangers

꙳

The *Century* articles in the "Battles and Leaders" series went on for two years, beginning in 1885. Aside from providing future Civil War historians with reliable military facts, the series served the present with its narratives, as one historian has put it, "of sectional reunion and harmony."[1] Grant had set this tone in his public statements after the war and up to the time of his death that year; his three essays in "Battles and Leaders" reinforced it. Indeed, it had been Lincoln's wish, and such a coming together of former enemies might have happened sooner without his assassination. His successor, Andrew Johnson, a Southerner suspected of regional sympathies by the victorious Radical Republicans, was unable to sustain Lincoln's view in Congress. "General Grant," the editors of *Battles and Leaders of the Civil War* wrote in the first volume, "in accord with the well-known purpose of President Lincoln, began at Appomattox the work of reconciliation." When he died, as a result of his conciliatory stance toward his defeated enemy, nobody was surprised to see Confederate generals among his pallbearers.

As close as Mark Twain had come to the general, he was not one of those pall bearers. Moreover, as mentioned above, his essay on "The Private History of a Campaign That Failed" was not included in the 1887 volumes. Readers were not disappointed with the original contribution because they had always expected Twain to be funny. And it wasn't simply because the essay *was* funny that it was omitted from the more somber accounts of war in the four-volume series. It was left out for a couple of other reasons. First, it had reduced deadly combat to a Tom Sawyer adventure in which a gaggle of untrained recruits essentially run around in circles in fear of an invisible enemy. As a farce, "The Private History" undercut the idea of the nobility of war, the oil that lubricated the other essays in the series. This, as another historian has wisely argued, was the central tenet of the series. Twain's rendering of his piece of the war failed to match "the heroic story and figures of the military authors in the *Century* series."[2]

The other reason Twain's essay got left out was that it came up short on the theme of national reconciliation. How could something so "funny" become a catalyst for overcoming such a bitter argument? Too many soldiers on both sides had died. There was something in Sam Clemens's Southern roots that kept him from fully embracing the national idea of letting bygones be bygones. He may have been, as Howells called him in *My Mark Twain* (1910), "the most desouthernized southerner" he ever met, but he was still a born and bred Southerner — not only just that, but one from Missouri, where the conflict over slavery went all the way back to the Missouri Compromise of 1820. He had also been a native of northern Missouri, a veritable peninsula of slavery, surrounded by the Free-Soil territory of Iowa, Illinois, and Kansas. Indeed, it was in neighboring Kansas that the first bloody conflict over slavery took place, five years before the Civil War began, over whether an American territory would come into the Union as a free or slave state.

When the war over the same issue finally broke out in 1861, Sam Clemens was a Confederate; he had clearly sided with the South and as a result joined the Marion Rangers. In fact, it wasn't until three years later, while hiding out in Nevada with other Southern sympathizers that he shifted allegiances, no doubt influenced by some of his "Yankee" colleagues on the *Virginia City Enterprise*. Indeed, before his conversion from secession to loyalty, he had published in that newspaper a cruel hoax depicting the Sanitary Commission (forerunner of the Red Cross) as a miscegenation society.

His niece, Annie Moffett Webster, the wife of Twain's publishing partner in 1885, recalled that when she was eight years old, in 1861, and living in St. Louis, her Uncle Sam had returned to the city, "his occupation of pilot lost forever. He came on the last boat from New Orleans to get through Union lines. He was obsessed with the fear that he might be arrested by the government agents and forced to act as pilot on a government gunboat while a man stood by with a pistol ready to shoot him if he showed the least sign of a false move." Moffett described her uncle as "almost afraid to leave the house." Sam was staying at the house of his sister Pamela and her husband, William A. Moffett, a merchant in the city. Sam's mother was also living with the family, and she gave strict orders "that if anyone called and asked for Mr. Clemens she was to be called first." One day in June, a caller from Hannibal appeared and was admitted to Sam's company. His name was Smith. According to Annie, "he had come with the wild project of forming a [military] company. . . . Uncle Sam accepted at once, and so began his three weeks' experience as a Confederate soldier."[3]

Two or three weeks later he deserted the war, but not necessarily the Confederacy. It hadn't been simply because he disliked the rigors of military life or its dangers that he left military service. Sam Clemens suffered from divided loyalties. Like Robert E. Lee, he loved the United States but felt, initially, that his allegiance belonged to his native state. When one of the neighboring youngsters in their St. Louis neighborhood was assaulted for waving a Union flag, Sam ran out of the house to protect him, thinking also that the lad should have better protected the national banner. In the words of his niece Annie, who also suffered from divided loyalties: "I knew [Uncle Sam] would have given his life for his country, but he was a southerner, his friends were all Southern, his sympathies were with the South." St. Louis itself experienced the same divided loyalties. Because of its large population of German immigrants that had voted for Lincoln, there was strong sympathy in Missouri for the North. But there were many, including the state's governor, who sided with the South. Just across the street from Annie's house in St. Louis, a neighbor woman spoke publicly and derisively of able-bodied young men who weren't already in the Confederate army, or Missouri state militia. "Charles Little," she announced, "does not like the smell of gunpowder. He would rather stay with his mother and make baking-powder bisquits."[4]

So there had been mixed feelings over the war both in St. Louis and throughout the state, at the beginning of the war and for its duration. Nothing in 1861 had been so clear as the Manhattan response that inspired Whitman to write his poem, "Beat! Beat! Drums!" Twain had tried to get this point across in "The Private History" before he broke into farce. "There was a good deal of confusion in men's minds during the first months of the great trouble — a good deal of unsettledness, of leaning first this way, then that, then the other way. It was hard for us to get our bearings." It was even harder to get his bearings in 1885 as the editor's deadline for his essay came due.

Writing his wartime essay must have been almost like coming back from the dead, like the man in that fall of 1885 who had reportedly survived a hanging (*New York Times*, November 5). For "The Private History" reported not only the death of a "mysterious stranger," it also recorded the disappearance of Sam Clemens, who afterward followed his brother, the Union-sympathizing Orion, out west. When Sam Clemens returned to the East five years later, he was Mark Twain, who hailed not from the South but the West and the Pacific Slope. As such, he avoided the shadow of defeat that hung over his homeland — that is, until 1885, when he was forced to reclaim, or at least acknowledge, those roots.

Sam's mission in "The Private History" was to pen a farcical account of his service, and in that endeavor he succeeded. Readers thought it was as funny as *Huckleberry Finn*, which by now had sold tens of thousands of copies. As previously noted, Mark Twain was not the only literary person asked to take part in this series on the Civil War. The *Century* editors also had asked, among other non-generals, Thomas Wentworth Higginson and Cable, but these well-known writers had actually fought in the war, both sustaining wounds. Hence, the pressure on Twain to survive the embarrassment of his actual military role still placed him in an awkward position.[5]

Beyond protecting that flank, Twain either consciously or unconsciously undercut in "The Private History" the traditional glory of war, burlesquing it in at least one of the illustrations in the *Century* that carried the same legend as one in Grant's *Memoirs*. This wasn't the first time Twain had lampooned a war. During the Franco-Prussian War of 1871, he had produced a similar caricature of a wartime map. "The Seat of War" illustration in "The Private History" surely had its origin in Grant's "Map of the SEAT OF WAR 1861–1865" in the *Personal Memoirs*. While Twain's depicted the counties the Marion Rangers roamed through in 1861, Grant's covered a vastly larger area in which terrible battles had actually been fought. As Grant's publisher and editor for the *Personal Memoirs*, Twain had the advantage of reading them before he wrote his own essay.[6]

Was he mocking Grant? Surely not, but it must be remembered that he was not below poking good fun at the general, as he had that night in Chicago. Indeed, while planning his essay, he wrote in his journal: "Put Huck & Tom & Jim through my Mo. campaign & give a chapter to the Century. Union officer accosts Tom & says his name is US Grant."[7] At heart, he meant no disrespect for Ulysses S. Grant, but he may have harbored subconscious feelings against the nature of Grant's fame, namely as Lincoln's killing machine in the war, a "machine" that had killed so many of his fellow Southerners. In the summer of 1884, we recall, Twain had tried to take his Mississippi trio out west in "Huck Finn and Tom Sawyer Among the Indians." That unfinished piece trails off in rape and murder. "The Private History" ends almost as badly, with the killing of an unarmed man.

He is shot off his horse by six of the Marion Rangers, including Clemens; hence, like a firing squad, no one shooter is forced to carry the burden of the deed alone. It is a metaphor for the legalized murder that is war itself. Yet the man Sam Clemens had become twenty-four years later confesses that at the time, "The thought shot through me that I was a murderer; that I had killed a man — a man who had never done me any harm." As Clemens approached the fallen man, he imagined that "the dying man gave me a reproachful look out of his shadowy eyes. . . . He muttered and mumbled like a dreamer in his sleep, about his wife and child." It occurs to him that the "killing of strangers" goes well beyond the individual person killed.

Compare this passage with similar ones in Erich Maria Remarque's *All Quiet on the Western Front,* and you begin to suspect this German veteran of World War I had been reading Mark Twain. At one point in the madness of the trench warfare (in chapter 9) Remarque describes the scene in which his protagonist, Paul Bäumer, jumps into a foxhole for cover. When an enemy combatant seeks out the same shelter, Bäumer fatally stabs him. His French foe, however, does not die immediately, but like the stranger in Twain's war story, appears to stare at his assailant. Paul thinks of the man's wife and imagines a letter her husband has written to her that is still in transit. "Forgive me, comrade; how could you be the enemy?" he asks in anguish. He even decides to write the soldier's assumed wife, and in searching the now dead man comes upon "portraits of a woman and a little girl, small amateur photographs taken against an ivy-clad wall."

Earlier, in chapter 8 of this classic war novel, Bäumer observes Russian prisoners of war. He finds it a strange and enlightening experience to see the enemy close up: "They look just as kindly as our own peasants." They are his enemies, like the Frenchman in the foxhole, at the command of their mutual leaders, who themselves do not take part in the actual slaughter: "At some table a document is signed by some persons whom none of us knows, and then for years together that very crime on which formerly the world's condemnation and severest penalty fell, becomes our highest aim. But who can draw such a distinction when he looks at these quiet men with their childlike faces and apostles' beards?"

Remarque had set out to condemn war by dashing its romantic abstractions. Mark Twain did the same in 1885. Whether or not he did so purposely in "The Private History," he repeated its antiwar pattern not only in *A Connecticut Yankee*, where his introduction of Gatling guns into the plot of the novel anticipated the trench warfare of World War I, but also in "The War Prayer" at the turn of the century, a piece that anticipates Remarque in shining a light on the humanity of the enemy. With its implicit argument that well over half a million Americans, more than in any other U.S. conflict, may have died merely because they were the "enemy," "The Private History" went against the *Century* series theme of reconciliation. Ultimately, Mark Twain was saying that warfare settles nothing that is chronically and designedly wrong with the human condition.

On a much broader canvas Stephen Crane would undercut the romance of war, and Ernest Hemingway would as well in *A Farewell to Arms*, where his protagonist comes to the same conclusion as his predecessors in the development of the antiwar theme in literature. When questioned by the carabinieri, the Italian police who suspect that the ambulance driver is German, Hemingway's Frederick Henry (a name taken from Crane's Henry Fleming in *The Red Badge*) comes to the sudden realization that all wartime actions are based not on any kind of virtue but blinding ideology about the enemy as "barbarians" and "the sacred soil of the fatherland." No wonder Hemingway insisted that all great American literature began with one book, *Huckleberry Finn*, which came out of the same phase of Twain's literary greatness as "The Private History of a Campaign That Failed."

In the aftermath of the slaughter that culminates the chapters of *Huckleberry Finn* about the feuding Grangerfords and Shepherdsons, we have yet another, perhaps the first, complaint about war, when Huck laments the bushwhacking of his new-found friend Buck Grangerford: "All of a sudden, bang! bang! bang! goes three or four guns." Surprised by the Shepherdsons, Buck and another jump in the river, only to be shot in the back, their murderers shouting, "Kill them, kill them!" "It made me so sick," Huck mourns, "I most fell out of the tree. I ain't agoing to tell *all* that happened — it would make me sick again if I was to do that. I wished I hadn't ever come ashore that night, to see such things. I ain't ever going to get shut of them — lots of times I dream about them." After describing the killing of the stranger in "The Private History," Twain concludes: "The thought of him got to preying upon me every night; I could not get rid of it. I could not drive it away, the taking of that unoffending life seemed such a wanton thing." And *that,* he admits, was "an epitome of war."

* * *

America under President Cleveland continued to grapple with social problems that would follow it into the twentieth century. On November 6, 1885, the Park Avenue Methodist Church celebrated the eighteenth anniversary of the founding of the Freedman's Aid Society with a number of speeches, which, rather than celebrating the condition of blacks, mainly bemoaned it. The pulpit was surrounded with posters, pictures, and maps suggesting the results of the society's labors. "Education is the Cheap Defense of Nations," read one prominent sign that carried a diagram showing the high illiteracy rate of various Southern states. A clergyman from Brooklyn spoke of the miserable state of both Southern blacks and poor whites. The Negroes, he said, needed most of the society's attention because the "white has privileges of franchise, jury, and church. The negro is a man and a citizen, but these are only his theoretical rights." Cable had argued the same point in "The Freedman's Case in Equity."

A New Orleans cleric gave the chief address, astutely predicting that the curse of "that sum of all villainies, slavery, would remain a curse for generations," and complaining that the nation seemed indifferent to the black dilemma. A black preacher from Newark, a graduate of Boston University, proved to be the most compelling speaker of the evening. He also echoed Cable. Declaring blacks to have the potential to become "the bulwark of American ideas," if only given their due as citizens, the Reverend J. W. E. Bowen assured his auditors that blacks would not want to mingle their blood with whites. "Believe me," he asserted, "the colored man regards the conservation of his blood. Education to him does not mean marrying a white lady."[8]

The president of the United States, however, considered "the Indian Question" much more pressing than the plight of the freedman. Having recently protected their lands from white cattlemen, Cleveland sought to bring American Indians more into the mainstream of American life. A delegation from a recent conference at Lake Mohonk in New York heartily agreed during its audience with the president at the White House. The delegation, the *Times* reported on November 11, 1885, "advocated the abolition of the present system of Indian reservations and favored the adoption of a policy in regard to [Indians] similar to that so successfully employed in the case of the colored population." Cleveland agreed but wondered how the government could get the Indians to mingle with the white population. "We certainly can't drive them off their reservations." Integration, it seemed clear, wouldn't work in either the case of the Indian or the black, not that the social intermingling of the latter was much of an issue twenty years after the end of the Civil War.

Getting blacks off the Southern plantations still seemed to be enough of a goal for the foreseeable future.

(Fast-forward to the year 2011. The word "nigger" has been expunged from a new edition of *Huckleberry Finn,* published in the Deep South of Montgomery, Alabama, where resistance to integration in the 1950s and 1960s had been the fiercest. Nonetheless, the substitution triggers universal condemnation in the national press. As ugly as the word has become, even in the South, there is a strong consensus in favor of literary integrity. Volume one of the latest edition of Mark Twain's autobiography has been on the *New York Times* best-seller list for months since its release in November 2010. A black man is president of the United States. Affirmative action is no longer effectively controversial.

And there is another anniversary in the history of the American civil rights movement. Celebrations for the fiftieth anniversary of the first freedom rides through the South in 1961 take place in Chicago and Jackson, Mississippi. The Chicago event is originally planned for Washington, D.C., where the historic invasions of the Jim Crow South began, but Oprah Winfrey, a black woman and one of the most powerful television celebrities on the planet, flies most of the former freedom riders to Chicago so that they can populate her audience during the taping of a show celebrating the same event. Many figures of the civil rights era participate in the national remembrance, but some — in scornful protest — do not. One of the most vocal, the Reverend Jim Lawson of the United Methodist Church in Los Angeles, had volunteered to be on the first bus to Jackson in 1961. Lawson complains that it is still too early to celebrate anything. "We did not dismantle the system. A lot has changed in the state, but be assured, racism is alive and well in Mississippi." He and others who boycotted the celebrations argue that the event in Mississippi amounts to nothing more than "stealing the legacy of the civil rights movement so they can profit from tourism." During the Mississippi part of the festivities, Governor Haley Barbour unveils a plaque at an old Greyhound station in Jackson, identifying it as one of the stops on the Mississippi Freedom Trail. It now forms a state triad with the Mississippi Blues Trail and the Mississippi Country Music Trail.[9])

When readers reach the chapters in *Huckleberry Finn* that Hemingway complained about, they must recognize that Mark Twain was in fact bringing his river romance back to the reality of the slaveholding South. With his final chapters of farce in which Tom Sawyer engages in every Sir Walter Scott tactic he can imagine in the alleged freeing of a free Negro, Twain also affirms the hard facts of race by depicting the contempt Southern whites harbored for blacks before the war, and by extension how most whites felt about freedmen in 1885. After the armed farmers are relieved of their fears that abolitionists have invaded their town, and Tom, who was shot by one of them, receives medical aid, the doctor tells the vigilantes not to be any rougher on the runaway Jim "than you're obleeged to, because he ain't a bad nigger." Jim could have run away again, but he had remained to assist the wounded Tom. So he suffers only their scorn — "They cussed Jim considerable, though, and give him a cuff or two." Earlier they thought to hang Jim as "an example to all the other niggers around there." But others warn that Jim isn't their property, "and his owner would turn up and make us pay for him, sure. So that cooled them down a little, because the people that's always the most anxious for to hang a nigger that hain't done just right, is always the very ones that ain't the most anxious to pay for him when they've got their satisfaction out of him."

As late as November 17, Clemens was still proofing volume two of Grant's *Personal Memoirs;* that day he did so at the New York City residence of Mrs. Grant. Two days later, on November 19, he visited the White House, accompanied by Johnson of the *Century* and George Walton Green of the American Copyright (a lobbying effort to achieve an international copyright agreement).[10] On Thanksgiving the vice president, Thomas A. Hendricks, died suddenly of a heart attack. The next day, November 27, Livy celebrated her fortieth birthday at their Farmington Avenue house in Hartford. The popular actor Joseph Jefferson happened to be in town that night for a performance of *Rip Van Winkle,* a popular play that rivaled the stage versions of *Uncle Tom's Cabin.* He was a guest of the Clemenses that evening at a table that numbered twelve, including the son of John Bright, the English liberal who had taken the side of the Union in the first years of the Civil War.

Three days later Livy's husband observed his fiftieth birthday.

Mark Twain's half century of existence was widely celebrated. The *Critic* published tributes from Joel Chandler Harris, Charles Dudley Warner, and Oliver Wendell Holmes. "I am glad he is fifty years old," Harris wrote. "He has put his youth in his books, and there it is perennial." "Few living men," Warner, Twain's coauthor in *The Gilded Age,* added, "have crowded so much into that space, and few have done so much for the entertainment and good fellowship of the world." Holmes, who had been one of Twain's targets in his Whittier birthday dinner speech in 1877, wrote a humorous poem that included the following verse:

So 50 years have fled, they say,
Since first you took to drinking
I mean in Nature's milky way
Of course no ill I'm thinking.

Holmes, according to his letter to Twain following the Whittier affair, had taken no offense at his remarks, but it was never altogether certain whether or not Twain had been under the influence during the delivery of his speech.[11] Moreover, Mark Twain's southwestern drawl made him sound inebriated to some. Publicly at least, Twain took no offense and heartily thanked Holmes, saying that the poem had "drawn the sting of my fiftieth year; taken away the pain of it, the grief of it, the somehow *shame* of it, and made me glad and proud it happened." To "Uncle Remus," he thanked Harris for his good word about Huck, "that abused child of mine who has had so much unfair mud flung at him."[12]

* * *

On December 1, 1885, Charles L. Webster & Company published the first volume of *Personal Memoirs of U. S. Grant*. It covered the late general's ancestry and boyhood, his time as a cadet at West Point, his participation in the Mexican War, and the first years of the Civil War, when the washed-up career officer had returned to the military and reinvented himself at the battles of Fort Donelson and Shiloh. Volume one consisted of 584 pages. In its front-page review of December 2, the *New York Times* quoted Grant that many in his hometown in Georgetown, Ohio, would have voted for Jefferson Davis over Abraham Lincoln, but Grant himself had always opposed slavery, even though he married a Kentucky woman whose father had owned many slaves. "The line between the rebel and Union element in Georgetown," he was heard to say, "was so marked that it led to divisions even in the churches."

The following day the newspaper reported that General Grant's book was expected to outsell any work ever issued except for the Bible and Shakespeare. The offices of Webster & Company at 42 East 14th Street were beset by agents and others anxious to purchase the first volume. Charley Webster compared the attention to that given to *Uncle Tom's Cabin* in 1852, when it had sold 300,000 copies in its first year. The Grant memoir, a set of two volumes when published in its entirety in the winter of 1886, had already received 825,000 orders. "We got out 375,000 copies [of volume one]," Webster confidently announced to reporters at the publishing office, "and the extra 50,000 will soon go off at the present rapid call for them. Eight binders have been and are now busy getting out the work, and 1,000 tons of white paper have been used in its complete make-up." Sales came from everywhere, including, notably, the South.

The *Chicago Tribune* of December 7 took note of the near miss between Colonel Grant's army and the Marion Rangers in 1861 by juxtaposing a passage from the *Memoirs* with one from "The Private History," which had appeared in the December issue of the *Century*. Grant's army, as noted earlier, had entered Missouri six weeks after the Rangers had broken up and Mark Twain had skedaddled. Grant had actually been wary of Colonel Tom Harris, the Rangers' leader whom Twain belittled as a former telegraph operator in Hannibal. Actually, Harris was no stranger to military activities. He had attended West Point and was a veteran of several military campaigns, including the Mexican War.[13] "In time," Twain wrote in a bald-faced lie, "I came to know that Union colonel whose coming frightened me out of the War and crippled the Southern cause to that extent — General Grant. I came within a few hours of seeing him when he was as unknown as I was myself."

On December 6, 1885, the wife of Henry Adams committed suicide in Washington, D.C. If he took notice, Mark Twain never mentioned it, even though the story concerned a noted acquaintance of his close friend Howells. Called "a perfect Voltaire in petticoats" by Henry James, who may have used her as a model for Isabel Archer in *The Portrait of a Lady*, Marian Hooper Adams had held court with her husband for the famous and influential in their Lafayette Square house across from the White House (today the site of the Hay-Adams Hotel). Her death devastated Adams, who became known as one of America's finest writers only after his own death in 1918. The famous gap of twenty years (1872 to 1892) in *The Education of Henry Adams* was due to his wife's suicide. Adams never referred to her death in public, and when he had a memorial erected in Rock Creek Park, created by his friend the sculptor Augustus Saint-Gaudens, he mandated that it was to bear no name, date, or epitaph — not even the identity of the sculptor.[14] To this day, there is no indication that Adams is also buried there as well.

Twain simply couldn't abide most highbrow writers. He rudely refused Julian Hawthorne's invitation to help start an "Authors' Club."[15] But he did seek to occupy the spotlight with Grant, whose humble beginnings he had shared. Grant wrote the same way he fought, going directly to the point. So it may have been painful when Twain was criticized for trying to capitalize on the war in "The Private History." Evidently, the criticism originated from veterans canvassing for a history of the war that took issue with some of Grant's alleged facts. In writing his wartime essay, Twain, they said, was merely trying to promote the *Memoirs,* of which he was the publisher. His critics viewed the killing of the stranger in "The Private History" as evidence that Twain had been a bushwhacker in the guerilla warfare that consumed Missouri during the war. "The account by the humorist of his campaign," they asserted, "seeks to turn the thing into ridicule, and make it out a mere holiday escapade of boys, with no seriousness of intention or consequences on the part of the fifteen members of the company. But Twain was then 21 years old, and the band of which he was Lieutenant did some quite wicked marauding."[16] Actually, Sam Clemens was twenty-six in 1861, but he too had misstated his age in the Civil War, claiming to have been twenty-four.

Twain's association with Grant produced another fallout when the sculptor Karl Gerhardt came back into the news for refusing to relinquish the death mask he had made of Ulysses S. Grant. At first, Clemens took Gerhardt's side in the dispute, thinking everything could be settled to the satisfaction of both parties. "I think I'll insist on Gerhardt yielding up the mask *unconditionally,*" he told Charley Webster, whose company was involved in producing the miniatures of Grant's bust that Gerhardt had also done. "Then if you get Mrs. Grant to allow Gerhardt the first or exclusive use of it for a time, she can do that as a favor to you or me, & maybe it will come easier. However, I'll see how Gerhardt feels about it."[17]

Gerhardt refused to listen to Clemens, his patron and sponsor, even though he had helped Gerhardt get the commission in the first place. "I have the death mask in a vault in New-York," Gerhardt solemnly told the *Times* of October 25, 1885. "It is my private property, but I have no intention of disposing of it. In fact, $10,000 has been offered for it and refused." The *Times* article asked by what right was it Gerhardt's property. "Because this young, unskilled workman happened to apply to the family first, the delicate operation of taking a death mask was entrusted to him. Nobody knows whether he did it well or ill. In either case, the mask belongs to the Grant family, not to Mr. Gerhardt."

Gerhardt finally relented and returned the mask to Julia Grant on December 21, 1885 (it wouldn't be discovered until 1896 that the sculptor had secretly made a duplicate). Twain may have compensated him by erasing all personal debts from Gerhardt to himself, which by that time amounted to around $17,000. The two stayed in touch socially and professionally (Twain even got the sculptor to invest $1,000 in the doomed Paige Typesetter), but by the early 1890s Gerhardt's commissions began to dry up in the Panic of 1893. He remained in Hartford until his wife Hattie died of tetanus in 1897 at the age of only thirty-four. Apparently, the sculptor who owed his Mark Twain connection and thus his once prominent career as an artist to his young and flirtatious wife never bothered to provide her grave with a memorial marker. The teenaged beauty, who had once "stripped" for Mark Twain, lies to this day in an unmarked grave in the Spring Grove Cemetery in Hartford. Karl Gerhardt, who had once seen his photograph on the cover of *Frank Leslie's Illustrated Newspaper,* eventually moved to Louisiana for the "warmer climate." His last public notice took the form of an entry in a New Orleans City directory, where his occupation is listed as a "bartender" in the French Quarter.[18]

* * *

In composing "The Private History," Twain had more to reveal (or conceal) than his military record. If he had fought for the Confederacy, no matter for how short a period, it also meant that the man who had married the daughter of an abolitionist had once stood up for the institution of slavery. Unlike his protagonist in *Huckleberry Finn*, who essentially becomes an abolitionist in his efforts to assist the fugitive slave Jim, the author of "The Private History" had apparently never seen the light that now supposedly shone down upon the entire country after the Emancipation Proclamation. Today, during the sesquicentennial anniversary of the Civil War, there still hangs over every celebration the fact that the South had fought to preserve slavery.

This wasn't the problem during the twentieth anniversary of the war in 1885. In the spirit of reconciliation, citizens from both the North and the South were in favor of forgetting that past. With it, they would also forget the future as well as the past of the freedman. Yet Mark Twain was the author of a work that *cared* about blacks. Its hero hadn't been an abolitionist who opposed the treatment of human beings as slaves, but he had been sensitive enough to recognize the humanity of at least one slave, whom he tried to free at the risk of becoming a hated abolitionist.

Several newspapers ran excerpts, some generously long, of "The Private History." It made for good copy because Mark Twain was always funny. One publication, however, focused on one of its more serious aspects. It wasn't the futility and cruelty of war, because nobody noticed that theme, or at least no one mentioned it. Instead, it was again the matter of slavery as the catalyst for the war. The *Christian Union*, coedited by Henry Ward Beecher, the brother of the author whom Lincoln had described as "the little woman" who sparked "the great war," quoted from the more serious part of "The Private History." Described as a "family magazine," the *Christian Union* had published such reformers of its day as Mrs. Stowe, John Greenleaf Whittier, and Helen Hunt Jackson. Under the title of "Magazine Miscellany," published on December 10, 1885, it described Twain's wartime article as a "ludicrous account" about "raw country lads" trying to partake of war.

Nonetheless, Mark Twain, America's funnyman, Grant's publisher, the author of the antislavery novel *Adventures of Huckleberry Finn,* does admit in the essay that his father had owned slaves. Actually, the Clemens family in Hannibal had been dirt poor and owned during Sam's youth no more than two or three, whom his father had to sell to make ends meet. Yet his family had still owned slaves. The gravity of his confession mustn't be thought to be anywhere as weighty as such a confession in either the twentieth- or the twenty-first century. In fact, Livy, fearing that her husband would be confused — mainly because of the first-person narrative — with the illiterate Huck and thus a "poor white," insisted, in a letter written by her daughter Clara, that any biographical magazine pieces include the "mention that his parents on both sides had been slave holders."[19]

As the author of *Huckleberry Finn,* Mark Twain felt it necessary in "The Private History" to remind his reader of the terrible ambiguity over the question of slavery in the South. "I was piloting on the Mississippi," he wrote, "when the news came that South Carolina had gone out of the Union on the 20th of December 1860. My pilot-mate was a New Yorker. He was strong for the Union; so was I. But he would not listen to me with any patience; my loyalty was smirched, to his eye, because my father had owned slaves. I said, in palliation of this dark fact, that I had heard my father say, some years before he died, that slavery was a great wrong, and that he would free the solitary negro he then owned if he could think it right to give away the property of a family when he was so straitened in means."

After revealing the "dark fact" of his family's involvement in slavery, the New Yorker, possibly Horace Bixby, who trained Clemens as a pilot and who acted as a pilot for Union troops during the war, retorts that "anybody could pretend to a good impulse; and went on decrying my Unionism and libeling my ancestry." Using his best weapon, humor, Mark Twain satirizes the inconsistency on both sides of the Mason-Dixon Line. "A month later [after the departure of South Carolina from the Union] the secession atmosphere had considerably thickened on the Lower Mississippi, and I became a rebel; so did he. We were together in New Orleans, on the 26th of January, when Louisiana went out of the Union. He did his full share of rebel shouting, but was bitterly opposed to letting me do mine. He said that I came of bad stock — of a father who had been willing to set slaves free. In the following summer he was piloting a federal gun-boat and shouting for the Union again, and I was in the Confederate army."

Although the *Christian Union* had quoted from the more humorous aspects of "The Private History," this part was funny, too, perhaps the funniest because the heart of humor is always incongruity. As in so many of his profiles in insincerity, Twain suggests here that the moralist, even the one condemning slavery, can be a fraud. "I held his note for some borrowed money," he concludes. "He was one of the most upright men I ever knew; but he repudiated that note without hesitation, because I was a rebel, and the son of a man who owned slaves."

It seems clear that "The Private History" was Mark Twain's effort to justify his past as Sam Clemens of Hannibal. Even though he had briefly served on the Confederate side, he could still present himself as one of those courageous enough to have taken up arms for the cause of one's country, regardless of which side. "No one, not even our sons," exclaimed one veteran, "can appreciate the memories of camp and the march, of bivouac and battle, as those who were participants therein; the scenes of the great struggle can never be to them what they are to us."[20] In the spirit of reconciliation in 1885 the color of the uniform wasn't that important — that is, as long as the veteran in gray took a subservient role in the celebration, as Twain did in "The Private History." The nostalgic watercolor entitled "Bygones," painted in 1911 in Philadelphia, captures the nature of the new Blue-Gray relationship in this spirit of forgiveness in 1885.[21] It depicts two veterans of officer rank, one uniformed in blue and the other in gray. Both are elderly men, sitting in what looks like a plantation garden, smoking cigars together and talking in earnest, clearly discussing the details of an old battle. The hatted Union veteran is relaxed and slightly reclined in his chair, while the uncovered Confederate leans toward his former foe, somewhat anxiously and respectfully. The Confederate veteran bears more than a slight resemblance to Mark Twain.

It had been easy to overlook his past in the years after the war, through the 1870s, when the nation was preoccupied with the problems of Reconstruction. Then with Union veterans vociferously demanding war pensions and the country in an economic downturn, people wanted to forget the war. But by the next decade, the mood had changed. Once veterans were recognized with pensions and the economy cleared up, they sought to consecrate the war as an almost sacred event. Like Grant, his brave soldiers in blue, the Grand Army of the Republic, had also saved the nation, and they didn't want it ever forgotten. The spirit of their claim came to fruition, in fact, with Grant's *Personal Memoirs*, which the Confederate deserter Clemens had published! Fading by then was the dreadful loss of war. Grant, whose initial essays set the tone for the other generals in the "Battles and Leaders" series, never alluded emotionally to bloodshed, except to establish a context for his terse statements of the facts. (Indeed, his taut prose style may have influenced Hemingway's journalistic style in *A Farewell to Arms*).

As Edmund Wilson remarks in *Patriotic Gore,* the "very objectivity" of Grant's descriptions of war "always seems to eliminate its tragedy." Young Stephen Crane, on his way to writing *The Red Badge of Courage,* read many of the essays in the *Century* series (which had doubled the magazine's circulation). He was looking not simply for facts but the human element that Grant and his compatriots carefully left out. The *Century* authors, Crane complained, never wrote of "how they *felt* in those scraps. They spout enough of what they *did,* but they're emotionless as rocks." "The thought shot through me," Twain had written in *his* essay on the killing of the stranger, "that I was a murderer." Twain's "The Private History" may have been the one essay in "Battles and Leaders" that revealed the emotion Crane sought for his novel. Crane and Twain may have spoken of the war if they met at the Lantern Club in New York City in 1895. It was a hangout for journalists and writers. Both authors are known to have visited the clubhouse on William Street in lower Manhattan. We don't know whether Twain ever read *The Red Badge of Courage,* which was published that year, but he owned a copy of Crane's *The Monster and Other Stories* (1899).[22]

* * *

There was a lot to write about in America, which was teeming with poor people struggling to survive hand-to-mouth existences. Crane focused on the Irish, such as the tragic heroine in *Maggie Girl of the Streets* (1893). Frank Norris based his Irish-bashing *McTeague* on an Irish ironworker who stabbed his estranged wife thirty times with a freshly sharpened pocketknife. Only Mark Twain turned in his fiction to the tragedy of the black. As he looked to their antebellum condition in his fiction, their stories filled the current days' newspapers in 1885 — "Lynched in Broad Daylight — The Penalty Paid by a Texas Mulatto" (December 21), "Burned at the Stake — A Negro Murderer Chained to a Tree and Roasted to Death" (December 29). Yes, Mark Twain's father had owned slaves, and his son had once held a strong prejudice against blacks. On the issue of race, he had been closer to Tom Sawyer, the son of middle-class slave owners, than to the underclass Huck Finn, who battled his conscience over that "peculiar institution."

On December 24, Twain wrote Francis Wayland, dean of Yale Law School, asking about a black student there. "Do you know him? And is he worthy?" he asked. "I do not believe I would cheerfully help a white student who would ask the benevolence of a stranger, but I do not feel so about the other color. We have ground the manhood out of them, & the shame is ours, not theirs; & we should pay for it." The crisis he faced in 1885 was full of irony. On the one hand, he had to admit that he deserted the ranks during the Civil War. On the other, he had to admit to himself that he had joined up to fight for slavery. Then, just as Huck Finn had lit out for the territory at the end of *Huckleberry Finn,* Sam Clemens had lit out for Nevada. He ran not only from the dangers of war but also from his past in slaveholding Missouri. Twenty-four years later, in 1885, he promised Dean Wayland to provide "6, 12, or 24 months' board, as the size of the bill may determine." The student, Warner T. McGuin (1859–1937), would become the mentor of Thurgood Marshall (1908–93), the first black member of the U.S. Supreme Court.[23]

Earlier that month, on December 15, 1885, Robert Augustus

Toombs died. Toombs had been a Confederate general and a member of Jefferson Davis's cabinet. Before the war, he had served as a U.S. senator from Georgia. In January 1885 Toombs had attacked Cable for his essay on the "Freedman's Case in Equity," published in the *Century*. The criticism came in the form of an interview with the *Atlanta Constitution,* which had published a number of similar attacks on Cable's article. "I have always maintained, and still hold," General Toombs was quoted as saying in the interview, republished by the *Constitution* on the sixteenth and reprinted in the *Times* the following day, "that so long as the African and Caucasian races coexist in the same society, the subordination of the African is the necessary, proper, and normal condition best calculated to promote the highest interest and greatest happiness of both races, and consequently the society at large."

Toombs's deeply racist remarks still sear today, and it is noteworthy that the *Times* reprinted the interview in full. The "Negro Problem" was making its way to the forefront of the American conscience, and it wasn't yet clear where the majority stood on the matter. After all, the North had never "voted" on the Emancipation Proclamation, and Lincoln in signing the document "freed" slaves in places — that is, the rebellious Confederate states — where he then lacked authority to do so. It was never, of course, a question of restoring slavery, but social bondage was still the order of the day. Subordination, Toombs argued (by then, thankfully, from his tomb), had to be the "status of the African in this mixed society." The general's condemnation was emphatic: "Annihilate the race to-day and not a single discovery, invention, or thought original with a black man would be left to be remembered."

In the meantime, Robert E. Lee's reputation grew and grew,

even before his opposite in the war got to his final resting place, "Grant's Tomb." Its completion came seven years after the monument of Lee astride his horse Traveler was erected in Richmond in 1890. A crowd estimated at between 100,000 and 150,000 was on hand for the unveiling of Lee's statue — an even larger gathering than those that had attended the unveiling of monuments of Lee in Lexington, Virginia, and New Orleans.[24] Toombs's characterization of the black had turned solidly into the "Negro Problem" by the middle of the 1890s. Frederick Douglass, whose remarkable odyssey from slave to statesman cuts to shreds Toombs's condemnation of the black man, stood before the congregation of the Metropolitan Methodist Episcopal Church of Washington, D.C., on January 9, 1894, and delivered his last important speech, a year before his death. In "Lessons of the Hour," he dismissed the "Negro Problem" as the latest misleading "misnomer," cooked up by Southern racists and "accepted by the good people of the North."

Douglass had spent his life fighting for Negro rights, and now he was tired and even feeling somewhat defeated. "Do not ask me what will be the final result of the so-called negro problem," he told the largely black audience. "I cannot tell you. I have sometimes thought that the American people are too great to be small." He hoped that his estimate "would soon cease to be contradicted," but for now he had to conclude that the "cause lost in war, is the cause gained in peace, and the cause gained in war, is the cause lost in peace." The Supreme Court had not yet delivered its "separate but equal" ruling of 1896 in Plessy vs. Ferguson, but the case was in the pipeline, clearly headed for that result. The Civil Rights Bill of 1865 had been "destroyed," and the Republican Party — the party of antislavery before the war — had become the "party of money rather than a party of morals." (Mark Twain had abandoned it in 1884 in voting for Grover Cleveland.)

Douglass had been right. Twisted language stood in the way of "equity" for freedmen and their descendants. Even the term "civil rights" was turned around to serve whites instead of blacks. On Christmas Day, 1885, the *Times* condemned segregation while also condoning it. "Nobody will deny that the exclusion of a colored concert company from a hotel in Troy is an outrage," the story entitled "Civil Rights" reported. But it went on to say, "neither in legislation nor in public opinion is there any hope of effectual redress." For it was unjust, it said, to blame the landlord of the Troy hotel, who had as a businessman to make his hotel attractive "by keeping out of it persons who, for any reason or for no reason, are offensive to the classes upon whose favor he must rely for his living." In other words, there were "very few landlords . . . who would turn away colored guests on account of their personal prejudices. . . . They dislike to receive them simply because they believe that by entertaining them they will lose more than they will gain." Thus, it was the landlord's "civil right" to discriminate against blacks.

A Thurgood Marshall was already needed, well before his time, to cut through the legal and linguistic morass. In "Civil Rights of Colored People," the *Times* of December 27, 1885, reported that the courts in Iowa had ruled that a "negro who was refused admission to a place of amusement because of his color" lacked any legal relief. "The act complained of by the plaintiff was the withdrawal by the defendants, as to him, of the offer which they had made to admit him, or to contract with him for admission. They had the right to do this, as to him or any other member of the public. This right is not based upon the fact that he belongs to a particular race, but arises from the consideration that neither he nor any other person could demand as a right under the law that the privilege of entering the place be accorded to him."

* * *

The lynching atrocities in America found the first spark of their literary dramatization hardly a week after Douglass's speech. In "Ten-Foot Drop," appearing in the *St. Louis Republic* of January 18, 1894, yet another lynching, this one in St. Louis, was vividly described in a newspaper. The reporter was Theodore Dreiser, still in his newspaper days, working his way east to a career, next, as a magazine writer, and ultimately as the author of *Sister Carrie* and other novels that would contrast the ever-widening gap between wealth and poverty in America. Before he wrote that book, his first and perhaps finest novel, he wrote "Nigger Jeff," based on the lynching of a black he reported for the *Republic*. He took his title from Twain — from the "Nigger Jim" of *Huckleberry Finn*. (In newspaper accounts "the nigger Jim" of the novel had morphed into "Nigger Jim.") Dreiser's use of what has become a racial slur eventually brought about the banning of his finest short story from all current-day high school and college anthologies.

Mark Twain's "The United States of Lyncherdom" would have to wait until 1923 to finally get published in a collection by his biographer, Albert Bigelow Paine. Paine was an "authorized" biographer, indeed one who literally lived with his subject for the last four years of his life and afterward *on* his posthumous fame. The twenty-two appendices to his 1912 biography included an excerpt from "3,000 Years Among the Microbes," but nothing from "The United States of Lyncherdom." Dreiser's "Nigger Jeff" first appeared in *Ainslee's* magazine for November

1901. "Don't kill me, boss," the accused rapist of a white woman is reported to plead in Dreiser's newspaper story in 1894, as the lynching victim is about to be executed. The fictional Jeff Ingalls says almost the same thing as he is dragged from his hiding place, tied in a sack, and transported to the bridge from which he will be hanged. "Then came the concerted action of a dozen men," Dreiser writes in "Nigger Jeff," "the lifting of the black mass into the air, and then Davies [the newspaper reporter] saw the limp form plunge down and pull up with a creaking sound of rope. In the weak moonlight it seemed as if the body were struggling, but he could not tell."[25]

Back in December 1885, Mark Twain had other fish to fry. He had already written his antilynching story; it was *Adventures of Huckleberry Finn.* "I am plotting out a new book, & am full of it," he told Webster at their publishing company. "So unless there is use for me down there, I shall not come yet awhile."[26]

EIGHT

><tt>><

Connecticut
Yankee

><tt>><

"The real war will never get into the books," Walt Whitman wrote in *Specimen Days* in 1882. "And so good-bye to the war." This part of the so-called Wound Dresser's autobiography revisited the same conflict that Mark Twain also sought to put to rest. To Whitman, who spent the war in the Union capital, visiting in the more than forty makeshift hospitals and attending to wounded and dying soldiers from both sides of the Mason-Dixon Line, the political significance of the war was less important than the personal losses and sacrifices — "the two or three millions of American young and middle-aged men, North and South, embodied in those armies." "So much of a race," he added parenthetically, "depends on how it faces death."

He was speaking mainly of the *white* deaths. Whitman was never an abolitionist, in spite of the fact that he was always against slavery. The difference lay in the degree of protest. An abolitionist in the 1850s was considered a radical, somebody who would risk even the dissolution of the Union for the emancipation of slaves. His close friend and fiery champion William Douglas O'Connor was a former abolitionist who favored giving the vote to freedmen in 1872, and O'Connor's difference with Whitman on this issue cost them their friendship for almost a decade. Outside of the Transcendentalist precincts of *Leaves of Grass,* Whitman also had difficulty accepting blacks as equals to whites. Few whites in the North could. For Whitman, the Civil War was fought to maintain the Union; emancipation was another important, but secondary concern. In the first year or two of the war, as the South seemed to have the edge and the Union wounded and dying poured into the Washington hospitals, the poet insisted, "This war must stop." For O'Connor it had to be continued until the issue of slavery had been "settled." Whitman then admitted that he didn't "care for the niggers in comparison with this slaughter."[1]

Even Lincoln, also firmly in the antislavery camp, hesitated in issuing the Emancipation Proclamation, which didn't become law (however unenforceable in the South) until January 1, 1863. He first tried to use the threat of the law to get the South to lay down its arms and keep its slaves (at least until the end of the century). Like Whitman, Lincoln considered the preservation of the Union the primary reason to fight the war. Whitman's "divine average" were largely white, though he reaches out to blacks in *Leaves of Grass.* In "Song of Myself" (section 10), the narrator even participates in the Underground Railroad. Christlike, he washes the feet of the runaway slave. In the reality of prose, however, when so many blacks, or "contrabands," from the South were flooding into the Union capital, he thought it boded ill for what was still called "these United States."

After the war, it became *the* United States, as the spirit of reconciliation washed away the blood of the mighty conflict. In the process, blacks — the real reason for the war — were forgotten. As a result, today, 150 years later, relatively few blacks visit the nation's Civil War battle sites and museums. Revisionists of the "Lost Cause," as one commentator recently put it, insisted that the South hadn't really lost the war but had merely been overwhelmed by the industrialized North. Lee became a "contemporary King Arthur," while Grant in the next century became a symbol of the absurdity and horror of war. "That [revisionist] interpretation served the North, too, for it elided uncomfortable questions about the profits reaped by the North from Southern cotton."[2]

The Southerner Mark Twain, who until his early twenties evidently approved of slavery, was one of the first major American writers to acknowledge the role of blacks in the war. In his first appearance in the *Atlantic Monthly,* in 1874, he wrote "A True Story, Repeated Word for Word as I Heard It." Written in the vernacular of an ex-slave woman, it told the story of her reunion near the end of the war with a son who as an adult had become a soldier in the Union army. In taking the point of view of the black, Twain was giving voice to this trampled minority. Such African American voices became an essential part of his greatest achievement in *Adventures of Huckleberry Finn.* There "the nigger Jim" tells Huck of his longing for his wife and children, and the tragedy of slavery is reinscribed for the next and subsequent generations of Americans.

Mark Twain's role in the aftermath of the Civil War was of course complicated. He had started out to fight for the South, which fought for slavery, but afterward he had slyly condemned that cause in works that led directly up to his magnum opus. In a way, his situation mirrored the conflicted state of his own Missouri during the war. While its governor had wanted to secede with the rest of the South, the state resisted and fell into guerrilla warfare. It became a land of bushwhackers, as guerrillas were known during the Civil War. And now with his confession in "The Private History," he too was called a bushwhacker. The

Chicago Tribune of December 13, 1885, noted in alluding to Twain's wartime essay, "The discussion of Mark Twain is raised by the disclosure of the fact, heretofore not generally known, that he was a Rebel guerrilla in Missouri early in the Civil War." Ultimately, few cared about what Mark Twain had done in the war. It was enough that he was funny, and most observers attributed any fuss to the competition between "war-book publishers," of which Twain was certainly one.

In fact, the revised history of the war took precedence over the real reason for it, in spite of emancipation jubilees held every New Year's Day in the South. In Nashville at the Colored Exposition Building, the former American minister to Haiti, John M. Langston, spoke of "The Future of the Negro," who was in "the second stage of his social condition since the time of reconstruction." The speech was vapid, according to its rather biased description in the *New York Times* of January 2, 1886. The great uncle of Langston Hughes, the poet of the Harlem Renaissance in the following century, Ambassador Langston had long been an activist in the black cause. He would later, in 1888, become one of the first African Americans elected to Congress, and the *last* one for nearly another American century. He told his mostly black audience in Nashville that the "colored man" could now study the question of civil rights and "settle it" so that "he may bring himself into such relationship with the people of the South, in whose midst he largely dwells, so as to blunt the edge of their past enmities toward him, and secure, if possible, through political action a condition of things which will . . . secure peace, through reconcilement and general amity to both classes of the South."

* * *

Having confronted the "race" question in *Huckleberry Finn,* Mark Twain shifted his attention to another kind of slavery. He was turning ever so gradually with the rest of the country to the growing labor crisis, to slavery in the workplace. Newspapers were full of stories about "socialists" and "anarchists." Eighteen eighty-six opened on New Year's Day with this headline in the *New York Times:* "Assaulted by Strikers/Obliged to Fight Their Way to the Factory through a Mob," reflecting the newspaper's tilt toward capital over labor. Striking box makers had violently confronted eleven "non-union" men who had taken the places of the strikers at a factory in Chicago. The violence was escalating every day. Saner voices called for compromise, but the mounting crisis was fueled by fear of socialists, especially in Chicago. They were suspected of manufacturing "dynamite bombs, and in experimenting with other infernal machines with the purpose, as they declare, of destroying the militia, and blowing up the large public buildings when the 'great revolution' begins."[3]

In focusing on the labor issue, Mark Twain turned, as he often did, to history, always his favorite subject. During their tour of 1884–85, Cable had presented Twain with a copy of Thomas Malory's *Morte d'Arthur.* It was in the sixth century that the writer found the basis for his next novel, because *A Connecticut Yankee in King Arthur's Court* would allow him to speculate on the serfdom or slavery of legendary England. In this dystopia about the Hartford man waking up in King Arthur's time, he would critique the motherland instead of the homeland.[4]

"For the first time in a long while," he told Charley Webster, who was putting the finishing touches on a book contract with Pope Leo XIII for his autobiography, "I am so situated that I can't well leave home." His daughter Clara had badly sprained her ankle in a toboggan accident, and her case was keeping them all "shut up in the house." "I have begun a book, whose scene is laid far back in the twilight of tradition."[5] During February, he wrote the first four chapters, from which he read nightly to his family. He thought that *A Connecticut Yankee* might well be his last book since he soon hoped to become rich as a publisher and perhaps retire from writing. Mrs. Grant had been paid the highest royalty ever, and Charles L. Webster & Company still had a cash balance of $260,000, with more coming in every day.[6]

Yet the work at hand drew him away from the present. The only item to prevent it was the continuing drama of the Paige Typesetter. He had already spent tens of thousands on the project, and on February 6 he signed a contract with its inventor Paige to pay him an annual salary of $7,000.[7] Eventually, this technical failure — and it would become clear in the ensuing year or two that it was indeed a failure — found its way into the plot of his novel, where technology cannot overcome either human mediocrity or religious ideology.

Mormons were also making their way into the news of the day in the winter of 1886, mainly because of the polygamy still practiced among their number in the territory of Utah. Twain had made fun of the practice in *Roughing It.* In chapter 15 he hilariously describes the typical Mormon polygamist as "some portly old frog of an elder" who "marries a girl — likes her, marries her sister — likes her, marries another sister — likes her, takes another — likes her, marries her mother — likes her, marries her father, grandfather, great grandfather, and then comes back hungry and asks for more." In January the Senate had passed the Mormon Bill, which added fourteen government-appointed trustees to the thirteen-member board of the Church of Jesus Christ of Latter Day Saints in order to outvote the church's will "on every question," including "plural marriage." There now existed the danger that the government was attacking religion, rather than punishing it for its inclusion of polygamy.[8] Known generally as the Edmunds Bill, it also forbade Mormons from serving on juries, thereby ensuring the conviction of polygamists.

In 1886, fifteen years after the appearance of *Roughing It,* Twain confessed that he was "no friend of the Mormon Religion." Raised a Presbyterian and by this time edging into agnosticism, he would have gladly seen it done away with. But he didn't approve of the government's heavy-handed tactics. "I would like to see it extirpated," he told the journalist Kate Field, who had heard that Twain disapproved of her anti-Mormon lectures, "but always by fair means, not [by] these Congressional rascalities. If you can destroy it with a book, — by arguments and facts, not brute force, you will do a good and wholesome work."[9] He even hinted that Charles L. Webster & Company might consider publishing such a book.

But he quickly rescinded the possibility of such an offer, saying that his publishing house was already "piled up with contracts which two or three years — and possibly four — will be required to fulfil." Contracts were indeed piling up, and the latest (to become a commercial failure) was just signed. Charley Webster had just returned from Rome, announcing to the national press "the book will be a genuine autobiography of the Pope, although of course not literally written by him. The ruler of the Catholic world cannot spend his time scribbling, but he is dictating a portion of the book."[10] This was Leo XIII, who would make a signal contribution to the rights of working people around the world, but few of them bought His Holiness's book in 1887. Clemens had foolishly thought that at least every Catholic would feel duty bound to purchase a copy.

Four years later, on May 15, 1891, Pope Leo XIII issued an

encyclical entitled "Rights and Duties of Capital and Labor." Also called *Rerum Novarum* (Of New Things), it addressed the plight of workingmen in the nineteenth century, the urban poor beset by the rise of industrialization and tempted by the growing popularity of socialism around the world. It called for social justice in an age of unrestricted capitalism and a fair wage ("sufficient to support a frugal and well-behaved wage-earner"), but at the same time reasserted the Church's teaching about the importance of private property. Pope Leo's concern for the worker may have been the main reason why the Protestant publisher Clemens chose to publish the autobiography.

Twain, as we said, was shifting his focus from black slavery to wage slavery. The Knights of Labor, which in 1886 combined all trades into a single union consisting of about 725,000 members, caught his attention and admiration. While testifying in favor of an international copyright law on January 29, 1886, he heard the speech of a printer, the president of the Philadelphia Typographical Union, No. 2, who wanted the copyright bill to require that all foreign books sold in the United States be printed in the United States. Twain may not have favored this particular stipulation, but he was impressed at the power of the people — what Whitman had called "the divine average." James Russell Lowell had also been on hand to support the bill, but his testimony paled in comparison to that of "a foreman of a printing office, clad in unpretending gray."

He expressed his admiration of this representative of labor in every trade in an article he read before the Monday Evening Club of Hartford on March 22, 1886. Entitled "The New Dynasty," it attests to Twain's mounting interest in the growing American labor movement. Based on the assumption that power corrupts, he struck out for the underdog — that category that had been prominently peopled in his mind by his own father and eldest brother. "I am not here," Twain quoted the representative worker that day before Congress, "as a printer; I am not here as a brick-layer, or a mason, or a carpenter, or as any other peculiar or particular handicrafts man; but I stand here to represent ALL the trades, ALL the industries, all brethren of ANY calling that labor with their hands for their daily bread and the bread of their wives and their little children."

Twain had been deeply impressed that January day before Congress, he told the Monday Evening Club members, by comparing the persuasive power of the workers in support of the copyright bill to that of the authors represented by Lowell. "The authors had with slender hopefulness indicated what they would like the Congress to do; in the other case, without any insolence of speech or bearing, but reposeful with the clear consciousness of unassailable authority, the five-million-voiced printer DICTATED to the Congress — not anything which it MUST do, but certain things which it must NOT do. And that command will be heeded."[11] The printer before Congress had egregiously exaggerated the number of members in the Knights, which would go into serious decline during the rest of the decade, mainly because of the Haymarket Affair in May of 1886.

Little wonder that in *A Connecticut Yankee* "Sir Boss" of Camelot tries to rearrange the relationship between noble and commoner in the sixth century. Capital and labor in the nineteenth century needed the same recalibration, but not everyone agreed with Twain's support of labor. This disagreement would be reflected in the development of his novel, which he completed in 1889, as the sixth-century Church defeats the Connecticut Yankee. Hank Morgan would wake up with his creator back in the nineteenth century, where a free-market economy would do the same thing to Sam's publishing business, which went into bankruptcy early in the next decade.

* * *

"Here was the nation in person speaking," he told the members of the Monday Evening Club that night, "and its servants, *real* — not masters *called* servants by canting trick of speech — listening. The like could not be seen in any other country, or in any other age." The image of that printer before the Senate Committee on Patents the past January 29 remained in his memory, eventually enriching the theme of *A Connecticut Yankee*. "They whom that printer represented are in truth the nation: and they are still speaking. Have you read their Manifesto of demands? It has a curiously worn and old and threadbare sound. And it is old. It is older than the Scriptures. It is as old as Tyranny — old as Poverty — old as Despair."[12]

When the Haymarket labor violence occurred in May of 1886, it is generally thought that Howells stood alone in his outrage at the way the alleged conspirators to murder were summarily tried and sentenced to death. Twain and other prominent authors supposedly paid no attention to the injustice. Yet in Twain's case his Monday Evening Club talk on "The New Dynasty" and the developing plot in *A Connecticut Yankee* suggest otherwise. If *Huckleberry Finn* was predicated on the injustices of slavery, *A Connecticut Yankee,* his next completed novel, took its cue from the American labor movement in 1886 and beyond, when the country was plagued by labor violence, culminating a few years later with the bloodshed emanating from the 1892 strike against Andrew Carnegie's steelworks in Homestead, Pennsylvania, just outside of Pittsburgh. Already in that part of the country, striking miners were battling with police. Three hundred strikers from the Coke Region, the *New York Times* of January 21, 1886, reported, "armed with bars, coke forks, and revolvers, started on a March and drove the men from the work at the Alice Mines."[13] This economic climate worked against the initial optimism in the plot of *A Connecticut Yankee*. Hank Morgan, the protagonist who wakes up the sixth century, sets out on a five-year plan to reorganize its economy on an equitable basis, but the pessimism would soon creep in.

In January of 1886, the first English translation of Leo Tolstoy's *War and Peace* (1867) became available. Howells talked about his reading of Tolstoy in his "Editor's Study" column in *Harper's Monthly*, characterizing the Russian's historic epic as "that great assertion of the sufficiency of common men in all crises, and the insufficiency of heroes."[14] Howells's reading of Tolstoy, which began with the English translation of 1886, influenced him profoundly. Earlier books, such as his greatest, *The Rise of Silas Lapham*, had addressed the moral challenges of the American middle class, but after reading Tolstoy he produced a number of "economic" novels dealing with the working class, including *A Hazard of New Fortunes*, published in the same year as *A Connecticut Yankee*.

Howells continued to believe, as his remark about *War and Peace* suggests, in the moral free will of the individual. Twain, on the other hand, was quickly turning into a determinist with *A Connecticut Yankee*, where most decisions depend on circumstance, or "training." In other words, we are the victims of our environment and thus subject to the inevitability of events. Whereas Howells picked up on Tolstoy's morality, Twain absorbed his naturalism. In the description of the newly translated *War and Peace* in the *Times* of January 31, 1886, a reviewer was clearly in the camp of Howells and his fellow social Darwinists.

He described the Russian author as a "stanch disciple of that new school of criticism which (as an eminent satirist has very aptly observed) 'turns history into an almanac' and supposes all great political changes to be merely recurring phenomena beyond human control as the succession of the seasons."

To the naturalist, war was a simply speeded-up version of peacetime in which life's loss is accelerated. In *War and Peace* Tolstoy defines war as an event "opposed to human reason and to human nature." In other words, life was unreasonable and amoral; it was opposed to *human* nature, but not biological nature, or the world in which humans must exist — and perish. In describing the defeat of Napoleon during his invasion of Russia in 1812, Tolstoy gives no more credit to the Russians than he does to the French. Both, he writes, were moved by either fear or vanity, "imagining that they knew what they were doing and did it of their own free will, but they all were involuntary tools of history."[15] Labor violence was simply on a lower plane, disparate activities that would coalesce in the "civil wars" of such climactic events as the Haymarket Affair and the Homestead Strike. "Joe, why do you want to save men?" he asked the Reverend Twichell, who had fought in the Civil War and had become known as "Mark Twain's clergyman." "You owe it to yourself, & to the powers that are in you, to reform."[16]

All great fiction reflects the life and times of its writer, whether it be in the nineteenth century of Huckleberry Finn or the sixth century of King Arthur. Regardless of whether or not Mark Twain became the richest robber baron on the planet with the Paige Typesetter, he would never be able to stop writing. He died in mid-sentence while trying to write a note to his surviving daughter, Clara. *A Connecticut Yankee* wouldn't come close to being his last book. He went on to write *The American*

Claimant, Pudd'nhead Wilson, Following the Equator, The Man That Corrupted Hadleyburg, and the posthumously published *Mysterious Stranger* manuscripts.

* * *

In 1886, betwixt and between black slavery and wage slavery, Mark Twain also turned his attention to the American Indian, whom he had denigrated in *Roughing It*. On February 23, he wrote to President Cleveland about the nation's mistreatment of indigenous peoples. His shift in attitude reflected the country's shift toward a more sympathetic view of what we now call the Native American. They were no longer dismissed as Stone Age savages that were simply in the way of western expansion. By the 1880s the nation had fought almost forty Indian wars. The prejudice against the Indians had reached its zenith in 1876 with the massacre of George Custer and his troops at Little Big Horn. The victorious Indian chieftain was Sitting Bull, whose crime was forgiven when he became the star of Buffalo Bill Cody's Wild West Show in 1885. Before that he was a fugitive whose cause was both condemned and celebrated by American poets. Whitman issued "A Death-Sonnet for Custer," which reflected the country's shock at the defeat — the consensus until then being that the "Indian problem" was under control.

But there was already emerging sympathy for the Indian. Perhaps as an answer to Whitman's support of the settler movement that the slain Custer had died for, Longfellow published "The Revenge of Rain-in-the-Face," implying that American troops in the West had it coming because of the already long history of Indian mistreatment. In his letter to the president, Twain enclosed a circular entitled "A Disgrace to Civilization." In manifesting his disapproval, it described a notice published in the *Southwest*

Sentinel that offered a $250 reward to any citizen for "each and every hostile renegade Apache killed." "You not only have the power to destroy scoundrelism of many kinds in this country," he told Cleveland, "but you have amply proved that you have also the unwavering disposition & purpose to do it."[17]

By this time the country had also been moved by Helen Hunt Jackson's *A Century of Dishonor* (1881). Emotional in its appeal but also factual in its argument, it described the mistreatment of Indians since the American Revolution, reviewing in its survey a succession of broken treaties with the nation's 300,000 Native Americans. Like Cleveland, Jackson much preferred the Indian cause to the black one, an affair she never embraced.[18] Already nationally known before this book as a writer and a poet (the "other poet of Amherst" who had grown up with Emily Dickinson), she became enthralled with the Indian question after marrying William Sharpless Jackson, president of the Denver & Rio Grande Western Railroad.

So there were three victims of the American Dream to worry about in the 1880s — the freedmen, the wage slaves, and the Indians, who were ultimately restricted to federal reservations in the twentieth century. Of these, the "white" immigrants of the labor movement would upstage the others. They also take the center stage in *A Connecticut Yankee*. Told from the perspective of a worker in the Colt Arms Factory in Concord who is knocked cold by a fellow worker and wakes up in Camelot, Twain's protagonist decides to democratize sixth-century England. He sets out to change a land "where a right to say how the country should be governed was restricted to six persons in each thousand of its population.... I was become a stockholder in a corporation where nine hundred and ninety-four of the members furnished all the money and did all the work, and the other six elected themselves a permanent board of direction and took all the dividends."[19]

The spark for Mark Twain's interest in the labor movement came initially from his interest in the Knights of the Round Table in his reworking of Camelot. On the eve of what has been termed "the Great Upheaval of 1885–86" in Chicago, the Knights of Labor came into prominence, almost exactly at the same time Twain took up *Morte d'Arthur* in writing *A Connecticut Yankee*. As this labor movement grew, reflecting labor unrest around the country, so did the plot of Twain's latest novel. Indeed, the plot may have turned deadly directly as a result of the Haymarket massacre and its fallout. As the Knights absorbed other labor groups in the city, consisting mainly of foreign-born or first- and second-generation members, largely German and Bohemian, the situation in Chicago grew more serious, especially in the spring of 1886. For the collective movement was also fueled by socialist and anarchist propaganda, published in numerous ethnic newspapers, in a city where between 1870 and 1900 at least forty percent of the residents were foreign-born blue-collar workers.[20]

It was a world otherwise quite removed from that of Mark Twain, who in 1885, long before the era of federal income taxes, had earned the combined sum of approximately $285,000 — from his lecture tour with Cable, royalties from *Huckleberry Finn,* income from Charles L. Webster & Company aside from his own royalties, and income from his wife Olivia's inheritance. While it wasn't *Downton Abbey,* the Hartford mansion brimmed with servants and class-conscious decorum, at least when the master wasn't making members of the household staff laugh. Even his friend Howells was earning only $10,000 or $12,000 a year, an amount that still dwarfed that of the average wage earner in the

United States. Yet like Hank Morgan of *A Connecticut Yankee,* Clemens was, as an American investor and businessman, more or less pulled into the fray. The news out of Chicago leading up to the May 4, 1887, "riot" made it impossible not to notice the labor rumblings. One report — in the *Times* of February 4, 1886 — put the annual wage figure for a laborer as low as $400. As one economist noted, "Possibly this was enough to live on, but men wanted more and became dissatisfied. To oppose the centralization of capital there came the organization of labor. At the present rate capital invested increased from 50 to 75 per cent. in a decade, while the wealth of the country increased only 10 per cent."

As he worked away on his construction of Camelot, Sam's own losses in the stock market of that day — direct investments — gave his narrative a ring of irritability. Not only was he losing with his investments, but he now had to pay Paige a salary to keep him working on the doomed typesetter, already his biggest investment at around $3,000 month. The result was a sort of a Jekyll and Hyde personality when it came to the labor question. On the one hand, he wanted to become the richest of the robber barons with the typesetter, which every newspaper in the world would have to either purchase or lease; on the other, he was capable of such screeds in favor the workingman as "The New Dynasty," the lecture he had given before the Monday Evening Club in Hartford that March in which he hailed workers who had banded together under the banner of the Knights of Labor. If only in his novel he could persuade himself that King Arthur's knights were capable of such noble action. If only he could stifle his growing suspicion about the "damned human race."

The day after the Haymarket Riot ("riot" mainly in the sense that the police panicked and starting shooting into the crowd of protesters after a dynamite bomb went off), the news of it had apparently not reached Sam in New York. He told his wife about the Webster contract with the pope. "I thought it would reconcile you to your costly sofa," he wrote on May 5, 1886, "you can order 1000 such sofas now, if you want to — the future bank account will foot the bill & never miss it." He thought, foolishly as it turned out, that the "Pope's book" would "sell a fleet load of copies."[21] His poor choice of books for his press mirrored his bad investments in other areas.

As he wrote Livy, he was on his way back to West Point, where he had just entertained the cadets in April with readings from *Huckleberry Finn*. He made a number of visits to the Point beginning in 1876. The senior captain of the cadets in the class of 1886 happened to be a fellow Missourian — John J. Pershing, future commander of the American Expeditionary Force in World War I. In the words of his biographer Frank Vandiver, "Pershing looked forward eagerly to each visit by Mark Twain [who in young Pershing's eyes may have loomed even larger because of his association with the late General Grant]. Twain apparently had a special affection for the Point and its men, and he visited often. Usually he came to lecture, but always he wandered off to a cadet room for private and hilarious story telling."[22] One room he was sure to visit was Pershing's. We must wonder whether the cadet had read "The Private History of a Campaign That Failed," and if so, what he thought of it. Of the 15,000,000 who died in the First World War, the number of American combat deaths reached well over 100,000. The "killing of strangers," of course, was central to the curriculum at the Point, indeed almost universally taken for granted until after the Great War in which Pershing inscribed his name in American military history.

In *A Connecticut Yankee,* Hank Morgan establishes a military academy that closely resembles the one that produced Pershing. In chapter 38 King Arthur and the narrator are rescued by knights on bicycles, not so anachronistic as it seems today because the American military was then experimenting with the newfangled devices.[23] Horses would continue to be used in combat, however, until World War I, when trench warfare, Gatling guns, and barbed wire made cavalry charges impossible.

World War I weakened the aristocratic class in Europe. In England, the Edwardian period was the last one named for a king or queen. After that, the chronological periods are generally named for their wars. Edwardian England went off to war with aristocrats as the military officers and the proletariat in the enlisted ranks, many of them former chauffeurs and valets on large country estates. During the war the czar and his family in Russia were executed. The days of the aristocrats and serfs that populated *War and Peace* were a thing of the past. Interestingly, the last vestige of the class system was — and is — to be found in the military. In the United States in 1886, still overwhelmed by the past of the Civil War, the new division in America was between capital and labor, between business owners and the working class, between economic princes and paupers.

The paupers consisted mainly of cheap European labor. When Mark Twain encountered his own economic problems in 1893, he took his family abroad to save money. He kept his family in luxurious hotels for relatively little (maintaining the Hartford mansion had cost much more) because their staffs were peopled by the poor, the very ones who worked in Europe for pitiful wages and were desperately crossing the Atlantic in search of a better life, only to be exploited by robber barons like Andrew Carnegie and Jay Gould. "We are not politicians or public thinkers," one of them confessed in the 1880s. "We are rich; we own America; we got it, God knows how, but we intend to keep it if we can."[24]

Twain himself would owe his own economic survival in the 1890s to one of these robber barons. Henry Huttleson Rogers, Rockefeller's vice president at Standard Oil, who once proudly told a government commission investigating the monopoly: "We are not in business for our health, but are out for the dollars."[25] Rogers was a heartless businessman, but his sympathy went out to Mark Twain, whose debts he reorganized, thus saving the writer from personal bankruptcy. One of Rogers's favorite books as a boy had been *The Adventures of Tom Sawyer.* Rogers probably had read all the river books — not only *Tom Sawyer,* but also *Life on the Mississippi* and *Huckleberry Finn,* if not *Pudd'nhead Wilson* — that invoked the nostalgia of the American boy and America's antebellum period. It is doubtful that he read *A Connecticut Yankee,* or if so if he approved of its antiaristocratic theme or especially its sympathy for thane, serf, or working man. Twain has been criticized for befriending — and defending against muckrakers and monopoly busters — such a plutocrat as Rogers. Yet it was these contradictions in the makeup of that Siamese twin known as Sam Clemens and Mark Twain that rendered the humorist so interesting. With Walt Whitman, he might have exclaimed: "Do I contradict myself? / Very well then I contradict myself."

Meanwhile the pauper in Chicago sought an eight-hour working day and better wages. Instead, he encountered stern resistance — fines instead of wage increases. There were fines for tardiness, fines for missing work without permission, for talking while working. If the workers didn't have enough to live on, to feed their families, their bosses blamed it on alcoholism, ignorance, and downright indolence. One industrialist declared that the basic cause of their "impecunious condition" lay in the workers' own improvidence. "Too many are trying to live without labor. . . . and too many squander their earnings on intoxicating drinks, cigars, and amusements, who cannot afford it."[26]

Often the problem was that the working hours were too few so that there was a corresponding reduction of wages. In 1886 nearly 40 percent of the working classes in Chicago were threatened with enforced idleness. That March, just a month before the Haymarket bloodshed, the Cook County poor farm was "literally overrun and infested by tramps from Chicago." On the other hand those who "owned" America sat back and basked in their success. They could afford to smoke cigars, good ones, or imbibe intoxicating drinks—Armour of meat packing, Beidler in lumber, McCormick in reapers, Crane in plumbing fixtures, Field in the department store, Pullman in railroad cars.[27] And soon, or so he was still dreaming, Clemens in typesetting machines.

* * *

The Haymarket bombing and its aftermath of judicial murder in Chicago marked a new era in America. It was the biggest thing since Lincoln's assassination. The incendiary device killed more than eight policemen and three or four civilians when it triggered an exchange of gunfire between police and protestors. It also set back the clock for European immigrants, who were tarred with the same brush that unjustly identified seven political activists with conspiracy to murder. Theodore Dreiser's eldest brother, Paul, the pre-ragtime songwriter who wrote "On the Banks of the Wabash," changed his German-sounding name to "Dresser." Most of the accused, who come down to us today as the Chicago martyrs for labor, were of German ancestry.

Of the eight put on trial for murder in the summer of 1886, five were German immigrants and one the son of German immigrants. The seventh was born in England, and the eighth could trace his lineage back to the American Revolution. He was Albert R. Parsons, who could have successfully run away like the suspected bomb thrower Rudolph Schnaubelt (never heard from again), but nobly turned himself in to the authorities to stand with his fellow socialists and labor activists. Interestingly, Parsons, who was older than most of the others by nearly a generation, had fought on the side of the South in the Civil War. Unlike Twain, he neither deserted military ranks nor gave up the cause after the defeat of what he liked to call "the slave-holders' Rebellion." It was only after attending Baylor College in Waco, Texas, and founding his own newspaper there that he saw the light and supported the ex-slaves in their fight for civil rights during Reconstruction. By the time he moved to Chicago in 1874, this cause had broadened into a lifelong campaign for the rights of the American worker. By 1884 he had founded the anarchist newspaper called *The Alarm*.

Parsons died for his outspoken reputation, and the others died for theirs—for their association with the labor cause, which became instantly unpopular after the Haymarket Riot and had to be punished. He was hanged on November 11, 1887, along with August Spies, George Engel, and Adolph Fischer. The fifth condemned man, Louis Lingg—the youngest at age twenty-three—committed suicide in his cell the day before. The other two, the only ones to plead for clemency, Samuel Fielden and Michael Schwab, had their sentences commuted to life imprisonment and were exonerated and released in 1893. By this time, the statute of limitations on the open secret that there had been no real evidence to connect any of the accused men to the crime had expired. As late as May 1986, the centennial anniversary of the Haymarket Riot, there were—and still are—two monuments. The first was established in 1889 in a local cemetery. It depicts Lady Liberty standing watch over the graves of the executed men. The other one, erected the same year, is a statue of a policeman with his hand upraised. It had to be removed to a precinct house after it was defaced in 1968 and then threatened by explosives in 1969 and 1970.[28]

Parsons and his compatriots died exactly thirty-one years before Armistice Day would bring an end to World War I. By that day, not only was the worst war up to that time at an end, but the labor wars had ended, too. The American Depression of the 1930s would drown out any of its death rattles. By the 1950s the unionization of (white) workers had been achieved. Only blacks remained forgotten, first in the spirit of reconciliation after the Civil War and then by the Jim Crow dominance in the South, with its abiding influence in the North, where so many blacks had relocated in the twentieth century. And then there was the civil rights movement of the 1960s. The rest of that story is still "to be continued" (as is perhaps the one about labor unions), but the latest marker in that redoubtable quest came with the 2012 groundbreaking for a black history museum on the National Mall. (There in 1862, at the Smithsonian Institution, Frederick Douglass was barred from speaking in favor of abolition because he was black.[29]) And so is Mark Twain's story "to be continued." *Adventures of Huckleberry Finn* persists as one of the most controversial books in American literature. First banned for its use of slang, now it is often banned (below the collegiate level at least) for its authentic use of language, or what we now know as the "N-word."

Back in 1886 Mark Twain had already given up the optimism of his greatest book and fallen into the pessimism of *A Connecticut Yankee*. He could no longer live in an antebellum past where the universe consisted of a boy and a raft and the river. When he returned to the Mississippi of his youth in *Pudd'nhead Wilson,* there was nobody like Huck to keep somebody like "the nigger Jim" from being sold down the river. In a way, Mark Twain sold himself down the river in his last river book. When his investments and his publishing house began to collapse in the 1890s, he kept writing to support himself and his family, who had become long accustomed to life in the upper crust.

He spent most of the last decade of the nineteenth century in Europe. By the time he returned permanently to the United States, on October 15, 1900, he had lost one daughter and discovered that his youngest suffered from epilepsy, an ailment that physicians then knew little about. His wife, Olivia, whose long history of asthma may have been connected to the fact of her husband's heavy cigar and pipe smoking, was by this time considered an invalid with a bad heart. She would die in 1904 well before reaching the age of sixty. Twain had also suffered bankruptcy since returning to America. It wasn't personal bankruptcy, but it may as well have been, for he alone became responsible for the indebtedness of his vanquished publishing company.

Mr. and Mrs. Clemens had already died once after the death of their eldest daughter Susy in 1896. The blow was made even heavier by the fact that neither parent had seen her for more than a year before her death. In the summer of 1895, back from Europe with the intention to remain in America, they embarked on a lecture tour around the world in order to pay off the Webster debts. These lectures became the substance of *Following the Equator* in 1897, something Twain wrote during the first year of his mourning for Susy, when he and the rest of the family retired to England and saw virtually nobody. Susy had died in the abandoned Hartford mansion. While visiting Hartford and their former neighbors, she and Katy Leary, their longtime housekeeper, entered the house. Susy, who was still an aspiring opera singer, practiced in the house. It was there that summer that she contracted spinal meningitis and died within days. She was twenty-four, her family's "prodigy." Had she lived, she might have become a writer like her father, having already begun a biography of "Papa" at thirteen. "It kills me to think of the books that Susy would have written," Twain lamented to his friend Rogers, "and that I shall never read now."[30]

Jean Clemens (1880–1907), named for the author's mother Jane, showed the first signs of epilepsy around the age of eleven. Twain thought it had been the result of a head injury she had suffered a couple of years before. While living with her family in Vienna and later England at the turn of the century, she was treated by various doctors. While in Vienna Twain could possibly have discussed her condition with Sigmund Freud, still relatively unknown before the publication of *The Interpretation of Dreams* (1899). Jean's condition was the main reason that the family remained in England until 1900, where Jean was undergoing treatment. After having given up her doctors in Vienna, who mainly dosed her with potassium bromide, the Clemens family turned to the counsel of Henrik Kellgren, first in Sanna, Sweden, and then in London. When Kellgren's course of "medical gymnastics" (chiropractic) appeared to keep away the seizures, the family went home. But Jean's attacks continued throughout the first decade of the twentieth century, for part of which she was institutionalized. She died of a seizure in her bath on Christmas Eve 1909, just four months before the death of her father. He once bitterly told her, "God Almighty alone is responsible for your temperament, your malady, and all your troubles and sorrows. I cannot blame you for them and I do not."[31]

The memory of the Civil War had faded with the Spanish-American War of 1898 and would soon (until its centennial) become even more obscured by World War I. The next book "by" Mark Twain would be his authorized biography by Albert Bigelow Paine in 1912. Paine would keep alive the name of Mark Twain with the help of Clara Clemens, the second daughter, who lived to 1962. When she died, she was nearly penniless, her first husband having died in 1936 and her second spouse having gambled away the assets from both the estates of her father and first husband, Ossip Gabrilowitsch, a pianist Clara had met in Vienna and who was the director of the Detroit Symphony at the time of his death. Mark Twain's only grandchild, Nina—born a few months after his death in 1910—became an alcoholic and a drug addict, who in 1965 may have taken her own life.

The spectacular life of Samuel Langhorne Clemens had climaxed as Mark Twain in 1885 with the American publication of *Huckleberry Finn,* that unstoppable book. That year its author had come to terms with his Civil War record as well as his history with slavery. Like Huck Finn, he had had nothing really against the "peculiar institution" and had gone along with it. But like Huck Finn, he also made amends by having Huck act from the heart instead of the head. As Mark Twain, he had also "apologized" by making public "The Private History of a Campaign That Failed." There he set out to make a joke out of war, but like all his jokes its implications were deadly serious.

Since 1861 this Confederate war veteran had been living out his life in a nation where the Union had vanquished his native South, and he had lived that life through a series of dazzling literary achievements. From the sudden success of "Jim Smiley and His Jumping Frog" in 1865 to the ultimate triumph of *Huckleberry Finn* in 1885, Mark Twain had not only hidden his military past but converted its sense of guilt into the grand irony that is found in his magnum opus. Indeed, *Huckleberry Finn* was the supreme expression of the former Confederate's personal growth, from his belief in slavery to his embrace of emancipation. The journey had begun in Marion County, going west to the territories and east to Europe and the Holy Land, finally landing in an heiress's mansion in Elmira that was an abolitionist household, which then morphed into another mansion in Hartford, where Sam Clemens became the most desouthernized Southerner that his friend Howells ever knew. All his adult life he had been obsessed by the war and his role in it. This obsession, along with his guilt about having been part of the very slavery the war supposedly fought to erase, became the foundation for an American classic and an antislavery novel in which the narrator decides to "go to hell" rather than turn in a fugitive slave. Sam Clemens was born to travel widely, and that he did.

ACKNOWLEDGMENTS

〉〈

As this story came out of the biographer's desire to spend more time on a single year in Mark Twain's life and career—the year in which he brought out the American edition of *Adventures of Huckleberry Finn*—I did not have to draw upon as many resources, both in terms of research documents and scholars in the field, as I did during the writing of *Mark Twain: The Adventures of Samuel L. Clemens* (2010). Nevertheless," as John Donne famously said, "no man is an island," and so no writer is ever alone in writing a book, especially one about a subject so famous and so widely written about. As I wrote this one, two people responded to each chapter and with their encouragement helped me to develop the whole story of Mark Twain's crisis over his involvement with the Confederate army and early association with slavery. The first was Philip McFarland, who was at the time writing his own book on Twain and Theodore Roosevelt. The second was my agent Don Fehr of the Trident Media Group, who by gentle prodding got me to develop the drama to its full significance. I also thank Stephen P. Hull, my editor at the University Press of New England. Other Twain scholars who read my manuscript and made invaluable suggestions were Alan Gribben and Forrest Robinson. Paul Sorrentino kindly provided me with information about Stephen Crane's connection to Twain. I thank Robert H. Hirst of the Mark Twain Project at the University of California at Berkeley for allowing me access to Twain's unpublished or obscurely published letters, and Patti Philippon of the Mark Twain House in Hartford and Barbara Schmidt for background material on the sculptor Karl

Gerhardt. As he has with a number of my books, Ed Folsom came to my aid in the final stages of writing this book, making excellent suggestions. Finally, I want to acknowledge the work of my research assistant for the last three years, Emily Sterling. This book is dedicated to the memory of yet another distinguished scholar of Mark Twain and American literature, James M. Cox, the author of *Mark Twain: The Fate of Humor*.

NOTES

>⊱━⊰

Abbreviations

HF   Mark Twain. *Adventures of Huckleberry Finn*. Ed. Victor
Fischer and Lin Salamo. Berkeley: University of California
Press, 2002.

LLMT   *Love Letters of Mark Twain*. Ed. Dixon Wecter. New York:
Harper & Brothers, 1949.

MT   Mark Twain.

MTB   Albert Bigelow Paine. *Mark Twain: A Biography*. New York:
Harper & Brothers, 1912.

MTDD   *Mark Twain, Day by Day*. Ed. David H. Fears. 2 vols.
Privately published, 2008.

MTHL   *Mark Twain–Howells Letters: The Correspondence of Samuel
L. Clemens and William D. Howells, 1872–1910*. Ed. Henry
Nash Smith and William M. Gibson. 2 vols. Cambridge:
Harvard University Press, 1960.

MTN   *Mark Twain's Notebook*. Ed. Albert Bigelow Paine. New
York, 1935.

MTP   Mark Twain Project/Papers. University of California,
Berkeley.

N&J   *Mark Twain's Notebooks & Journals, 1855–1891*. Ed.
Frederick Anderson et al. 3 vols. Berkeley: University of
California Press, 1975–79.

OLC   Olivia Langdon Clemens.

Introduction

1. J. Stanley Mattson, "Mark Twain on War and Peace: The
Missouri Rebel and 'The Campaign That Failed," *American Quarterly*
20 (Winter 1968): 783–94.

2. "The story ["The History of a Campaign That Failed"] might have been still better if he had not introduced the shooting of a soldier in the dark. The incident was invented, of course, to present the real horror of war," *MTB* 2:169.

PRELUDE *"Mark Twain's War Experiences"*

1. "The famous Ancient and Honorable Artillery of Boston selected Hartford as the place for the annual field day, October 1st, 1877, that day being the 241st anniversary of that venerable company. Hearing this the Phalanx tendered the visitors an escort and other courtesies for the occasion, which were gladly accepted. Invitations were also sent to all other military organizations in the city to participate. The "Ancients" arrived in this city about 3 o'clock in the afternoon of October 1st and were agreeably surprised by the reception which they received. The parade was reviewed Governor Hubbard, Generals Hawley and Franklin and others. In the evening a grand complimentary ball was tendered the visitors at Allyn Hall. On the following day at noon the commands again assembled and proceeded to Allyn Hall where a banquet was served. Among the guests on this occasion were ex-Governor Banks of Massachusetts, Mark Twain, Governor Hubbard, General Hawley and the Hon. Henry C. Robinson. The entertaining of the Ancients and Honorables was the last noteworthy incident of the Putnam Phalanx during the year of 1877" (*New York Times*).

ONE *On the Eve of* Huckleberry Finn

1. *MTH L*, 1:350–53.

2. Barbara Schmidt, "Mark Twain & Karl Gerhardt," http://www .twainquotes.com/Gerhardt/gerhardt.html.

3. *Shreveport Times*, May 8, 1940.

4. *Autobiography of Mark Twain*, ed. Harriet Elinor Smith et al. (Berkeley: University of California Press, 2010), 1:87.

5. *MTHL,* 1:354.

6. Henry B. Wonham, "'I Want a Real Coon': Mark Twain and Late Nineteenth-Century Ethnic Caricature," *American Literature* 72 (May 2000): 117–52; and Beverly David, *Mark Twain and His Illustrators* (Albany, N.Y.: Whitston Publishers, 2000).

7. E. W. Kemble, "Illustrating Huckleberry Finn," *Colophon: A Book Collectors' Quarterly* (February 1930), etext.lib.virginia.edu /twain/colophon.html.

8. Quoted in *Mark Twain, Adventures of Huckleberry Finn,* ed. Victor Fischer and Lin Salamo (Berkeley: University of California Press, 2002), 374–75.

9. Jerome Loving, *Mark Twain: The Adventures of Samuel L. Clemens* (Berkeley: University of California Press, 2010), 280–81.

10. Thomas A. Bailey, *The American Pageant: A History of the Republic* (Lexington, Mass.: D. C. Heath and Company, 1975), 524–25, 540–42.

11. Kenneth R. Andrews, *Nook Farm: Mark Twain's Hartford Circle* (Cambridge: Harvard University Press, 1950), 115.

12. *MTHL,* 2:501–2n4.

13. Susan Goodman and Carl Dawson, *William Dean Howells: A Writer's Life* (Berkeley: University of California Press, 2005), 252.

14. Quoted in Andrews, *Nook Farm,* 115.

15. *Mark Twain, Huck Finn and Tom Sawyer Among the Indians and Other Unfinished Stories,* ed. Dahlia Armon and Walter Blair (Berkeley: University of California Press, 1989), 33, 35, 79.

16. *MTHL,* 2:513.

17. *MTB* 1:100–101.

18. Terrell Dempsey, *Searching for Jim: Slavery in Sam Clemens's World* (Columbia: University of Missouri Press, 2003), 27–38, 257.

19. MT to Olivia Susan (Susy) Clemens, November 23, 1884 (MTP).

20. Arthur Lawrence Vogelback, "The Publication and Reception of *Huckleberry Finn* in America," *American Literature* 11 (November 1939): 260–72.

21. http://etext.virginia.edu/twain/hfinn283.jpg.

22. *N&J*, 2:567–69.

23. Henry Nash Smith, "'That Hideous Mistake of Poor Clemens's,'" *Harvard Library Bulletin* 9 (Spring 1955), 156.

24. *MTHL*, 1:412.

25. MT to Thomas Nast, December 4, 1884 (Kelvin Smith Library, Case Western Reserve University, Cleveland, Ohio); MT to OLC, December 6, 1884; and MT to OLC, December 8, 1884 (MTP).

26. MT to Charles L. Webster, December 23, 1884 (Vassar College Library, Poughkeepsie, New York).

27. *N&J*, 3:63, 80–81.

28. *MTB*, 2:787–90.

TWO   *Skirting the Mason-Dixon*

1. Fred W. Lorch, *The Trouble Begins at Eight: Mark Twain's Lecture Tours* (Ames, Iowa: Iowa State University Press, 1966), 165; and *LLMT,* 223; and "Teaching the Negro," *New York Times,* March 19, 1885.

2. *LLMT:* 224.

3. *Cincinnati Commercial Gazette,* December 25, 1884.

4. *LLMT:* 225.

5. MT to Estes & Lauriat, January 7, 1885 (University of Virginia Library); and "Against Mark Twain," *Hartford Daily Courant,* February 11, 1885.

6. MT to Mrs. Whiteside, January 11, 1885 (MTP).

7. MT to OLC, February 3, 1885 (MTP).

8. "Amusements," *Chicago Daily Tribune,* January 17, 1885.

9. Arlin Turner, *George Washington Cable: A Biography* (Durham, NC: Duke University Press, 1956), 181.

10. Chicago's Rabid Socialists," *New York Times,* January 20, 1885.

11. "Strikes Among Workingmen," *New York Times,* February 7, 1885.

12. Émile Zola, *Germinal,* trans. Havelock Ellis (1894; reprint, New York: Barnes and Noble, 2005), 415.

13. MT to Olivia Susan (Susy) Clemens, January 23, 1885 (University of Virginia Library).

14. "Mark Twain's Book Condemned," *New York Times,* March 17, 1885.

15. MT to Frank A. Nichols, March 28, 1885 (MTP).

16. "Gen. Grant's Book—Mark Twain Secures the Job of Publishing It—How the Ex-President Looks When Writing," *Chicago Daily Tribune,* March 8, 1885.

17. "'Huckleberry Finn' in Concord," *New York Herald,* March 18, 1885.

18. "Trashy and Vicious—From the Springfield *Republican*," *New York Times,* March 19, 1885.

19. "Fenimore Cooper's Daughter Dead," *New York Times,* March 24, 1885.

20. MT to Charles L. Webster, April 4; and MT to Charles L. Webster, April 5, 1885 (Vassar College Library).

21. MT to Charles L. Webster, April 4; and MT to Charles L. Webster, April 6, 1885 (Vassar College Library).

22. MT to Charles L. Webster, March [28] and April 5, 1885 (Vassar College Library).

23. "Ferdinand Ward's Ways—What Gen. Grant and Mr. Fish Knew of Them," *New York Times,* March 28, 1885; and MT to OLC, April 8, 1885 (MTP).

24. "A Steamboat Explosion," *Chicago Daily Tribune,* March 28, 1885.

25. H. L. Mencken, *The American Language* (New York: Alfred A. Knopf, 1936).

26. "Bartholdi's Statue of Liberty," *New York Times,* April 8, 1885.

27. William H. Bishop, *Detmold: A Romance* (Boston: Houghton, Osgood, & Company, 1879), 159.

THREE *The Greatest General Who Ever Lived*

1. *Autobiography of Mark Twain,* ed. Harriet Elinor Smith et al. (Berkeley: University of California Press, 2010), 1:74.

2. Barbara Schmidt, "Mark Twain & Karl Gerhardt," (http://www.twainquotes.com/Gerhardt/gerhardt.html).

3. *Autobiography of Mark Twain,* 1:397, 609n.

4. *Autobiography of Mark Twain,* 1:348.

5. *Mark Twain in Eruption,* ed. Bernard DeVoto (New York: Harper & Sons, 1940), 201.

6. MT to Edward H. House, May 13, 1885 (University of Virginia Library).

7. "A Short Talk with Grant," *Philadelphia Times,* April 24, 1885.

8. MT to James Redpath, May 7, 1885 (University of Michigan, Michigan Historical Collection, Ann Arbor, Mich.).

9. Jerome Loving, *Walt Whitman's Champion: William Douglas O'Connor* (College Station: Texas A&M University Press, 1978), 104–8.

10. MT to Charles L. Webster, May 5, 1885 (Vassar College Library).

11. "Anecdotes of Grant," *New York Times,* May 23, 1885; and "Vila's Eulogy of Grant," *New York Times,* May 3, 1885.

12. *The Education of Henry Adams,* ed. Ira B. Nadel (Oxford: Oxford University Press, 1999), xv, 382.

13. *Mark Twain's Mysterious Stranger Manuscripts,* ed. William M. Gibson (Berkeley: University of California Press, 1969), 404–5.

14. MT to Charles Warren Stoddard, June 1, 1885 (University of Notre Dame Library).

15. "Man Upraised of God—Mr. Beecher's Sermon on Evolution in Religion," *New York Times,* June 1, 1885.

16. "To the Sun-set Breeze" in *Walt Whitman, Leaves of Grass: Comprehensive Reader's Edition* (New York: New York University Press, 1965), 546.

17. *MTHL,* 2:530–31.

18. "The Rights of Colored People," *New York Times,* June 5, 1885.

19. "Souvenirs of the Statue—Perfect Models Offered to the Public for One Dollar," *New York Times,* June 5, 1885.

20. MT to Karl Gerhardt, June 26, 1885 (Boston Public Library).

21. *N&J,* 3:139n; and Schmidt, "Mark Twain & Karl Gerhardt" (http://www.twainquotes.com/Gerhardt/gerhardt.html).

22. *The Education of Henry Adams,* 106.

23. "Gen. Grant's Trophies—Removing the Swords and other Relics to Washington," *New York Times,* June 12, 1885.

24. *LLMT:* 243; Justin Kaplan, *Mr. Clemens and Mark Twain* (New York: Simon and Schuster, 1966), 225; and Schmidt, "Mark Twain & Karl Gerhardt," http://www.twainquotes.com/Gerhardt /gerhardt.html.

25. *Battles and Leaders of the Civil War,* ed. Robert Underwood Johnson and Clarence Clough Buel (New York: Century, 1887), ix.

26. *Autobiography of Mark Twain,* 1:77.

27. "Mark Twain—Literary Man with a Good Business Talent," *San Francisco Chronicle,* June 15, 1885.

28. MT to the Editor of the *Boston Herald,* July 6, 1885 (MTP); and *Autobiography of Mark Twain,* 1: 81.

29. MT to Karl Gerhardt, July 18, 1885 (Mark Twain House Hartford).

30. Schmidt, "Mark Twain & Karl Gerhardt," http://www. twainquotes.com/Gerhardt/gerhardt.html.

31. MT to OLC, July 24, 1885 (MTP).

32. "Walt Whitman Prostrated," *New York Times,* July 24, 1885.

33. "The Hero's Pall Bearers," *New York Times,* July 31, 1885.

34. *Personal Memoirs of U. S. Grant,* ed. E. B. Long (New York: Da Capo, 1982), 126–27.

35. "Gen. Grant's Funeral," *New York Times,* August 5, 1885.

36. "Riverside Park Chosen—A Tomb at the End of the Drive for Gen. Grant," *New York Times,* July 29, 1885.

FOUR *March of the White Man*

1. Arlin Turner, *George Washington Cable: A Biography* (Baton Rouge: Louisiana State University Press, 1956), 194–97.

2. The rationale for the substitution of "slave" for "nigger" in Alan Gribben's NewSouth edition of *Adventures of Tom Sawyer and Huckleberry Finn* (2011) is to enable high school teachers to focus on the story as literature instead of spending all their time defending

Twain's historical use of the N-word. Moreover, because of the word, Twain's classic is increasingly not taught at the pre-college level.

3. Turner, *George Washington Cable*, 208–12; and MT to George Washington Cable, May 17, 1885 (Tulane University Library).

4. *MTHL*, 2:528–29n.

5. Ibid., 2:533–34.

6. "Art; Why It Has Declined," *New York Times*, July 26, 1885.

7. *MTHL*, 2:586–88n.

FIVE *"The Private History of a Campaign That Failed"*

1. MT to Robert Underwood Johnson, July 28, 1885, printed in *Mark Twain Journal* 7 (Summer–Fall 1945): 24.

2. "Mark Twain As a Pensioner," *St. Louis Post-Dispatch*, July 27, 1885.

SIX *The "Private" History and the "Personal" Memoir*

1. *MTB*, appendix 5.

2. Annie Dillard, *Pilgrim at Tinker Creek* (New York: HarperCollins, 1975), 169, 177.

3. *MTN*, 372.

4. "Mark Twain's Home," reprinted in *Hartford Daily Courant*, September 23, 1885.

5. "The Rock Spring Massacre," *New York Times*, September 26, 1885.

6. "Four Negroes Lynched—Suspected of Murder, But Their Guilt Not Clearly Established," *New York Times*, September 30, 1885; and "Cable on Woman Suffrage," *New York Times*, September 23, 1885.

7. MT to Charles L. Webster, December 14, 1884 (Vassar College Library); and MT to Chatto & Windus, September 8, 1885 (British Library, London, England).

8. "Mark Twain to Robert Underwood Johnson, *Mark Twain Journal* 7 (Summer–Fall, 1945): 24.

9. MT to Henry Ward Beecher, September 11, 1885 (MTP).

10. Ibid.

11. *Lectures and Orations by Henry Ward Beecher,* ed. Newell Dwight Hillis (1913; repr., New York: AMS Press, 1970), 7, 237.

12. *Civil War Letters of George Washington Whitman,* ed. Jerome M. Loving (Durham: Duke University Press, 1975), 71.

13. *N&J*, 3:147.

14. "Current Criticism," *Critic,* October 17, 1885, p. 94.

15. MT to William Tecumseh Sherman, September 19 and October 5–6, 1885 (Library of Congress).

16. Mark Twain, "The Private History of a Campaign That Failed," in *Merry Tales,* ed. Shelley Fisher Fishkin (New York: Oxford University Press, 1996), 44.

17. *Walt Whitman's Memorandum During the War,* ed. Peter Coviello (New York: Oxford University Press, 2004), 124.

18. William S. McFeely, *Grant: A Biography* (New York: W. W. Norton, 1982), 168–69; and *Walt Whitman: The Correspondence,* ed, Edwin Haviland Miller (New York: New York University Press, 1961), 1:223.

19. "Mr. Beecher's Anticipations—Reforms He Expects to See Effected Before His Death," *New York Times,* October 10, 1885.

20. "Thousands Turned Away—Great Crowds Gather to View the Dead Cardinal's Body," *New York Times,* October 15, 1885.

21. "Riotous Car Strikers—Fighting and Bloodshed in the Streets of St. Louis," *New York Times,* October 10, 1885.

22. "High-Minded Texans—Their Attempt to Justify the Lynching of a Defenseless Negro," *New York Times,* October 12, 1885.

23. MT to Frank Bliss, August 29 and September 8, 1901 (University of Texas Library).

24. Terry L. Oggel, "Speaking Out about Race: 'The United States of Lyncherdom' Clemens Really Wrote," *Prospects: An Annual of American Cultural Studies* 25 (2000): 115–58.

25. "Ferdinand Ward Married Again," *New York Times,* March 22, 1894.

26. Thomas M. Pitkin, *The Captain Departs: Ulysses S. Grant's Last*

Campaign (Carbondale: Southern Illinois University Press, 1973), 60.

27. Ibid., 117–29.

28. MT to Olivia L. Clemens, November 12, 1879 (MTP).

29. *MTHL*, 1:278–80.

30. *MTB*, 2:915.

31. *MTHL*, 1:280.

32. Twain, *Merry Tales*, 9.

SEVEN *The Killing of Strangers*

1. Timothy P. Caron, "How Changeable Are the Events of War: National Reconciliation in the *Century Magazine*'s 'Battles and Leaders of the Civil War,'" *American Periodicals* 16 (2006): 169.

2. Joe B. Fulton, *The Reconstruction of Mark Twain: How a Confederate Bushwhacker Became the Lincoln of Our Literature* (Baton Rouge: Louisiana State University Press, 2010), 18.

3. Samuel Charles Webster, *Mark Twain, Business Man* (Boston: Little, Brown and Company, 1946), 60.

4. Ibid., 62.

5. *N&J*, 3:106n.

6. Fulton, *The Reconstruction of Mark Twain*, 24–25.

7. *N&J*, 3:105.

8. "What the Colored Man Needs," *New York Times*, November 7, 1885.

9. Calvin Trillin, "Back on the Bus: Remembering the Freedom Riders," *New Yorker*, July 25, 2011, 36–42.

10. *N&J*, 3: 211.

11. *MTDD*, 2:1076.

12. *Mark Twain's Letters*, ed. Albert Bigelow Paine (New York: Harper & Brothers Publishers, 1917), 2:466; and MT to Joel Chandler Harris, November 29, 1885 (Emory University Library).

13. Fulton, *The Reconstruction of Mark Twain*, 31.

14. Joseph Gallagher, "A Wordless, Anonymous Memorial," *New York Times,* December 1, 1985.

15. *MTDD,* 2:1082.

16. "Bush-Whacker Mark Twain" (a gossip column), *Chicago Daily Tribune,* December 13, 1885.

17. MT to Charles L. Webster, December 10–13? 1885 (Vassar College Library).

18. Barbara Schmidt, "Mark Twain & Karl Gerhardt," http://www.twainquotes.com/Gerhardt/gerhardt.html.

19. Jerome Loving, *Mark Twain: The Adventures of Samuel L. Clemens* (Berkeley: University of California Press, 2010), 280–81.

20. Stuart McConnell, *Glorious Contentment: The Grand Army of the Republic, 1865–1900* (Chapel Hill: University of North Carolina Press, 1992), 204

21. "Bygones" (1911), published in McConnell, *Glorious Contentment,* 191. See http://www.usgennet.org/usa/ne/topic/military/GAR/bygones.html.

22. Wilson is quoted in McConnell, *Glorious Contentment,* 169. See also *Stephen Crane Remembered,* ed. Paul Sorrentino (Tuscaloosa: University of Alabama Press, 2006), 105; see also *Mark Twain's Library,* 164.

23. *MTDD,* 2:1083.

24. Gaines M. Foster, *Ghosts of the Confederacy: Defeat, The Lost Cause, and the Emergence of the New South, 1865–1913* (New York: Oxford University Press, 1987), 101.

25. Theodore Dreiser, *Free and Other Stories* (New York: Boni and Liveright, 1918), 105.

26. Mark Twain to Charles L. Webster, December 16, 1885 (Vassar College Library).

EIGHT *Connecticut Yankee*

1. Jerome Loving, *Walt Whitman's Champion: William Douglas O'Connor* (College Station: Texas A&M University Press), 86–87.

2. Ta-Nehisi Coates, "Why Do So Few Blacks Study the Civil War," *Atlantic Monthly* (Civil War Special Issue, 2011), 142–46; http://www.theatlantic.com/magazine/archive/2012/02/why-do-so-few-blacks-study-the-civil-war/8831/.

3. "The Chicago Socialists," *New York Times,* January 15, 1886.

4. *MTHL,* 2:550.

5. MT to Charles L. Webster, February 13, 1886 (Vassar College Library).

6. *MTDD,* 2:21

7. *MTDD,* 2:16

8. *Roughing It,* ed. Harriet Elinor Smith and Edgar Marquess Branch (Berkeley: University of California Press, 1993),127; and "The Mormon Bill," *New York Times,* January 9, 1886.

9. Lilian Whiting, *Kate Field: A Record* (Boston: Little, Brown and Company, 1899), 448. Also quoted in *MTDD,* 2:24.

10. *MTDD,* 2:25.

11. Paul J. Carter, Jr., "Mark Twain and the American Labor Movement," *New England Quarterly* 30 (September 1957): 382–88.

12. Ibid., 386.

13. "The Strike in the Coke Regions," *New York Times,* January 23, 1886; and "The Labor Question," *New York Times,* February 4, 1886.

14. William Dean Howells, "Editor's Study," *Harper's* 85 (July 1887): 10–11; reprinted in William Dean Howells, *Prefaces to Contemporaries,* ed. George Arms, et al. (Gainesville: University of Florida Press, 1957).

15. Leo Tolstoy, *War and Peace,* trans. Louise and Aylmer Maude (New York: Simon and Schuster, 1941), 667, 761.

16. MT to Joseph H. Twichell, February 18, 1886 (MTP).

17. MT to Grover Cleveland, February 23, 1886 (Library of Congress).

18. Helen Hunt Jackson, *A Century of Dishonor,* ed. Andrew F. Rolle (New York: Harper & Row, Publishers, 1965), xiii.

19. Quoted in Carter, "Mark Twain and the American Labor Movement," 382.

20. Bruce C. Nelson, *Beyond the Martyrs: A Social History of Chicago's Anarchists, 1870–1900* (New Brunswick: Rutgers University Press, 1988), 4.

21. MT to Olivia L. Clemens, May 5, 1886 (MTP).

22. Frank E. Vandiver, *Black Jack: The Life and Times of John J. Pershing* (College Station, Tex.: Texas A&M University Press, 1977), 1: 41–42.

23. Philip W. Leon, *Mark Twain and West Point* (Toronto: ECW Press, 1996), 92.

24. Quoted in Henry David, *The History of the Haymarket Affair* (1936; repr., New York: Russell & Russell, 1958), 10.

25. Justin Kaplan, *Mr. Clemens and Mark Twain* (New York: Simon & Schuster, 1966), 321.

26. David, *The History of the Haymarket Affair,* 10.

27. Nelson, *Beyond the Martyrs,* 11–14.

28. Ibid., 2.

29. "Black History Museum Rising on National Mall," Associated Press Report, February 23, 2012.

30. *MTHHR,* 235.

31. MT to Jean Clemens, June 1907 (Mark Twain House, Hartford).

INDEX

⤙⤚

Adams, Henry, 78, 84, 179; *The Education of Henry Adams,* 78, 179

Adventures of Huckleberry Finn, xi, xii, 6–7, 11–13, 16–17–20, 23–26, 28–29, 34, 38–40, 43, 45–48, 50, 54–56, 59, 64, 66–67, 71, 78–80, 88, 93–94, 98, 101–4, 109, 135–36, 152–53, 155, 182–83, 187, 192, 195–96, 209, 211, 214, 217–18; and autobiography, 20–21; banning by Concord Public Library, 51–52, 61, 63; defaced illustration, 24–25; ending, 18, 95, 175; frontispieces, 11, 65; Grangerford episode, 171–72; "Jim's Investments and King Sollermun," 38; NewSouth edition, 97, 174; "Prefatory Remark," 57–58; reviews, 43, 49–50, 55–58, 147; "Royalty on the Mississippi: As Chronicled by Huckleberry Finn," 47, 49, 88; sales, 75, 138, 168, 207; slavery, xiv, 18, 69;

Adventures of Jimmy Brown, The, 64,

Adventures of Tom Sawyer, 7, 17, 23–24, 27, 43, 49, 56, 70–71, 98, 102–3, 108, 110, 211

Allen, James Lane, 12

American Claimant, The, 18, 96, 204–5

American Copyright League, 99–100, 176

American Publishing Company, 154

Ancient and Honorable Artillery Company of Massachusetts, 1

Armour, Philip Danforth, 212

Army of the Tennessee, the, 76, 159, 162

"Assaulted by Strikers," 197

Atlanta Constitution, 96, 188

Atlantic Monthly, 17, 29, 56, 70, 98, 195

autobiography of Mark Twain, 73–74

Bachelder, R. N. (Colonel), 84

Balzac, Honoré de, 56; *Human Comedy,* 56

Barbour, Haley (Governor), 175

Bartholdi, Frédéric Auguste, 64

Battles and Leaders of the Civil War, 139

Baylor College, 213

Beauregard, P. G. T. (General), xiii

Beecher, Henry Ward, 41, 69, 77, 79, 140–42, 150, 182

Beidler, Henry, 212

Billings, Josh, 146, *Farmer's Almanac,* 146–47

Bixby, Horace, 184

Black, John C., 106